Diversity, Innovation and Clusters

NEW HORIZONS IN REGIONAL SCIENCE

Series Editor: Philip McCann, *Professor of Urban and Regional Economics, University of Sheffield, UK*

Regional science analyses important issues surrounding the growth and development of urban and regional systems and is emerging as a major social science discipline. This series provides an invaluable forum for the publication of high quality scholarly work on urban and regional studies, industrial location economics, transport systems, economic geography and networks.

New Horizons in Regional Science aims to publish the best work by economists, geographers, urban and regional planners and other researchers from throughout the world. It is intended to serve a wide readership including academics, students and policymakers.

Titles in the series include:

Diversity, Innovation and Clusters

Spatial Perspectives

Edited by

Iréne Bernhard

PhD, School of Business, Economics and IT, University West, Sweden

Urban Gråsjö

PhD, School of Business, Economics and IT, University West, Sweden

Charlie Karlsson

Professor Emeritus of the Economics of Technological Change, Jönköping International Business School, Jönköping University and Professor Emeritus of Industrial Economics, Blekinge Institute of Technology, Sweden

NEW HORIZONS IN REGIONAL SCIENCE

Cheltenham, UK • Northampton, MA, USA

Published by
Edward Elgar Publishing Limited
The Lypiatts
15 Lansdown Road
Cheltenham
Glos GL50 2JA
UK

Edward Elgar Publishing, Inc.
William Pratt House
9 Dewey Court
Northampton
Massachusetts 01060
USA

A catalogue record for this book
is available from the British Library

Library of Congress Control Number: 2019956679

This book is available electronically in the **Elgar**online
Economics subject collection
DOI 10.4337/9781789902587

ISBN 978 1 78990 257 0 (cased)
ISBN 978 1 78990 258 7 (eBook)

Typeset by Servis Filmsetting Ltd, Stockport, Cheshire

Printed and bound by CPI Group (UK) Ltd, Croydon CR0 4YY

Contents

v

Contributors

Tobias Arvemo is an Assistant Professor of Mathematical Statistics at the School of Business, Economics and IT, University West, Sweden. His research interests include regional studies of economic growth and of economic development. He has also applied statistical methods to various other applied fields such as pedagogics and marketing.

David Bartlett is Professorial Lecturer in the Department of Management at the Kogod School of Business, American University in Washington, DC, USA. He previously held faculty positions at the University of Minnesota and Vanderbilt University, and visiting professorships in Taiwan, Armenia and Uzbekistan. He has published and consulted on international corporate strategy, global sustainability, and economic development in emerging markets. His current research focuses on innovation ecosystems and technology cluster formation.

Karin Berg is a PhD student at the Institute of Innovation and Entrepreneurship, Department of Economy and Society, School of Business, Economics and Law, University of Gothenburg, Sweden. In her research she addresses questions related to innovation and university–industry interactions and she is particularly interested in capabilities for innovation, knowledge networks and innovation management. In 2018, she received the 'Best PhD Candidate Paper Award' at the 21st Uddevalla Symposium.

Iréne Bernhard is Assistant Professor in Informatics at the School of Business, Economics and IT, University West, Sweden. She holds a PhD in Planning and Decision Analysis with a specialization in urban and regional studies from the Royal Institute of Technology, Stockholm, Sweden. She has published more than 30 journal articles, book chapters and books. Her research focuses on digitalization, e-government, social media, inclusiveness, urban regeneration, work-integrated learning, networking and women's entrepreneurship.

Urban Gråsjö is an Assistant Professor in Economics at the School of Business, Economics and IT, University West, Sweden. He holds a PhD in economics with a specialization in regional studies from Jönköping International Business School, Jönköping, Sweden. His research focuses on knowledge production, innovation, entrepreneurship and economic development. He has edited books and is the author of more than twenty journal articles and book chapters. His recent publications deal with economic activity in border regions and indicators of economic development.

Terje Grønning received his PhD in applied sociology from Ritsumeikan University, Kyoto, Japan, and is Professor in Work, Society and Learning at the Department of Education, University of Oslo, Norway. He is the Director of Studies of the master's degree programme in knowledge development and learning within working life and teaches organizational learning, innovation processes, competence development, and research methodology both at postgraduate and undergraduate levels. He has previously published works focusing on innovation and organizational learning in automobile and biotechnology firms.

Masashi Imase is an Associate Professor at the Faculty of Business Administration, Aichi Toho University, Nagoya City, Japan. He specializes in regional revitalization, NPO management, and corporate management. His philosophy is to fulfil both the roles of 'research and education' and 'practical activities for social contribution'. He is a representative or director of various NPOs and academic societies. He conducts a variety of research and policy planning in central and local government.

Ivar Jonsson is Professor of Innovation and Entrepreneurship, Østfold University College, Norway. He has previously held professorships at: Nord University, Norway, political science; Bifröst University, Iceland, innovation and entrepreneurship. Associate professor (docent) of Human Work Science at Luleå University of Technology, Sweden; Associate professor at the University of Greenland. He has published various articles and books on regional, social and economic development. He is author of *The Political Economy of Innovation and Entrepreneurship: From Theories to Practice*, Routledge 2016.

Charlie Karlsson is Professor Emeritus of Economics at Jönköping International Business School, Jönköping, Sweden and Professor Emeritus of Industrial Economics at Blekinge Institute of Technology, Karlskrona, Sweden. He is also affiliated to the Institute of Innovation and Entrepreneurship at Gothenburg University, Gothenburg, Sweden. In 2009–2013 he was President of the European Regional Science Association (ERSA).

Nobuyuki Kishida is Professor of Entrepreneurship and Corporate Venturing at NSG Graduate Institute for Entrepreneurial Studies, Japan. He had a successful career in the venture capital industry for fifteen years before achieving an MBA and a Doctor of Commerce degree from Waseda

University, Tokyo. As well as participating in entrepreneur education for regional innovations, he is involved in innovation management research for healthcare information networking and international chemical warfare disposal. He is also a Fuji Pharma Valley R&D Forum member in Shizuoka.

Ulrika Lundh Snis is Associate Professor in Informatics with a specialization in work-integrated learning. She has conducted several research projects in collaboration with both industrial and public organizations. Her research focus is on collaboration and learning in relation to digitalization from the perspectives of innovation, management and work practice. She is head of the group Industrial Work-integrated Learning at University West in Sweden and is responsible for the third cycle of PhD education in informatics with a specialization in work-integrated learning.

Maureen McKelvey is Professor of Industrial Management at the Institute of Innovation and Entrepreneurship, School of Business Economics and Law at the University of Gothenburg, Sweden. She has published extensively in journals such as *Research Policy* and *Applied Economics* as well as books with Routledge, Oxford University Press, Cambridge University Press, and Edward Elgar Publishing. Winner of the Schumpeter Prize in 1994 and 2017, she was awarded the Swedish Research Council Distinguished Professor Programme. Professor McKelvey has had leading positions in expert groups for various Swedish organizations, the OECD and the EU.

Takashi Maneo is a Professor of the Graduate School of System Design and Management in Keio University, Tokyo, Japan. He received his BS and MS in Mechanical Engineering from the Tokyo Institute of Technology, Tokyo, Japan in 1984 and 1986, respectively. He received his PhD in Mechanical Engineering from the Tokyo Institute of Technology in 1993.

Lilja Mósesdóttir is Professor II at the Faculty of Business, Languages, and Social Sciences, Østfold University College and senior policy advisor at the Association of Social Scientists in Norway. Lilja was a professor in the Department of Business Administration at Bifröst University, Iceland until 2008. After the financial crisis, she was a Member of Parliament and chaired the committee on business and banking. She has published widely on labour market issues, welfare state models and gender from international, national and regional perspectives.

Tomasz Mroczkowski is a Professor of Management at the Kogod School of Business, American University, Washington, DC, USA. He writes about innovation, the management of change, and economic transitions. He is the author of over 100 works published in a variety of countries and languages including articles in such journals as *California Management Review*, *Academy of Management Executive* and *Journal of Product Innovation Management*. He has lectured on innovation at universities in France, Germany, Japan, India and Poland.

Gordon F. Mulligan is Professor Emeritus of Geography and Development at the University of Arizona, USA. He was previously Editor of the *Journal of Regional Science* and a Fellow of the Regional Science Association International. He has published extensively on regional and urban issues, with special interests in location theory, spatial competition, demography, multipliers, and metropolitan labour markets.

Mutsumi Okuyama is a doctoral student of the Graduate School of System Design and Management, Keio University, Japan. She received a bachelor's degree from Musashino Art University, Kodaira, Japan, in 1982. She has been CEO of Will Inc., an editorial production company, since 1990. In September 2011, she earned a master's degree in Policy Studies from Hosei University in Tokyo. She is currently a visiting professor at Shizuoka University and a part-time lecturer at Japan Women's University.

Anna Karin Olsson is an Assistant Professor in Business Administration at the School of Business, Economics and IT, University West, Sweden. Her recent publications cover issues such as place development, urban regeneration, networking, stakeholder collaboration, cultural heritage, women entrepreneurs and social media.

Kyosuke Sakakura is an Associate Professor of the Faculty of Urban Life Studies, Tokyo City University, Japan. He received his PhD in Media and Governance from Keio University, Tokyo, in 2019. He was an Assistant Professor of Keio University from 2007 to 2014 (Research Institute for Digital Media and Content, Global Security Research Institute). His fields of interests are community design and management based on sociology and urban design. He has been the Board Chairman of the Mitanoie LLP since 2008.

Toshiyuki Yasui is a Guest Professor of the Graduate School of System Design and Management, Keio University, Japan. Following his 35 years of distinguished public service for the Japanese Government, he earned his PhD at the International Christian University, Mitaka, Japan, in 2011. His research topics are innovation design theories and social system methodologies. He has published more than 13 books and 40 academic articles, including articles in *Systems Engineering Journal* and *Systems Research and Behavioural Science*.

1. Introduction: diversity, innovation and clusters – spatial perspectives

Iréne Bernhard, Urban Gråsjö and Charlie Karlsson

1. INTRODUCTION

Regions, and especially urban regions, are increasingly considered to be the areas driving economic development in the global economy (Malecki, 2007). The innovations and the entrepreneurship that these regions have the capacity to give rise to are increasingly seen as a key factor that lays the foundation for future growth (Fritsch and Mueller, 2004). Innovations require knowledge, and urban regions have become incubators of new ideas in the modern knowledge economy and provide opportunities for the discovery of new valuable knowledge (Huggins and Williams, 2011). Today, more and more researchers emphasize the link between, on the one hand, regional diversity and, on the other, regional knowledge, innovation and entrepreneurship (Özgen et al., 2011; Rodriguez-Pose and Hardy, 2015).

In regional and urban economics, it has been shown that there is a fundamental relationship between market size and diversity. For example, in spatial models based on the general model of monopolistic competition (Dixit and Stiglitz, 1977; Chamberlain, 1933), the diversity of inputs generates increasing returns at the aggregate level (Fujita and Thisse, 2002). By increasing the return on diversity at intermediaries, companies clustered in a region with a variety of input goods suppliers will have higher productivity than similar companies in a region with a less varied range of input goods.

Diversity in urban regions is the characteristic that is often highlighted in explaining why these regions are prosperous and have long-term economic development and growth (Jacobs, 1969; Florida, 2002). Jacobs argues that cultural heterogeneity in the labour market expands the collective diversity of skills, knowledge and ideas and thus becomes an important and valuable economic asset for a region's economic development.

Jacobs' explanation of the drivers of regional growth is in line with those found in more modern models of endogenous economic growth, where the generation, transfer and use of knowledge within and across regional economies are increasingly seen as the main drivers of regional economic growth (Antonelli et al., 2011). Jacobs claims that urban development and growth largely derive from the possibility that individuals can combine different sources of knowledge and interact with individuals who have other experiences and backgrounds. Consequently, increased diversity can benefit regional economies by broadening the regional knowledge base and improving their absorption capacity (Cohen and Levinthal, 1990), which in turn develops the ability to identify, evaluate, assimilate and utilize new knowledge (Hong and Page, 2001).

A region where the population is diversified and where people have different backgrounds is likely to offer a wide and varied range of available knowledge as well as many ways of combining existing knowledge in the region (Qian, 2013). The geographical proximity offered by the region also facilitates communication as the transfer of knowledge between individuals can take place face to face. Interestingly, there is some recent research stating that geographical proximity eases knowledge exchange via digital communication (via Twitter) (Delbaggio et al., 2018). Feldman et al. (2016, p. 10) captures the essence of how diversity, innovation and clusters are related: 'Despite the pervasive image of the lone genius, innovation is a social activity that requires a mix of individuals with different skills to collaborate to create value. Rather than distributed uniformly through time and across geographic space, innovation tends to cluster both temporally and spatially.'

2.   DIVERSITY AND INNOVATION IN URBAN REGIONS

Innovations play a crucial role in the renewal and growth of regional and national economies. In particular, more pervasive innovations tend to be the result of the establishment of new companies (Aghion et al., 2009). This means that the fundamental factor in an innovation often comes from companies and/or basic research laboratories in technology-related industries and not from existing companies (Winter, 1984). Since innovation is a complex process that often requires knowledge and expertise from other economic agents, contacts with other economic agents are crucial for a successful innovation process (Bergenholz and Waldstrøm, 2011). The links between economic agents facilitate the flow of ideas, R&D, knowledge, technology, skills and competence, and include both supplier–customer links and links to competitors, consulting companies, R&D companies and research universities (Andersson and Karlsson, 2007). Although innovation collaborations often exist in local networks, they also need global knowledge links to stay updated (Ter Wal and Boschma, 2011).

The introduction of new products can be expected to be more common in large urban regions where it costs less to develop networks for innovation cooperation and where access to networks with the right knowledge and competence profile exists (Grant and Baden-Fuller, 2004). Of course, innovative companies and especially those belonging to a multinational company will also be able to obtain knowledge from other regions (Davenport, 2005). For companies in smaller regions, interregional sourcing can act as a substitute when local knowledge is not available (Drejer and Vinding, 2007).

Although it may be possible to obtain knowledge inter-regionally, companies that participate in regional knowledge networks have a competitive advantage in that the knowledge network is likely to contain a variety of diversified knowledge-producing organizations, a large and diversified range of highly qualified workers and a diversified set of qualified partners. All in all, this can be expected to have a positive impact on companies' innovation ability, as a wider range of complementary and collaborative knowledge expansion can generate synergies (Lavie, 2009).

Typically, larger urban regions are characterized by more entrepreneurs and more innovating firms, which may explain the high likelihood that companies supplying new products will be located in such regions (Johansson and Andersson, 1998). Another reason why companies that are more innovative are located in large urban regions is that the companies are likely to meet customers who, together, have a broader and more diversified demand. During the innovation phase of a product cycle, it is assumed that each supplier communicates with its customers. This can be regarded as a distance-sensitive activity, since communication must, to a great extent, be face to face so that one can fully understand the other. Moreover, for every new product, only a small proportion of all potential customers are willing to test the new product (Vernon, 1966). This small proportion will only constitute enough demand in large urban areas.

Urban regions, especially large urban regions, offer a diversified access to knowledge and a sufficiently large and diversified internal market potential to make the launch of innovations profitable. In addition, geographical transaction costs are low in these regions, which is crucial in reducing the interaction costs of entrepreneurs who develop innovations. Thus, innovative activities show a strong tendency to cluster, especially in large urban regions (Karlsson, 2016) and the knowledge-intensive and high-tech industry tends to be localized in larger urban areas where there is a diversified set of higher education and research. Several studies from both the US and Europe provide empirical evidence for a link between diversity in urban regions and innovative activity (Peri, 2007; Özgen et al., 2011).

3.   DIVERSITY AND CLUSTERS IN URBAN REGIONS

Porter (1998) highlights the role of clusters for economic development, as proximity, achieved through co-location of companies, customers, suppliers and other institutions, increases the ability to innovate. The existence of a well-developed cluster offers great benefits for productivity and the ability to innovate that are difficult to match by companies based elsewhere.

It is possible to assume that the larger the region, the greater the opportunity to combine internal and external economies of scale, which also gives an increased economic density. Especially for large urban regions, economies of scale provide a place advantage for those products where demand is 'thin' and therefore clusters in these industries are formed mainly in such regions. Thus, large urban regions can specialize in 'cluster diversity' and benefit from the dual power of internal and external economies of scale. However, economies of scale represent an equally important phenomenon for industrial clustering in regions of all sizes. Hence, clusters can also be developed in smaller regions, but in this case the development is limited to a set of closely related products in the same industry with low geographical transaction costs supported by localization economies (Karlsson, 2007).

Large and dense urban regions have many advantages that are not present in other types of regions. As larger regions not only generate more entrepreneurial opportunities but also have a larger stock of entrepreneurial human capital and have richer potential entrepreneurs, these regions will not only experience more entrepreneurial events, but will also experience a superior build-up of entrepreneurial human capital, as there are more entrepreneurial activities to learn from in such regions (Karlsson and Gråsjö, 2019). Successful entrepreneurial activities and innovations stimulate growth and structural change in these regions, which in turn will generate even more entrepreneurial opportunities and innovations. The structural change involves the formation of new clusters at the expense of older clusters, as resources will be allocated to the new and growing clusters. The new and growing companies operating in markets characterized by monopolistic competition can generally offer higher payments. Incumbents in declining clusters must become more productive and perhaps also must move their production to other smaller regions that offer lower production costs if they want to stay in business.

Porter (2003) argues that knowledge spillovers that affect innovation and performance ought to be strongest within a cluster and among related industries. Hence, specialization in clusters, and not in industries, should lead to higher performance. A diverse range of overlapping clusters should cause better performance than a diversity of clusters that are unrelated. Of course, these overlapping clusters are mainly found in regions of a particular size, that is, in large urban regions.

4. CONCLUSIONS

The discussion above demonstrates that to increase the understanding of the multifaceted dynamic relationships between diversity, innovation and clusters, there is a strong need to further focus on and investigate the spatial perspectives of these relationships. Such investigations include identification and empirical testing of the mechanisms that may explain possible causal relationships. This is necessary from a scientific point of view, but also from the need to provide policy makers with a better and more comprehensive basis for decision-making, since the spatial perspectives are crucial in understanding what drives economic development. We hope that this book will make a small contribution to 'the economy of spatial diversity'.

5. THE CONTRIBUTIONS IN THIS BOOK

In this section the contributions are summarized following their appearance in the book in order for the reader to plan their reading experience.

In Chapter 2 Grønning contributes empirically and conceptually to the studies of technological trajectories, that is, the paths by which innovations in a given field occur. Hitherto technological trajectories have mostly been treated as constructs at the global level, whereas there has been relatively little attention on how various locations relate to such trajectories except for a focus on the presumed advanced locations of a trajectory. The analysis concludes that for firms, there was a period of initial emergence and first results, followed by periods of consolidation and contradictions. For policies, there was a period of policy formation followed by a period of mainly basic research and marine biotech focus and a period with a new pluralistic policy. As seen through the relations between business and policies, the country's part in the global biotechnology trajectory has not yet reached a mature phase.

Tentative indices for regional economic development using Swedish municipal data from 2015 are explored by Arvemo and Gråsjö in Chapter

3. The authors use variable selection methods and examine variables potentially suitable as indicators for different dimensions of economic development. Since potential factors for measuring economic development typically will differ greatly over large geographical areas, the study uses indicators at municipality level to avoid large geographical units of analysis. An extensive search yielded a number of prospective indicators to use even though the official data gathered in Sweden are not particularly suitable for investigating the softer dimensions of economic development. The results of the study suggest that the indicators of economic development can be categorized into five dimensions/indices that represent 'Quality of Living', 'Economic Capacity', 'Wealth and Stability', 'Growing Worries' and 'Gross Municipal Product per inhabitant' in the municipality.

In Chapter 4, Bernhard, Olsson and Lundh Snis contribute knowledge on the nature and challenges of stakeholder inclusion within local community regeneration in order to identify innovative, collaborative approaches at work in smaller cities through case studies in Norway and Sweden. Place innovation perspectives are applied to address issues of diversity and collaborative approaches in the renewal of a small city centre or district based on cultural heritage. The results reveal stakeholders' views on challenges related to collaborative approaches for place innovation. The complex nature of the two cases is characterized by diverse perspectives, conflicts and attitudes; limited inclusion of stakeholders; lack of communication and information; and indistinct place identity. Findings indicate that place innovation requires an integrated approach based on including diverse stakeholder perspectives, common communication, common physical and digital platforms, cultivating place identity and applying a step-by-step regeneration.

In Chapter 5, by Mulligan, the incidence of (utility) patents across US metropolitan areas during the period 1990–2015 is examined. Patent volumes are shown to have become increasingly concentrated in the nation's largest metropolitan areas during this period. Next, following an earlier study, estimates of these volumes are made every five years using only population size as an explanatory variable. Then other patenting estimates are made for the years 2000, 2005, 2010 and 2015 using more than twenty different metropolitan attributes. Besides population size, these other attributes include education of the workforce, industrial specialization, location (climate), average wages, per capita GDP, and various human-created amenities. A multivariate approach, which reflects differences in metropolitan innovation ecosystems, replaces the list of variables with six orthogonal factors. A performance score is provided for each metropolitan area on each of the six factors and, together, these (ordinal) scores provide a time-specific performance vector for each economy. Linear regression next indicates that three factors – Economic Size, Location, and Industrial Specialization – have become especially important in US metropolitan patent generation in recent times. The pattern of estimates for patent densities, or per capita patenting volumes, is shown to be remarkably similar.

Mósesdóttir and Jonsson aim in Chapter 6 to contribute to further development and 'progressive problem shift' of the neo-Schumpeterian research programme by theorizing the role of actors in real critical junctures. The authors argue that on a global scale, societies are facing a technological revolution that is expected to have a fundamental impact on their social, economic and political foundations. Theoretical frameworks analysing technological change seldom include political agency and rarely consider outcomes in terms of socio-economic inequality. In the context of the present cybernetic, bio-technological revolution, various stakeholders and actors struggle for alternative forms and content of what has been termed 'transformative change' involving capacity building to turn opportunities created by technological revolution into socio-economic progress. The authors claim that transformative change requires transformative innovation involving cooperation of different actors around mission-oriented and experimental policies in various constellations at the micro-, meso- and macro levels. How the actors shape transformative change depends on the challenges and opportunities created by context of critical juncture, the balance of power and their capacity to collaborate on restructuring society.

Chapter 7 relates to the larger question of how academic engagement with industry through collaborative research between universities and firms can influence firm innovation. Berg and McKelvey explore industrial PhD students and perceptions of their impact on firm innovation. Specifically, they explore university–industry collaboration from the perspective of industrial PhD students, who in the present case are simultaneously PhD students and firm employees. The empirical context is collaborative research in the engineering field in Sweden. Given the lack of previous relevant research, the authors first explore the conditions of industrial PhD students, leading to a definition. They then present an existing conceptual framework for academic engagement and elaborate on it by detailing the micro-level activities of these PhD students in order to understand their perceived contribution to firm innovation during their education. Their results suggest that industrial PhD students are more involved in developing firm capabilities for innovation than they are directly involved in developing product innovations or patents.

In Chapter 8 Bartlett and Mroczkowski examine the growing visibility and importance of start-up companies in the global economy. Drawing on field research in the San Francisco Bay Area, they examine the role of four types of business development organizations in spurring the globalization of high potential start-ups: Business Incubators, Business Accelerators, International Bridge Organizations, and Corporate Innovation Centres. The chapter augments the scholarly literature on global start-ups by (1) developing a typology of business development organizations dedicated to speeding the globalization of start-up companies; (2) using the results of preliminary field research to assess the relative effectiveness of these organizations; and (3) formulating a conceptual model to guide future research on start-up globalization.

Chapter 9, by Imase, reports on IT business case studies which have been created by the citizen/non-profit sector. This sector has a function as an 'economic entity' as well a 'public interest entity' and has been creating new business in regions. In regions with deep seated problems, innovation becomes easy to create, resulting in emerging new businesses. Activation of local contribution initiatives by citizen/non-profit sectors and their 'businessization' will make local needs more achievable. In the fields of products and services where market mechanisms have been difficult to actualize, companies have also started to do business, with the expectation that new products and service fields will mature. Through such processes, new markets and industries are created. Regionally, the citizen-based/ non-profit sector performs a 'seedbed function' for new industry. Furthermore, considering the role played by the citizen/non-profit sector, the author clarifies 'input resources' of regional innovation clusters and the process of new industry creation.

In Chapter 10, Kishida analyses a sake brewing cluster which has emerged since the 1980s. The results reveal that successful open innovations require not only new technologies from outside, but also good enough skills inside. The author bases the results on three factors that are relevant to regional inputs in this case: (1) Human resources: the sake brewing technologies have been supported by several seasonal migrant sake artisans' groups called Toji. There was Shida Toji in Shizuoka, but most of them worked only in Shizuoka and ceased migrant works in remote breweries at that time. (2) Inputs other than human resources: the Shizuoka yeast is one of the premium sake yeasts available only for Shizuoka breweries. (3) Sharing of the industry-specific technology and knowledge: in the early 1980s, Tojis from different regions tried to brew unique sakes with Shizuoka yeast. Kawamura formulated the standard process for the Shizuoka yeast sake with character and introduced it to Shizuoka breweries. The efficient brewing skills of ex-Shida Tojis would contribute to Shizuoka sake success in 1986.

In the last chapter, Chapter 11, authored by Okuyama, Yasui, Maneo and Sakakura, knowledge creation in the industrial cluster in the Sumida Ward in Tokyo is analysed. The Sumida Ward was selected for this research because the concentration of SMEs in industrial clusters is the highest in Japan and the spatial clusters are remarkable. The study uses and expands the design-driven innovation theory applied to cases of horizontal and co-creative networks of SMEs. The results show that the development of a dialogue between various stakeholders became an opportunity to give a new 'meaning' to the product, leading to the possibility of creating a new industry.

REFERENCES

Aghion, P., R. Blundell, R. Griffith, P. Howitt and S. Prantl (2009), The Effects of Entry on Incumbent Innovation and Productivity, *Review of Economics and Statistics*, **91**, 20–32.

Andersson, M. and C. Karlsson (2007), Knowledge in Regional Economic Growth: The Role of Knowledge Accessibility, *Industry and Innovation*, **14**, 129–49.

Antonelli, C., P. Patrucco and A. Quatraro (2011), Productivity Growth and Pecuniary Knowledge Externalities: An Empirical Analysis of Agglomeration Economies in European Regions, *Economic Geography*, **87**, 23–50.

Bergenholz, C. and C. Waldstrøm (2011), Inter-Organizational Network Studies: A Literature Survey, *Industry and Innovation*, **18**, 539–62.

Chamberlain, E.H. (1933), *The Theory of Monopolistic Competition*, Cambridge, MA: Harvard University Press,

Cohen, W. and D. Levinthal (1990), Absorptive Capacity: A New Perspective on Learning and Innovation, *Administrative Science Quarterly*, **35**, 128–52.

Davenport, S. (2005), Exploring the Role of Proximity in SME Knowledge-Acquisition, *Research Policy*, **34**, 683–701.

Delbaggio, K., Hauser, C.J. and Kaufmann, M. (2018), The Proximity Bias of Communication Recorded on Twitter in Switzerland, in Gråsjö, U., Karlsson, C. and Bernhard, I. (eds), *Geography, Open Innovation and Entrepreneurship*, Cheltenham, UK and Northampton, MA, USA: Edward Elgar Publishing, pp. 190–220.

Dixit, A.K. and J.E. Stiglitz (1977), Monopolistic Competition and Optimum Product Diversity, *American Economic Review*, **67**, 297–308.

Drejer, I. and A.L. Vinding (2007), Searching Near and Far: Determinants of Innovative Firms' Propensity to Collaborate across Geographical Distance, *Industry and Innovation*, **14**, 259–75.

Feldman, M., T. Hadjimichael and L. Lanahan (2016), The Logic of Economic Development: A Definition and Model for Investment, *Environment and Planning C: Government and Policy* 2016, **34**, 5–21.

Florida, R. (2002), *The Rise of the Creative Class*, New York: Basic Books.

Fritsch, M. and P. Mueller (2004), The Effects of New Business Formation on Regional Development over Time, *Regional Studies*, **38**, 961–76.

Fujita, M. and J.-F. Thisse (2002), *Economics of Agglomeration – Cities, Industrial Location and Regional Growth*, Cambridge: Cambridge University Press.

Grant, R. and C. Baden-Fuller (2004), A Knowledge Accessing Theory of Strategic Alliances, *Journal of Management Studies*, **41**, 61–84.

Hong, L. and S.E. Page (2001), Problem Solving by Heterogenous Agents, *Journal of Economic Theory*, **97**, 123–63.

Huggins, R. and N. Williams (2011), Entrepreneurship and Regional Competitiveness: The Role and Progression of Policy, *Entrepreneurship and Regional Development*, **23**, 907–32.

Jacobs, J. (1969), *The Economy of Cities*, London: Vintage.

Johansson, B. and Å.E. Andersson (1998), A Schloss Laxenburg Model of Product Cycle Dynamics, in Beckmann, M. et al. (eds), *Knowledge and Networks in a Dynamic Economy*, Berlin: Springer, pp. 181–219.

Karlsson, C. (2007), Clusters, Functional Regions and Cluster Policies, *Working Paper Series in Economics and Institutions of Innovation 84*, Royal Institute of Technology, CESIS – Centre of Excellence for Science and Innovation Studies.

Karlsson, C. (2016), Clusters, in *The New Palgrave Dictionary of Economics*, London: Palgrave Macmillan, pp. 1–16.

Karlsson, C. and U. Gråsjö (2019), Knowledge Flows, Knowledge Externalities and Regional Economic Development, in Fischer, M.M. and P. Nijkamp (eds), *Handbook of Regional Science*, Berlin: Springer, pp. 1–28.

Lavie, D. (2009), Capturing Value from Alliance Portfolios, *Organizational Dynamics*, **38**, 26–36.

Malecki, E.J. (2007), Cities and Regions Competing in the Global Economy: Knowledge and Local Development Policies, *Environment and Planning C*, **25**, 638–64.

Özgen, C., P. Nijkamp and J. Poot (2011), Immigration and Innovation in European Regions, *IZA Discussion Paper 5676*, IZA, Bonn.

Peri, G. (2007), Higher Education, Innovation and Growth, in Brunello, G., P. Garibaldi and E. Wasmer (eds), *Education and Training in Europe*, Oxford: Oxford University Press, pp. 56–70.

Porter, M.E. (1998), Clusters and Competition: New Agendas for Companies, Governments, and Institutions, in Porter, M.E. *On Competition*, Boston, MA: Harvard Business School Press, pp. 197–287.

Porter, M.E. (2003), The Economic Performance of Regions, *Regional Studies*, **37**(6/7), pp. 549–78.

Qian, H. (2013), Diversity Versus Tolerance: The Social Drivers of Innovation and Entrepreneurship in US Cities, *Urban Studies*, **50**, 2718–35.

Rodriguez-Pose, A. and D. Hardy (2015), Cultural Diversity and Entrepreneurship in England and Wales, *Environment and Planning A*, **47**, 392–411.

Ter Wal, A. and R. Boschma (2011), Co-Evolution of Firms, Industries and Networks in Space, *Regional Studies*, **45**, 919–33.

Vernon, R. (1966), International Investment and International Trade in the Product Cycle, *Quarterly Journal of Economics*, **80**, 190–207.

Winter, S. (1984), Schumpeterian Competition in Alternative Technological Regimes, *Journal of Economic Behaviour and Organization*, **5**, 287–320.

2. A high-tech trajectory in a commodity-dependent economy: modern biotechnology in Norway

Terje Grønning

INTRODUCTION

Technological trajectories are "the paths by which innovations in a given field occur. The emergence of technological trajectories can be explained by the interplay between scientific advances, economic factors and institutional variables" (Innovation Policy Platform, 2013, p. 1, paraphrasing Dosi, 1982). But what happens when a location proven to be a latecomer to a developing global technological trajectory attempts to participate in the emerging high-tech trajectory?

Modern biotechnology may be perceived as one form of technological trajectory. It is a so-called "high technology" in the sense of being characterized by "research and development (R&D) expenditures, the use of scientific and technical personnel relative to total employment, and product sophistication" (Riche et al., 1983, p. 50). A fully-fledged participation in the global modern biotechnology trajectory would thus necessitate major investments and changes to a country's economy and to its knowledge practices related to research, development and education. Norway is in many accounts considered to be a highly developed country, but it is also a fact that large parts of its economy are dominated by activities geared towards the extraction of natural resources in the form of oil and gas, fisheries and hydroelectric power (Grønning et al., 2008; Ville and Wicken, 2012). In spite of Norway being recently classified as a "strong innovator", the cited classification exercise also points to weaknesses such as "lowest indicator scores . . . on Medium and high-tech product exports, Design applications, and Sales of new-to-market and new-to-firm product innovations" (European Commission, 2019, p. 74). Indeed, as of 2019, Norway has even been classified as a commodity-dependent country by the United Nations Conference on Trade and Development (UNCTAD, 2019).[1] There has thus been a debate for quite some time about how the country will accommodate an era when revenues from oil and gas extraction will diminish, and when a possible transition towards high-tech fields will be necessary (see e.g. OECD, 2018).[2] A case study of Norway regarding latecomer participation in an ongoing high-tech global trajectory may thus be illustrative.

Such research is important also in theoretical terms since the tradition of focusing on technological trajectories tends to operate on the global level, and focuses less on how actors at a national level perform within a trajectory (Dosi and Nelson, 2018). Such research may also be important for a practice and policy-related context, since many nations and regions aspire to partake in knowledge-intensive activities and strive for knowledge about cases where transitions from a focus on "low" technology to "high" technology may have occurred.

The focus within this chapter is, however, not entirely new, since it has been the focus within studies of advanced versus basic sectors or industries (Pavitt, 1984; Souitaris, 2002), of advanced versus laggard clusters (Avnimelech and Teubal, 2008; Bagchi-Sen, 2007; Powell et al., 1996), and of advanced versus laggard regions (see e.g. Isaksen and Trippl, 2014). I am indeed inspired by these studies, but aspire at the same time to contribute by way of consciously basing the study within the technological trajectory framework, rather than within the sector, cluster or region frameworks. One special rationale behind choosing this approach is that a technological trajectory may envelop several sectors at once in contrast to the sector level, which is delimited to the products and services pertaining to the particular sector. Studies of clusters and regions, which indeed often illuminate the understanding of how technologies evolve, may de-emphasize the way national-level institutions and policies influence a nation's economic direction. It appears to be especially relevant to contextualize policies at the national level regarding the fostering of particular technologies (Lall, 1992), and the location-related decisions of a firm also tend to include national-level factors according to whether these factors allegedly enable or discourage the activities the firm attempts to undertake (see e.g. List and Co, 2000). Within such a theoretical context my perspective is on a systemic level, and focuses on the institutions, policies and environmental prerequisites that new, small biotechnology firms appear to crave (de la Mothe, 2000). The overall research question is thus: How do scientific advances, economic factors and institutional variables impact firm formation within a new technological trajectory in a relatively laggard region?

However, in relation to the overall and wide research question, I have devised a delimited approach consisting in revealing only selected aspects of the emerging Norwegian part of the global biotech trajectory, since a comprehensive investigation would cover an extremely broad scope of variables. The following questions guide the delimited focus of the chapter:

1. How many firms have been created, what are their fields of activity, and how have they evolved?
2. What kinds of legislation and policies have existed, and have there been any changes as for legislative and policy contents?
3. What have the relations been, if any, between firms and policies?

Whereas the two first research questions are empirically oriented, it is especially the third research question that aims at a methodological and theoretical contribution by way of theorizing the way relations between firms and policies may be conceptualized as stages of development at the national trajectory level. I am, as mentioned, inspired by several of the preceding contributions regarding the way clusters and regions may be seen as undergoing stages or phases of development (Avnimelech and Teubal, 2008; Bagchi-Sen, 2007; Isaksen and Trippl, 2014; Powell et al., 1996). In this chapter, I conduct a translation of the insights from these previous cluster and region-level contributions to the national-level trajectory. However, the delimitations made within the current study result in illuminating only selected aspects, and I may subsequently offer merely a modest and tentative explanation as for the emergence and development of a nation's participation in a global trajectory.

The chapter's sections start with an overview of key theoretical perspectives relevant to the study followed by sections explaining the chosen methodology and presentations of findings regarding the number and character of firms, key legislative framework conditions and the number and character of policies. The final sections consist of a discussion and conclusion.

THEORETICAL PERSPECTIVES

The key concepts and theoretical perspectives of relevance to this study are, first, the notion of technological trajectories; secondly, the notions of trajectory phases at the national level; thirdly, periphery and center when it comes to participants within global technological trajectories; and fourthly, the character and roles of policies relevant for technological and economic development as well as the notion of co-evolution between policies and business segments.

A technological trajectory is, as mentioned, defined as "the paths by which innovations in a given field occur" (Innovation Policy Platform,

2013). The originator of the concept invariably links a trajectory to the corresponding concept of paradigm in the sense that the trajectory constitutes "the direction of advance within a technological paradigm" (Dosi, 1982, p. 148). A technological paradigm laying the foundation for the technological trajectory is explained as a "'model' and a 'pattern' of solution of *selected* technological problems, based on *selected* principles derived from natural sciences and on *selected* material technologies" (Dosi, 1982, p. 152, author's italics). The term "technological trajectory" thus refers within this tradition to the path of evolution emerging and developing after the initial emergence of a technology in a given field. Examples include the technological trajectories of aircrafts, helicopters, automobiles, and so on (Dosi and Nelson, 2018). Elsewhere, Dosi (1982) exemplifies the corresponding concept of technological paradigm as "'cluster of technologies', e.g. nuclear technologies, semiconductor technologies, organic chemistry technologies, etc." (Dosi, 1982, p. 152).

Adapted to my study, the modern biotechnology technological trajectory thus consists of a diverse portfolio of products and services, whereas the underlying modern biotechnology technological paradigm is the set of principles underlying modern biotechnology. A prevalent single definition of biotechnology that includes both traditional and modern biotechnology is that it is the "application of science and technology to living organisms, as well as parts, products and models thereof, to alter living or non-living materials for the production of knowledge, goods and services" (OECD, 2005, p. 9). In order to distinguish modern biotechnology developed from the latter half of the 20th century and onwards, the OECD has specified (and updates regularly) various techniques associated especially with modern biotechnology, that is, "DNA/RNA; proteins and other molecules; cell and tissue culture and engineering; process biotechnology techniques; gene and RNA vectors; bioinformatics; and nanobiotechnology" (OECD, 2005, p. 9).[3]

A related theoretical approach theorizes the emergence and evolution of regions as founded on one out of several knowledge bases, for example knowledge bases governed by analytical (or science based), synthetic (or engineering based) or symbolic (or creativity based) modes of knowledge creation (Boschma, 2018). The approach has been applied while analyzing, for example, biotechnology as representing a science-based knowledge base within a region crossing national borders (Moodysson et al., 2008), and knowledge bases and their skill requirements in the case of urban as well as rural Norwegian regions (Fitjar and Timmermans, 2018). This approach could have been feasible and interesting within studies discussing the evolution of technological trajectories at the national level. However, the ambition within this chapter is to cover the entire modern biotechnology business segment, and the knowledge bases approach has not been included due to the analytical difficulties pertaining to defining the knowledge bases in question in this particular case. In other words, the case could to some extent have been analyzed and discussed as a predominantly science-based case, but such a discussion would nevertheless be misleading since the business segment overall covers multiple knowledge bases.

In relation to the technological trajectories discourse, I thus focus on how nations attempt to take part in the global trajectory of modern biotechnology. One advantage when applying this concept at the national level is that it enables us to include all kinds of modern biotechnology firms and policies, as opposed to concepts such as industry or sector, which invariably presuppose specific or related products or services. Empirical research on technological trajectories has been based on quantitative analyses of, for example, patent citations, bibliographic citations or other types of quantitative indicators (see e.g. Verspagen, 2007). A few instances, however, include conceptualizations of a wider landscape constituting the trajectories at the intra-national level, including the notions of "specialized trajectories" (Grønning et al., 2008), "layers of national innovation systems" (Wicken, 2009), "innovation by co-evolution" (Sæther et al., 2011), and "industrial paths" (Altenburg et al., 2016). The current study will be an addition to this latter type of emerging literature.

Phases: within the technological trajectories tradition the notion of phases or stages has not, to the best of my knowledge, been utilized hitherto, with the exception of usage within the dominant design literature concerning "technology battles" (Suarez, 2004). However, in the literature focusing on the cluster level there have been a number of contributions attempting to theorize evolutionary patterns (see e.g. Belussi and Sedita, 2009; Fornahl and Hassink, 2017; Menzel and Fornahl, 2009; Trippl et al., 2015). One such contribution discusses the evolution of entrepreneurial clusters as three phases, where the first is the emergent phase characterized as entrepreneurial innovation ignited by exogenous events (Feldman et al., 2005). The second phase is characterized by self-organization in the sense of self-reinforcing feedbacks among actors as well as institutions and resources, and the third phase is maturation as a "rich innovative and entrepreneurial system" (Feldman et al., 2005, p. 132). The similar phase-based model proposed by Carlsson (2006) ranges from a latency phase, "in which a strong base of labor skills or human capital, or a significant research infrastructure is created in a region" (Carlsson, 2006, p. 251), via a second phase when "the cluster evolves further as entrepreneurs establish their own networks and build deep institutional infrastructures that constitute the industrial system or supply architecture of a region" (Carlsson, 2006, p. 251), to a final stage where "there is a fully functioning entrepreneurial environment where the success of the initial start-ups creates additional possibilities" (Carlsson, 2006, p. 252). Subsequently, the role of policies and policy instruments is likely to be adapted to the stage of evolution, with, for example, support for upgrading knowledge infrastructure having a greater role in the initial compared to later stages, whereas support for networking and so on attains a greater role in the second phase (Carlsson, 2006).

Trippl et al. (2015) divide in a similar fashion between the phases of emergence, growth, maturation and possible reinvigoration. In this model, the growth phase after the emergence phase is identified by strong growth of leading firms and entry of new firms, whereas the third phase may be envisioned as a phase of stagnation or even decline. However, the cluster may in a fourth phase reinvigorate itself, with new uses of skills and new actors. Also in a much similar vein an approach theorizes the five phases of background, pre-emergence, emergence, crisis and restructuring, and consolidation (Avnimelech and Teubal, 2008; Rosiello et al., 2011; Vence et al., 2013), thus covering from the background "before an industry appears when the initial conditions are present or being formed", to the consolidation in the form of "a potential reshaping and expansion of an established sector" (Vence et al., 2013, p. 873).

When borrowing from these insights and applying them analytically and hypothetically to the case of a technological trajectory at the national level, I find it useful to theorize in terms of the four potential phases of "latency", "self-organization and growth", "maturation", and "reinvigoration (or, eventually) decline". In other words, the gradual way of subdividing between the initial phases as proposed by, for example, Feldman et al. (2005), Carlsson (2006) and Vence et al. (2013) may be informative, at the same time as the inclusion of possible decline phases as proposed by Trippl et al. (2015) may be relevant. In addition, it appears as logical that one includes the possibility of abrupt decline or stagnation immediately after the first latency or second self-organization and growth phase.

Periphery versus center has been a prevalent issue in connection with research into why and how modern biotechnology firms succeed and how they tend to be situated in specific locations, and concerns mainly whether the biotechnology firm's environment is favorable to the firm (as it allegedly is in the "center") by way of potentially supplying towards its knowledge creation and development. Most biotechnology firms appear to require access to external knowledge, and in this regard the presence of public knowledge sources such as universities and government laboratories is stated to be vital (Owen-Smith and Powell, 2006). The presence of such world-class public knowledge institutions can contribute to scientific and technological developments by attracting the most talented students, researchers, academics and entrepreneurs (Kenney and Patton, 2006). The presence of local and large established firms within the industry as "anchors" (Feldman, 2003), and the possibility of interaction with other similar firms through networks may also act as enablers (Oliver, 2009).

Again, the level of analysis tends to be the cluster or the network (see e.g. Karlsen et al., 2011; Varis et al., 2014), whereas I propose that it should to some extent be possible to adapt this perspective to the national trajectory level.

Policies are goals formulated by policy-makers in order to influence the development of a society (Edler and Fagerberg, 2017), and may support firms in a variety of ways. Examples are policies that may function as support for basic research through, for instance, leveraged funds, tax benefits, and support for patenting and other intellectual property rights (IPR) activities, while having national capabilities in mind when setting the directions (de la Mothe, 2000). The *techniques*, for example leveraged funds mentioned previously, that are developed in order to achieve the policy goals are called *policy instruments* (Edler and Fagerberg, 2017, p. 11, my italics). In the section below on policies and policy instruments, I treat developments in Norway according to this vocabulary, however, while distinguishing further between policies on the one hand and institutions on the other hand. For instance, the example of tax benefits mentioned above may be part of a policy if it is a temporary measure specified with certain goals, but may be more fruitfully assessed as an institution when it is embedded within legislation and of a long-term nature. In addition, of special relevance within this chapter is the issue of whether a policy should be broadly encompassed, i.e. "horizontal", versus "targeted" at, for example, a particular sector, sub-sector or cluster. Avnimelech and Teubal (2008) define such targeting of policy as "triggering, reinforcing and sustaining the market-led evolutionary processes of the emergence of multi-agent structures (clusters, sectors, markets, product classes)" (Avnimelech and Teubal, 2008, p. 151). There may be four different types of targeting, where two are according the dimension of strong versus weak targeting (targeting of new fields versus support and upgrading of existing fields) and two are according to the dimension of direct versus indirect engagement (create parts of a system versus overcoming existing system failures) (Rosiello et al., 2013, p. 754). Referring back to the notion of stages or phases above, one might envision or expect that certain constellations of strong/weak and direct/indirect targeting appear to be suitable or logical within particular stages or phases of development.

One may furthermore attempt to describe how policies may be seen as *co-evolving* throughout time together with a technology or industry. There have been varying conceptions of co-evolution within the innovation and technology literature, ranging from a narrow conception to broader conceptions. The perhaps most noted example of a narrow conception is the work by Murmann (2003), where he links particular organizational features to particular national institutions. The notion of co-evolution is in this case thus laden with causal connotations. More often, studies applying the notion of co-evolution identify more broadly developments which occur in parallel (see e.g. Fagerberg et al., 2009; Murray, 2002; Nelson, 1995). There may also be causally or sequentially oriented relationships in these cases; however, rather than identifying specific causations the ambition in such studies becomes descriptive and analytical in the sense of providing a basis for discussing possible relationships and plausibilities. In the context of this study, co-evolution is understood in the broad tradition and concerns "how private and public institutions, and public programs and policies co-evolved with a technology and industry", and nations may subsequently "differ in their pace and pattern of institutional response to the birth and development of an industry" (Nelson, 1995, p. 171).

METHODOLOGY

The methodological challenge of this chapter has consisted in mapping in an adequate manner the actual extent and character of biotechnology firms on the one hand, and the extent and character of relevant institutions and policies on the other hand.

Regarding firms, the narrative covers the entire period from the first relevant firms emerging in the mid-1980s until 2017, whereas the main portion of the findings focuses on the situation between 2007 and 2017. The latter technique was due to the need to demonstrate any evolutionary trends in a consistent way. The specific year of 2007 was chosen because of the existence of some mapping exercises focusing on the period around 2005–2007 (Grønning, 2009; Innovation Norway and the Research Council of Norway, 2007; Marvik, 2005). In the same vein as preceding register-based studies conducted in Sweden (Sandström, 2014; Waxell and Malmberg, 2007), I first extracted from the government's publicly available register on business units in Norway as of 2017 (Brønnøysund Register Centre, 2018), and subsequently sorted extracted data through several steps. After having narrowed down to specific forms of incorporation, that is, including shareholding firms but excluding the self-employed, I first made a list of companies in NACE Rev 2 categories I deemed as most relevant to modern biotechnology, e.g. Code 72.11 Research and experimental development on biotechnology, and so on. Secondly, since I wanted to apply one of the most widespread and broad definitions of biotechnology (OECD, 2003) while restricting my survey to modern biotechnology, after careful consideration I eliminated those deemed as irrelevant to the study (e.g. eliminating firms within traditional biotech, such as bakeries and breweries, and firms within traditional pharmaceuticals). Thirdly, I checked my preliminary list against existing historical and contemporary reports or mapping exercises which included company-level information in order to ensure that there were no omissions from my sample. Fourthly, I identified and included as one single firm all business units which were established as projects or separate firms while being fully or majority owned by their mother firm in order to gain an accurate, rather than a nominal, overview of actual firms.[4]

Next, I downloaded the annual accounts for 2017 and 2007 (when applicable) for each of the firms remaining in the above mentioned list from the government's publicly available register of annual accounting reports (Brønnøysund Register Centre, 2019). Based on information in these annual accounts, I eliminated further firms found as irrelevant, as well as (1) dividing the remaining 310 firms into dedicated and partial biotech firms according to whether they conduct a majority or minority of their activities within modern biotech, and (2) collecting and sorting information regarding year of establishment, number of employees, and accumulated capital.[5]

The 310 firms regarded as relevant for analysis were then divided into one out of five firm categories organized according to whether they were assumed to aim at long-term (therapeutics; diagnostics) versus shorter-term (technology services; healthcare; industrial biotechnology) development time for products or services. The first two types, therapeutics and diagnostics, should be self-explanatory, whereas technology service provision covers platform technologies (including bioinformatics), informational services including breeding technologies, and contract research organizations (CROs). Healthcare covers food additives (e.g. development of omega 3 oils etc.) and cosmetics including wound care. Industrial biotechnology covers environmental biotechnology and bioproduction. Within the sample study there is a group of 16 companies denominated as therapeutics, partial. These firms are not analyzed in full, but are included as a point of reference and comparison. They are firms within pharmaceuticals, mostly subsidiaries of foreign firms focusing on distribution and sales and some smaller firms originating in Norway within traditional pharmaceuticals.

Regarding institutions and policies, my focus has been on major institutions, relevant policies and several policy instruments that may influence the development of an environment hospitable or hostile to the modern biotechnology sector. The policies have either been applied throughout the country or directed at specific regions. Furthermore, some of the selected policies and policy instruments are only semi-targeted in the sense of covering various sectors, whereas others are targeted at biotechnology. Primary sources regarding policies have been strategy documents, white papers and reports from the government and its affiliated main agencies, Innovation Norway and the Research Council of Norway. After listing policy instruments chronologically and according to their degree of relevance to the trajectory, I assessed them according to their potential impact or significance in terms of funding sizes as well as for the way they target either basic science and technology, applied science and technology, or commercialization of scientific and technological activities.

A third source of information was three 1–1.5 hour interviews in May–June 2019 with three persons deeply involved in various roles within biotechnology-related matters in Norway. The interviews concerned both factual circumstances of key events identified within the chapter as well as opinions about business and policy developments.

I next turn to the empirical results, which are presented in two successive sections focusing on the number and character of firms and on the number and character of relevant legislations, policies and policy instruments.

NUMBERS AND TYPES OF FIRMS

I present here the findings regarding presence or absence of firms active within modern biotechnology. These findings concern the number and types of biotechnology-related firms in Norway, the timing of entries and exits, examples of successful or potentially successful products and services, and the situation as for firms organizing themselves in networks.

Of the 280 firms existing in 2017 (Table 2.1), 237 of the firms may be classified as *dedicated* to activities within modern biotechnology, compared to 115 in 2007, indicating a net increase of 122 firms in about a decade. There were 43 firms which I deem as being only *partially* involved in biotechnology in 2017 (including an extra-sample group of therapeutics, partial, companies as explained below), compared to 37 firms in 2007, a net increase of 6 firms. These figures include 16 selected firms within the reference segment of therapeutics, partial, and the net figures for the remaining four segments ranging from diagnostics, partial, to industrial biotechnology, partial, were 21 and 27 firms in 2007 and 2017.

As for dedicated firms, most firms as of 2017 were within healthcare (67 firms). A majority of these have activities within marine-related products, for example omega 3, whereas a select few operate within other food additives, cosmetics and wound care. Therapeutics was next (64 firms),

Table 2.1   Selected characteristics of sample firms

	Firms existing in:		Evolution 2008–2017		
	2007	2017	Established	Dissolved	Increase
Therapeutics	24	64	42	2	40
Diagnostics	12	26	18	4	14
Technology services	28	45	28	11	17
Healthcare	39	67	35	7	28
Industrial biotech	12	35	29	6	23
Sub-total	115	237	152	30	122
Therapeutics, partial	16	16	0	0	0
Diagnostics, partial	4	4	0	0	0
Tech-services, partial	7	9	2	0	2
Healthcare, partial	4	7	0	0	3
Industrial, partial	6	7	1	0	1
Sub-total	37	43	3	0	6
Total	152	280	153	30	128

Notes: Dissolved firms also include those both established and dissolved in 2008–2017. One industrial biotech firm was first dissolved and then immediately re-established and is thus not included in the "Dissolved" column. One healthcare and one technology service firm existing in 2007 were relocated overseas and are thus not included in the "Existing in 2017" or "Dissolved" columns.

Source: Constructed based on Brønnøysund Register Centre (2019).

including a number of firms specializing in oncology (see below) and firms within veterinary medicine (e.g. vaccines for the aquaculture industry). Technology services was represented with 45 firms, and is a segment with both human-oriented services as well as technologies for veterinary purposes including, for example, testing for the aquaculture industry and livestock breeding-related services within agriculture. Industrial biotech was represented with 35 firms, whereas diagnostics including drug delivery stands out as the smallest segment in terms of firm numbers (26 firms).

Employment in the firms as of 2007 and 2017 calculated as the number of full-time equivalent (FTE) employees each year (i.e. the number reported by companies in their annual report submitted to the register) was as shown in Table 2.2. Although the category "therapeutics, partial" is, as mentioned, included only as a reference, the total number of employees in these firms surpasses all the others followed only by "diagnostics, partial" firms. Within the former group one may find, for example, the firm Takeda's subsidiary, and in the latter group one may find, for example, the GE Healthcare subsidiary in Norway. It is, however, noteworthy that the

Table 2.2	*Number of employees per segment (and average employees per firm in segment)*

Year	Firm types	Therapeutics	Diagnostics	Tech.services	Healthcare	Industrial biotech
2007	Dedicated	351 (15)	117 (10)	179 (6)	755 (19)	100 (8)
	Partial	2008 (126)	1655 (414)	327 (47)	201 (50)	1913 (319)
2017	Dedicated	611 (10)	104 (4)	325 (7)	1188 (18)	237 (7)
	Partial	1541 (96)	1172 (293)	315 (35)	355 (51)	1111 (159)

Notes:	Figures are rounded up or down to closest full FTE. 2007 data for one Healthcare partial firm are for 2008, not 2007 (see endnote no. 5).

Source:	Compiled from data retrieved from Brønnøysund Register Centre (2019), Aker Biomarine (2008), and Orkla (2008).

total number of employees within both "therapeutics, partial", as well as "diagnostics, partial", has decreased between 2007 and 2017.

As for the dedicated sub-groups in focus within this chapter, the number of employees is highest within healthcare, with 1188, an increase from 755. Therapeutics follows, with 611, an increase from 351. Dedicated industrial biotechnology appears to struggle, with 100 employees in 2007 and 237 employees in 2017.

The average number of employees per firm is also a matter of concern (Table 2.2). Due to the large influx of new firms (see Table 2.1 and also Figure 2.1), the total number of employees has increased, while the average number of employees per firm has decreased within all categories of dedicated firms except in the case of technology services. Assuming, as mentioned in the section on methods, that the categories of therapeutics, diagnostics and technology services might contain most R&D-intensive activities, it follows that it might be unfortunate to have very limited resources in terms of FTEs at the same time as there are high levels of ambition.

Although somewhat dated, figures from Sweden and Denmark show that the average number of employees in these types of firms are not particularly high there either, but they are nevertheless considerably higher than Norway (see Table 2.3).

A similar reflection arises from the overview of equity (Table 2.4).[6] Although the total amounts of equity accumulated might seem impressive, including increases from 2007 to 2017, the average of equity per firm appears to be modest, especially in assumedly resource-intensive categories of dedicated firms such as therapeutics, diagnostics and technology services. Incidentally, firms within these three categories will presumably

Table 2.3   *Number of companies and employees in Swedish and Danish life science industries, selected years*

Survey	Year	Companies	Employment	Av. employees per firm
Sweden, survey I	2006	809	34 427	43
	2009	851	31 776	37
	2012	791	29 652	37
Sweden, survey II	2014	890	28 948	33
	2016	1101	Ca. 30 000	27
Denmark, survey I	2006	280	39 375	141
	2009	325	36 384	112
Denmark, survey II	2005	349	65 192	187
	2005	561	67 640	121

Notes: Includes life sciences, and thus excludes environmental biotechnology etc. and includes e.g. medical technology and some pharmaceuticals not included in the present study on Norway.

Sources: Compiled based on Sandström (2014, p. 133) regarding Sweden survey I and Wadell (2016, p. 6, 2018, pp. 16–17) regarding Sweden survey II; Gestrelius et al. (2008, p. 33) and Sandström et al. (2011, p. 41) regarding Denmark survey I; and IRIS Group (2017, p. 5, apparently including sales firms) regarding Denmark survey II, while calculating and adding rounded average employees per firm.

Table 2.4   *Total equity (and average equity per firm) for each segment, 2007 and 2017 (NOK million)*

Year	Types of firms	Therapeutics	Diagnostics	Tech. services	Healthcare	Industrial biotech
2007	Dedicated firms	950.3	330.5	245.2	2102.8	10.6
		(39.6)	(27.5)	(8.8)	(53.9)	(0.9)
	Partial firms	2141.6	746.3	228.4	992.5	3706.8
		(133.9)	(186.6)	(32.6)	(248.1)	(617.8)
2017	Dedicated firms	3691.6	746.6	306.4	3684.9	274.1
		(57.7)	(28.7)	(6.8)	(55.0)	(7.8)
	Partial firms	6362.7	9662.2	329.1	1770.6	4282.2
		(397.7)	(2415.6)	(36.6)	(252.9)	(611.7)

Note: Average figures are calculated based on raw data full figures, while final total and average figures in the table are rounded up or down to the nearest 100 000.

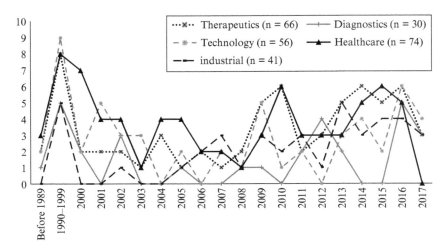

Note: Shows the dedicated firms existing in 2017 as well as firms dissolved before 2017.

Source: Constructed based on Brønnøysund Register Centre (2019).

Figure 2.1   Year of establishment of dedicated firms

have the longest development times before receiving any revenues from sales, and a modest amount of equity therefore signals that feasibility for long-term survival of the firm may be in jeopardy. As for the last two categories of firms, healthcare and industrial biotechnology, there are also cases (although not rendered explicitly in Table 2.4) where firms have taken out loans in addition to raising equity through investments.

Entries of new firms 2007–2017 are most numerous in the case of therapeutics, with 42 new establishments (Figure 2.1; see also Table 2.1). Healthcare had, as mentioned, the top notch in terms of the total number of firms, but had fewer new establishments (35 firms). Technology services had somewhat fewer new entries than healthcare (28 firms), whereas industrial biotech had 29 entries and diagnostics 18 new entries. In the case of firms being only partially involved in biotechnology, the movements are less dramatic as there are only three new establishments across all segments.

I have identified three waves or sudden outbursts of new firms' entries (2000–2001, 2008–2009 and 2012–2013; see Figure 2.1). First and perhaps most noteworthy is the therapeutics trend around 2010 when several immunology-related companies were established, including: Nordic Nanovector (est. 2009), Nextera (2009), Targovax (est. 2010), Oncoinvent (est. 2010) and Ultimovacs (est. 2011). These firms constitute as of 2018 the Norwegian Immuno-Oncology Consortium, together with the firms PCI

Biotech (est. 2000), Lytix Biopharma (est. 2003), Vaccibody (est. 2006), BerGen Bio (est. 2007), as well as the bioinformatics firm Oncoimmunity (est. 2014). Technology services had in contrast many early establishments (i.e. before 2000).

Exits, on the other hand, may be divided into the two categories of negative exits (bankrupt or otherwise dissolved) and positive exits (acquired, merged or transferred abroad). Addressing only the segment of dedicated firms, I have identified most negative exits within technology services (11 firms), diagnostics (4 firms), and healthcare (7 firms). Most of these firms were, as far as I could find, micro firms at the time of dissolution. Exceptions include the firms Mole Genetics and LingVitae within technology services, which both at one time had employment at the two-digit level. Lifandis, also within technology services, was aimed at commercializing genetic data as a biobank venture in collaboration with one of the universities in Norway (5 employees at the time of dissolution in 2016). Incidentally, two other firms in biobanking or related activities, Bovibank and Genova, were both dissolved in 2015. Three larger dissolutions concern the healthcare firm Zymtech Production, with nine employees at the time of their bankruptcy in 2016, the therapeutics firm Clavis Pharma, which had about 30 employees at the time it ceased to operate as a biotech firm in 2013, and the diagnostics firm Diagenic, which went from 17 employees in 2012 down to 11 in 2013 at the time of its dissolution (Bakke, 2013; DiaGenic ASA, 2014; Heitkøtter, 2016). Incidentally, both Clavis Pharma and Diagenic had before their demise often been mentioned during the 2000s as among the most promising within Norwegian biotech (see e.g. Innovation Norway and the Research Council of Norway, 2010). In the case of both firms, their demise was immediately preceded by disappointing results from clinical or exploratory studies of their core projects.

Acquisitions by foreign firms, albeit with a continuation of activity in Norway and included as 2017 firms in Table 2.1, are 2013 cases within therapeutics, with the firm Algeta Innovations being acquired by Bayer and the healthcare firm Pronova Biopharma being acquired by BASF.

In order to determine whether the influx of new firms to this technological trajectory is high or low, the developments within the smaller industries like, for example, mining and utilities rendered within Table 2.5 might be of some indication. There are some fluctuations throughout the years in question, but both of these smaller industries end up with a somewhat higher figure than at the outset. A similar trend is observed for the other examples as well, although on another scale in terms of numbers. However, these examples are allegedly not of particular relevance to policy preferences within the country, with the possible exception of the utility example's relevance in terms of recent policy focus consisting in fostering a bio-economy.

Table 2.5　Number of businesses within five business segments, 2010–2018

	2010	2011	2012	2013	2014	2015	2016	2017	2018
Mining	73	85	92	92	110	81	69	87	94
Manufacturing	1439	1371	1616	1539	1589	1893	1888	1893	1765
Utilities	159	153	172	152	167	180	174	169	208
Construction	6632	6885	8516	8040	8046	8120	7850	7371	7393
Business services	3193	3298	3749	3560	3723	3901	3976	4187	4411

Source:　Central Bureau of Statistics in Norway.

Firms' associations started out from a relatively early stage in the form of the Norwegian Bioindustry Forum established in 2001. The Forum had membership fees and regular meetings and served as the coordinator when answering relevant calls for opinions launched by the authorities in connection with planned changes in legislation or policy. However, it had ceased activities by 2015, and biotechnology firms are currently represented by conventional Norwegian Employers' Federation sub-federations, mainly within the federation Norwegian Industry. Networks for firms and public institutes interested in particular fields include the Norwegian Immuno-Oncology Consortium and The Life Science Cluster. The latter is a collection of interested parties associated with the research park in the vicinity of the University of Oslo and was later (in 2019) converted into a formalized cluster under the auspices of Innovation Norway's cluster program. A network for industrial biotechnology functioned for several years with funding from Innovation Norway, but was eventually discontinued. On the other hand, regional associations focusing on cancer therapies, agricultural biotechnology and marine biotechnology respectively have eventually led to the formation of four different cluster constructs under the cluster policy program as described below within the sub-section presenting policies and policy instruments (see next section).

I find that biotechnology-related business in Norway has evolved in terms of three phases. The first period was the *period of emergence and first results (1986–2005)* starting with the very first dedicated biotech firm Dynal AS established in 1986 (later acquired by a foreign company). There were relatively few firms overall (Marvik, 2005 lists only 110 firms in his overview), albeit also a couple of cases of success in terms of firms (as in the case of Dynal) being internationally acquired. This phase was superseded by a *period of attempted consolidation (2006–2012)*, when two of the segments were consolidated in terms of having new central firms established which continue to be central to the trajectory (a new healthcare, partial, firm called Aker Biomarine established in 2005) and a number of therapeutics firms specializing within onco-immunology established between 2006 and 2011. The third phase denominated a *period of contradictions (2013–)* is characterized as being a period of contrasts between additional successes and failures. Two of the firms within therapeutics and diagnostics respectively, which had been highlighted as high potential firms during the preceding period and had significant (in this context) numbers of employees were discontinued in 2013. At the same time there were the large mergers and acquisitions of the formerly indigenous firms Algeta and Pronova Biopharma, and a significant influx of new firms.

INSTITUTIONS, POLICIES AND POLICY INSTRUMENTS

In this section I first give a brief overview of the legislation relevant to biotechnology and to selected general activities that enhance increasing knowledge intensity, since an insight into this institutional setting is indispensable for understanding the context of firms and policies presented in the subsequent sub-sections. Secondly, I review policies and policy instruments relevant to biotechnology.

Brief Overview of Legislative Setting

Legislation as well as other framework conditions may obviously enable or restrict the activities of the firms and give direction to the policy activities. Overall, the institutional environment specific to biotechnology has been relatively stable throughout the period in question, whereas the broad legislation includes a number of more recent additions (Table 2.6).

The first modern biotechnology legislation consists of the Gene Technology Act (1993) and the Biotechnology Act (1994). The former concerns the production and use of genetically modified organisms and so on, and the latter provides the legal framework for organizations that are operating within biotechnology. A rough assessment with comparison to more liberal examples of legislation such as, for example, USA would find that legislation in Norway is comparatively restrictive with, for example, prohibitions regarding both genetically modified organism (GMO) research as well as research on embryonic stem cells while being more or less on a par with most EU countries. There have afterwards been only a few minor revisions in the Act, but legislation is as of 2019 up for revision in order to accommodate recent developments within biotechnology. The implication for biotechnology firms already located in or contemplating

Table 2.6   Legislation and policies relevant to biotechnology (1990s–2017)

	Horizontal and semi-targeted	Targeted
Legislation	The budgetary rule concerning the usage of capital gains from the Government Pension Fund Global (2001) Skattefunn ("Tax Find") (2002) University Act (2002) Aim to use 3% of gross domestic product (BNP) for R&D (2005)	Gene Technology Act (1993) Biotechnology Act (1994)
Policies	White Paper on higher education (1985) Strategy plans "Research for future" including action plans for biotechnology (1994 & 1998) White Paper on research advocating expanded support for marine-based industries (1999) Five-Year Plan to overturn the negative growth in the field of natural science studies (2002–2007) White Paper "The Will to Research" (2004–2005) White Paper "Climate for Research" (2008–2009) National strategy for natural sciences (2015)	National strategy for biotechnology (1998) National Biotechnology Strategy (2011–2020) National strategy for bio-economy (Nov. 2016) HealthCare21 (HelseOmsorg21) (2013–)

Note: There were no major policies specific to biotechnology during 1999–2010. An additional semi-targeted White Paper was issued in 2019 entitled "Health Businesses".

a move to Norway is, however, that it is impossible to conduct the most advanced or controversial types of R&D as part of their activities.

There are in addition several major horizontal or semi-targeted legislations that may influence biotech activities within the country, including the Tax Find (i.e. SkatteFUNN) arrangement in operation since 2001. This institution gives firms conducting R&D a 20 percent (in the case of small firms) or 18 percent (for large firms) tax deduction from R&D project costs. The University Act of 2002 gives universities the right to benefit from commercialization of their researchers' scientific inventions, and has therefore facilitated the establishment of technology transfer offices (TTOs) at all the major universities and hospitals.

A practice unique to the Norwegian context is a budgetary rule executed since 2001 and subsequently embedded in a 2005 Act concerning how the state may use the state's revenues from oil and gas extraction activities

(Government of Norway, 2005). Normally, an annual maximum of 4 percent of the capital gains within government budgets from the country's oil revenues may be consumed, and this rule subsequently regulates the way the Government can spend this extraordinary income on both ordinary expenditures (e.g. welfare) as well as on extraordinary measures such as, for example, innovation policy instruments. Related to this rule are instructions regarding the way the country manages its direct revenues from oil and gas extraction activities through placements in a huge investment fund. The state owns shares in a number of domestic firms, such as within the oil and gas industry. But it should be noted that in order to avoid favoritism towards specific sectors and corporations, these "new" funds based on the generation of state wealth may not be invested directly in domestic corporations or sectors (Government of Norway, 2010). Subsequently the state does not channel funds directly into domestic sectors or technologies such as biotechnology-related activities, except for delimited inputs into select seed funding schemes.

An institution which may function as a constraint towards investing in high risk endeavors is the existence of a so-called wealth tax on a corporation's capital and on the shares an individual holds in, for example, start-ups.[7] This is an institution which as of 2018 exists only in Norway, France, Spain and Switzerland among OECD countries (Government of Norway, 2018), and may function as a disincentive regarding long-term private investments in highly insecure projects (Kreutzer, 2018; Sasson, 2011). The government recently asked an expert group for advice regarding the continuation or abolishment of this institution (Government of Norway, 2018), but as of 2019 de-institutionalization has not yet taken place.

Policies and Policy Instruments

Horizontal policies on innovation and entrepreneurship may sometimes be interpreted as being related to biotechnology in the sense of containing a component of biotechnology or acting as an enabler for biotechnology-related activities. The very first horizontal policy may be traced to a Government White Paper on higher education from 1985 (see Table 2.6), in which biotechnology became one of the five main target areas (Government of Norway, 1985).[8] Subsequently, the Research Council of Norway (RCN) created in 1994 its first strategy plan named "Research for Future" (later revised in 1998), followed by the 1999 government White Paper on Research. The latter advocated expanded support for marine industries. From the 2000s a series of follow-up policies include a Five-Year Plan to overturn the negative growth in the field of natural science studies (2002–2007), the White Paper "The Will to Research" (2004–2005), the White Paper "Climate for Research" (2008–2009), and a National strategy for natural sciences (2015). The several general policy instruments that were developed during this period include the programs administered by the Research Council of Norway FORNY (translated "Renew", 1995–2004, later prolonged as FORNY2020 (2011–)) for financing start-ups and young firms via TTOs, and a user-driven research-based innovation program called BIA (2006–) for providing financing for R&D projects. The latter program has developed into a sizable and main component within innovation enabling measures, and had a budget of NOK 670 million in 2016 alone (Røtnes et al., 2017). The program was supplemented with a similar program especially targeting the business located in rural regions called VRI (2007–17).

Horizontal programs administered by the agency Innovation Norway include a scheme consisting in providing low-risk loans which allocated NOK 2498 million in loans in 2017, more innovation- or risk-associated loans (NOK 1352 million in 2017), and startup loans (NOK 108 million in 2017). In addition, Innovation Norway's several support schemes include pre-seed funding (NOK 50 million in 2017), grants to Phase I startups (NOK 40 million in 2017), grants to Phase 2 startups (NOK 242 million in 2017), R&D contracts (NOK 298 million in 2017), a program called guarantee for growth (NOK 142 million in 2017), guarantees for working capital (NOK 20 million in 2017), and miscellaneous other grants (NOK 2224 million in 2017) (Kreutzer, 2018).

Targeted policies and policy instruments for biotechnology emerge from the early 1990s in the wake of the horizontal 1985 White Paper and other White Papers mentioned above, and led first, as mentioned, to more emphasis on marine industries. There were initiatives which focused especially on the promotion of marine ("blue") biotech, such as the establishment of the Council on Marine Value Creation (RMV) in 2003 and the Marine Biobank in 2005, both directed to improve access to expertise in this area. There was also a focus on life sciences broadly conceived, as seen in some of the programs mentioned below. Later, a National Biotechnology Strategy (2011–2020) targeted the four areas of (1) aquaculture, seafood and marine; (2) agriculture-based food and biomass production; (3) environmentally friendly industrial processes and products; and (4) healthcare.

In Table 2.7 showing the expenditures of public R&D funding channeled through the Research Council of Norway in 2007 and 2017 respectively, the amounts for R&D support specified as biotechnology-related constitute relatively small parts of the annual budgets. However, biotechnology-related projects could also be funded through other pro-

*Table 2.7   Research Council of Norway budget subdivided into purposes
(2007 and 2017)*

	2007	2017
"Food"	503 000	–
"Ocean"	251 700	1 019 236
"Energy and environment" (2007) / "Climate, environment and environmentally friendly energy" (2017)	722 300	1 193 747
"Health" (2007) / "Improved public services" (2017)	484 200	845 462
ICT	315 900	329 375
Biotechnology	347 200	169 950
"New materials/nanotechnology" (2007) / "Nanotechnology" (2017)	104 800	146 586
"Research for entrepreneurship and innovation" (2007) / "An innovative and change receptive business environment" (2017)	1 976 400	1 550 436
"Basic research" (2007) / "World leading scientific milieu" (2017)	1 708 600	2 242 808
"Internationalization" (2007) / "Other themes" (2017)	361 600	2 107 713
Total	6 775 700	9 605 312

Note: Million NOK. 2007 figures are planned estimates based on 2006 expenditures, and 2017 figures are revised budgets.

Source: RCN 2007 and 2017 budgets.

grams including, for example, "Food" in 2007 and "Ocean" in 2007 and 2017. Under the labels "Food" and "Ocean" and so on the RCN organized calls for applications ordered into specific programs. A series of smaller-scale targeted programs were organized, including the establishment of the European Laboratory for Marine Biology in Bergen (1994) and the establishment of a user-driven program targeting the process and mineral industry (PROSMAT, 1996–2000).

A five-year program called BIOT2000 (2000–2005) with an approximate NOK 142.2 million budget aimed at creating competent experts within the industry and increasing research quality, whereas the GNBIO program (2001–2008) aimed at accelerating basic nutritional biotechnology research. The NOK 200 million PROSBIO program (2002–2005) targeted R&D in biomedicinal companies, and a NOK 120 million program encouraging activities within marine bioprospect was initiated (and later incorporated within the FUGE program; see below). Somewhat later, a series of still comparatively small programs included the establishment of Norway Biobank (2011–2018), a Stem Cell Program (2013–2017), the establishment of the Norwegian Centre for Digital Life (2016) focusing on biotechnology research, innovation and education, and the BIONÆR program (2012–2021) that had its major focus on fostering Norwegian bio-based industries. Furthermore, the NevroNors (2006–) network for facilitating research funding for neuroscience research relevant to healthcare, the Centre of Molecular Inflammation Research (CEMIR) in 2013, the Centre for Cancer Biomarkers (CCBIO) in 2013, and Hamar BioSmia bio-economy center were established in order to improve skills and to improve systemic capability. The Norway Food from Land and Sea program (MATPROGRAMMET, 2006–2008) by RCN, and the Innovation Norway administered an environmental technology-oriented MILJØTEKNOLOGI program (2010–) primarily as a means of improving access to expertise.

In our context, however, the largest RCN administered programs have been the Functional Genomic Research program (FUGE, 2002–2011) providing major support in knowledge and innovation development within biotech (ca. NOK 1.6 billion total expenditure) and the ongoing (as of 2019) BIOTEK2021 program (2012–2021, with an estimated budget of ca. NOK 1.45 billion). Both of these programs targeted basic research, however. Firms could obviously participate in conjunction with research institutes or universities, but they were expected to submit applications to a more horizontal program such as BIA or the measures administered by Innovation Norway in the cases where they were the lead applicant.

During roughly the same period Innovation Norway initiated a policy orientation consisting in fostering clusters of businesses, research organizations, universities, and so on. Especially relevant to the context of this chapter are the clusters Oslo Cancer Cluster (2006–), Blue LegaSea (2009–) in North-West Norway, which involves, for example, healthcare-related businesses based on marine resources as well as other marine-related industries, Biotech North in Northern Norway (2010–), and the Heidrun Biocluster in Eastern Norway (2018–) focusing mainly on agricultural biotechnology.

In the later parts of the period there has been renewed attention on health issues as well as a focus on participation in the so-called bio-economy. The HelseOmsorg21 (2013) initiative is one of the country's several 21st-century oriented councils discussing possibilities for creating a total value chain for various domains, in this case healthcare. National Strategy for Bio-economy (2016) calls for climate change rectifying measures including bioprocessing, for example. In addition, there has been continued attention on "blue" industry during this period with, for example, the program HAVBRUK2 (2015–), which was initiated to increase R&D in fisheries and aquaculture.

The authorities' strategizing and policy creation towards biotechnology from the late 1980s until 2017 can thus be roughly divided into three periods based on how the focus of the policies changed. *The policy formation period (1985–2000)* consisted mostly of policies which were of a horizontal nature, albeit with a national strategy for biotechnology that was issued close to end of this period in 1998 as the only targeted policy in this field. *The basic research and marine biotech policy focus period (2001–2010)* can be identified by the commencement of horizontal policies focusing on expansion of research and creating business infrastructure, especially in marine industries. *The new pluralistic policy strategy period (2011–)* has had semi-horizontal policies and policy instruments with a broad focus as well as a recent focus on the bio-economy in its broader sense, simultaneous with some focus areas such as life science and a continued focus on marine resources.

It is obviously beyond the scope of this chapter to present a comprehensive comparison with Sweden and Denmark, but it is noteworthy that the developments within the policy realm appear to be rather different. In the case of the two neighboring countries there appears to have been a larger set of horizontal policies supplemented with cluster policies in early stages, then increasing targeting of specific clusters (e.g. "Medicon Valley" in the Copenhagen and Scania area) during the early 2000s (Pålsson and Gregersen, 2011; Vence et al., 2013; Waxell and Malmberg, 2007) and finally more recent semi-targeting processes enveloping the entire spectrum of life sciences entitled Growth Plan for Life Science in the case of Denmark (2016–) and Life sciences road map in the case of Sweden (2018–). While the latter semi-targeting of life sciences is also included in the Norwegian new pluralistic policy strategy period from 2011 and onwards, the semi-targeting appears to cover more broadly in the Norwegian case in the sense of spanning the entire bio-economy and reflects the absence of a strong pharmaceutical basis in this country.

DISCUSSION

In this section, I look at the way the Norwegian trajectory appears when comparing the evolution of the business and policy spheres, that is, whether they evolved in parallel or according to some co-evolutionary mechanisms. I leave the sphere of biotech-specific legislation out of the discussion due to its relatively stable character throughout the period. Next, I look at the findings while utilizing the theoretically based model distinguishing between the four phases of latency, self-organization/growth, maturation and decline/reinvigoration, as well as revisiting the classic technological trajectory perspective as proposed by Dosi (1982) in order to theoretically evaluate my findings.

I find that biotechnology-related business in Norway has evolved in terms of three phases: a period of emergence and first results (until 2005), a period of attempted consolidation (2006–2012), and a period of contradictions (2013–) characterized as contrasts between simultaneous successes and failures. As for policies, I find it relevant also to distinguish between three phases in this case, however with a slightly different kind of dating. The period of policy formation (1985–2000) contains the first few attempts of formulating a targeted policy during the 1990s. There were still relatively few policy instruments in the first period, while the second period (2001–2010) consisted of increased basic research and marine biotech targeting. The third period of new pluralistic policy on biotech (2011–) starts with a revised National Biotechnology Strategy for 2011–2020. Rather than continuing the targeting of mainly therapeutics and marine biotech, the policy recommends the strengthening of the four sub-fields of marine, biomass, industrial, and health simultaneously, and I have hence denominated it as a pluralistic policy due to its semi-targeted/horizontal nature. Moreover, additional policies supporting the second, third and fourth of these fields even further were launched in the form of a policy on bio-economy mainly involving agricultural and industrial biotechnology in 2012 and 2016 and an awareness initiative on health and welfare-related innovations during 2013–2018.

In terms of parallel evolutions versus the possibility of co-evolutionary mechanisms, I interpret my findings as partial support of both cases. Evidence of parallel evolution includes the limited success of industrial biotechnology in spite of increasing policy focus on this sub-field. There have been several new firms, albeit with relatively small volume, within this field, and some firms are in addition represented in the bankruptcy statistics. There has been limited continuation, and in a sense an actual decline in terms of employee numbers, when it comes to diagnostics in spite of this field normally being referred to as one of the sub-areas in which Norway has the longest traditions and potential (Grønning, 2009). Within technology services, policy emphasis and the failure of biobank-related business activities appear to be a case of disharmony. There is also a contradiction between the dissolution of the bioindustry association in 2015 during a phase where there should be policies encouraging precisely this type of self-organization.

On the other hand, I find traces of possible co-evolution especially in the case of cancer focused firms and, to some extent, healthcare and technology services linked to aquaculture and agriculture. Whereas the first generation of cancer-related firms such as Photocure (est. 1993), PCI Biotech (est. 2000) and Algeta (est. 1997) had been established by 2000, several of the firms specializing within onco-immunology emerged between 2006 and 2011, that is, during or immediately after the period which included a policy focus on science-based, medically related activities. Other examples of possible co-evolution include the growth in this period of the part of the healthcare segment focusing on marine-based products and firms servicing the aquaculture industry either within therapeutics or within technology services in correspondence with the policy focusing on these areas.

Next, I turn to the exercise of comparing the phases formulated on the basis of empirical observations with the pre-existing theoretical notions of phases characterized as latency, self-organization/growth, maturation or decline/reinvigoration. I find that this issue can be discussed at two different levels, where the first level is to attempt to conceptualize the trajectory's firms and policies comprehensively and overall (Figure 2.2, third column "Theorized phases – Overall").

There have been pockets of success where individual firms as well as entire segments of firms have evolved further than others. The way policies

Business phases	Policy phases	Theorized phases	
		Overall	Segmental
Emergence and first results (1986–2005)	Policy formation (1985–2000)	Latency	Self-organization and growth in diagnostics firms; otherwise latency
	Mainly basic research and marine biotech focus (2001–2010)		From policy formation (latency) to targeting (maturation)
Attempted consolidation (2006–2012)		Latency evolving into some self-organization and potential growth	Self-organization and growth (parts of therapeutics, healthcare and technology services); Latency (industrial biotech): Maturation/decline (diagnostics)
Contradictions (2013–)	New pluralistic policy (2011–)		Persisting limited results in terms of most firms' growth, coupled with a change to broader (semi-targeted) policies

Figure 2.2   Business and policy phases compared to theorized phases

have been formulated and directed has also changed throughout the years. Nevertheless, I find that the trajectory in overall appears to have been within the latency phase for a prolonged period of time until around 2010, whereas the phase thereafter may be characterized as a possible transition between this latency phase and a second phase consisting in some self-organization and possible growth. However, when moving on to the second level of analysis, that is, each of the segments (Figure 2.2, fourth column "Theorized phases – Segmental"), I find a more complicated picture, where one of the segments (i.e. diagnostics) had first entered into a maturation phase and later appears to have devolved into a phase which may even be interpreted as decline. This was already at a time when other segments were either still in a latency phase (e.g. industrial biotechnology) or were gradually entering a self-organization and growth phase (e.g. cancer-related therapeutics, portions of healthcare and therapeutics and technology services linked to aquaculture).

As for an assessment vis-à-vis the original framework concerning technological trajectories as proposed by Dosi (1982), the findings may be interpreted as a case of country-level firm activities and policies attempting to partake in the global overreaching trajectory, albeit with somewhat mixed results. The mixed results, consisting in persistent latency coupled with partial self-organization and growth on the one hand simultaneously with maturation or even decline on the other hand, may perhaps be explained by the fact that the overall modern biotechnology trajectory is after all heterogeneously composed. The five categories within the "list-based definition" of biotechnology as proposed by OECD (2005) range, as mentioned previously, widely from DNA to sub-cellular organisms. My study identifies areas which appear to transition towards self-organization and growth, first and foremost within two sub-trajectories corresponding basically to the categories of cell and tissue culture and engineering (anti-cancer-related firms and policies focusing on immunology) and parts of the category called process biotechnology (omega 3-related healthcare and "blue" biotech policies). The more generic activities within diagnostics and the portion of the category process biotechnology concerning industrial biotechnology are, according to my analysis, either in possible decline or still within a latency phase in spite of having been highly focused on within policy. On the other hand, it is perhaps not to be expected that a small country like Norway will excel in all of the five sub-trajectories of modern biotechnology.

It is somewhat surprising that, having arrived at some distance into the process, the policies became more horizontal and in a sense more impatient in spite of the fact that the achieved number of established new firms and level of employment was still moderate and fragile. For public policy to have a decisive influence, it would perhaps have made more sense to focus on specific parts of the trajectory for longer periods until the trajectory showed that it was sustainable, instead of diversifying policies into a number of other areas at a relatively early stage.

CONCLUSION

In this study I have provided an overview of how modern biotechnology firms and policies have evolved in the case of Norway, and have in addition mentioned the situation regarding biotechnology relevant legislation. Several phenomena, such as limited success of industrial biotechnology and non-aquaculture technology services in spite of enabling policies also for these sub-fields, demonstrate that firms and policies have to some extent evolved separately from each other. However, other aspects, such as the growth of cancer research-related firms and of some of the marine bio-technology-based healthcare, therapeutics and technology services firms, may be interpreted as cases of co-evolution between firms and policies.

I have characterized the Norwegian part of the modern biotechnology trajectory as having evolved overall from a latency phase to a potential self-organization and growth phase, but cannot find enough evidence to characterize the trajectory as having entered a mature phase. In order to arrive at this conclusion, I have applied a framework for analysis inspired by both theorizations on the meso-level of cluster evolution and on the various facets of innovation policy. The resulting framework has been eclectic and tentative, but contributes as a methodological addition to analyses of technological trajectories as they may manifest themselves at the national level. As for insights into the technological trajectory approach, my study has demonstrated that it might be useful to investigate how a global trajectory manifests itself in the case where actors, that is, firms and policy makers, attempt to partake in the ongoing global trajectory.

However, the study also contains shortcomings and suggests potential for further research activities. In this study I can only provide part of the answer to what happened when biotechnology established itself in an economy heavily dominated by other incumbent sectors, This is due to the lack of more detailed data on business performance and a lack of attention to other parts of the trajectory, such as, for example, increase or decrease of biotechnology-related R&D within the public and semi-public sectors and the character of the nation's workforce, and so on. Furthermore, the project has had limited resources, and a more thorough review of the motivations of firms for having activities in Norway has been only partially, and not systematically, covered.

My aim has been to contribute with empirically based understanding of how national-level policies targeting a particular technology evolve in parallel or together with the evolution of a business segment which applies the technology targeted within policy. I find that there has been a process which is partly dominated and led by policies, a process which may be partly characterized as co-evolution between policies and firms, and a process where the firms partly appear to behave endogenously from policy. The study's findings and suggestions regarding theory and methodology may, in spite of having a highly tentative character, serve as a reference for practitioners and policy makers in a range of countries where incumbent natural resource extraction trajectories are being challenged by new knowledge-intensive trajectories.

ACKNOWLEDGEMENTS

I am grateful to interviewees Thor Amlie, Ole J. Marvik, and Tom E. Pike for sharing their profound insights about biotechnology in Norway, to Parisa Afshin for assistance in connection with initial data collection and analysis, to Yukie Hara for assistance in connection with initial data collection, to two anonymous reviewers and to discussants Hege Y. Hermansen and Dina M. Mansour for comments on early drafts, and to the Department of Education, University Oslo, for a travel grant in connection with an early draft conference presentation.

NOTES

1. "Export-commodity-dependent" is when a country is considered to have more than 60 percent of its total merchandise composed of commodities (UNCTAD, 2019, p. iv; for the case of Norway, see p. 155).
2. According to the OECD; "For Norway's society to remain inclusive as its petroleum resources decline and its population ages, the business sector will have to diversify to non-oil sectors and continue to exploit opportunities from globalisation and technological change" (OECD, 2018, p. 14).
3. When applied to agriculture and the environment, modern biotechnology has been defined as "the application of: a. In vitro nucleic acid techniques, including recombinant deoxyribonucleic acid (DNA) and direct injection of nucleic acid into cells or organelles, or b. Fusion of cells beyond the taxonomic family, that overcome natural physiological reproductive or recombination barriers and that are not techniques used in traditional breeding and selection" (Secretariat of the Convention on Biological Diversity, 2000, p. 4), with genetic engineering used to create GMOs as a prevalent example, whereas biotechnology in general is defined as "any technological application that uses biological systems, living organisms, or derivatives thereof, to make or modify products or processes for a specific use" (United Nations, 1993, p. 3).
4. All cases of small interrelated entities were counted as only one firm, except in a few

cases where the subsidiaries have attained a status and business model of their own differing from the mother firm by way of, for example, being listed on the stock exchange as separate business units. Orchestration firms (e.g. consultants) are not included in the study. For further details, see document "Data for publication 'A high-tech trajectory in a commodity-dependent economy: Modern biotechnology in Norway'", as uploaded to Zenodo (https://zenodo.org/).

5. For two firms, Borregaard within industrial biotech partial and Aker Biomarine within healthcare partial, some deviation from this approach was necessary since they experienced a change of status (and hence book-keeping practice) from 2007 to 2017. Thus, the source for 2007 figures regarding employees and equity are different for Borregaard (Orkla, 2008) and Aker BioMarine (2008) respectively. Moreover, the figures for Biomarine are for 2008 and not for 2007, due to a major reorganization of the latter in 2007.

6. In the tables and elsewhere in the chapter the real time amounts are inserted, meaning that 2007 figures should be incremented by 24.4 percent in order to be comparable with 2017 figures, since according to the Central Bureau of Statistics' consumer price index there was a 24.4 percent increase from 2007 to 2017 (https://www.ssb.no/kpi).

7. I am indebted to one of the interviewees for bringing to my attention the issue of wealth tax as a potentially significant factor.

8. That is: "Technically-oriented studies must be further expanded, and the following may be mentioned: high technology within computer subjects and physics, geology, geophysics, biotechnology (especially related to marine resources), mathematics and mathematical informatics" (Government of Norway, 1985, p. 59, my translation).

REFERENCES

Aker BioMarine (2008). *Årsrapport 2008*. Oslo: Aker BioMarine.

Altenburg, T., Sagar, A., Schmitz, H. and Xue, L. (2016). Guest editorial: Comparing low-carbon innovation paths in Asia and Europe. *Science and Public Policy*, **43**(4), 451–3.

Avnimelech, G. and Teubal, M. (2008). Evolutionary targeting. *Journal of Evolutionary Economics*, **18**(2), 151–66.

Bagchi-Sen, S. (2007). Strategic considerations for innovation and commercialization in the US biotechnology sector. *European Planning Studies*, **15**(6), 753–66.

Bakke, K.A. (2013). Kroken på døra for Clavis Pharma. *Dagens Medisin*, 2 April.

Belussi, F. and Sedita, S.R. (2009). Life cycle vs. multiple path dependency in industrial districts. *European Planning Studies*, **17**(4), 505–28.

Boschma, R. (2018). A concise history of the knowledge base literature: Challenging questions for future research. In: Isaksen, A., Martin, R. and Trippl, M. (eds), *New Avenues for Regional Innovation Systems: Theoretical Advances, Empirical Cases and Policy Lessons*. New York: Springer, pp. 23–40.

Brønnøysund Register Centre (2018). *Enhetsregisteret – Åpne Data*. Accessed 26 September 2018 at: https://data.brreg.no/enhetsregisteret/oppslag/enheter.

Brønnøysund Register Centre (2019). *Regnskapsregisteret*. Accessed 31 May 2019 at: https://www.brreg.no/om-oss/oppgavene-vare/alle-registrene-vare/om-regnskaps registeret/.

Carlsson, B. (2006). The role of public policy in emerging clusters. In: Braunerhjelm, P. and Feldman, M. (eds), *Cluster Genesis: Technology-Based Industrial Development*. Oxford: Oxford University Press, pp. 264–78.

de la Mothe, J. (2000). Biotechnology and policy in an innovation system. In:

de la Mothe, J. and Niosi, J. (eds), *The Economic and Social Dynamics of Biotechnology*. New York: Springer, pp. 215–33.

DiaGenic ASA (2014). *DiaGenic Annual Report 2013*. Oslo: Diagenic ASA.

Dosi, G. (1982). Technological paradigms and technological trajectories: A suggested interpretation of the determinants and directions of technical change. *Research Policy*, **11**(3), 147–62.

Dosi, G. and Nelson, R.R. (2018). Technological paradigms and technological trajectories. In: Augier, M. and Teece, D.J. (eds), *The Palgrave Encyclopedia of Strategic Management*. London: Palgrave Macmillan, pp. 1708–19.

Edler, J. and Fagerberg, J. (2017). Innovation policy: What, why, and how. *Oxford Review of Economic Policy*, **33**(1), 2–23.

European Commission (2019). *Biotechnology innovation scoreboard*. Accessed 2 February 2019 at: https://ec.europa.eu/docsroom/documents/36281.

Fagerberg, J., Mowery, D.C. and Verspagen, B. (2009). The evolution of Norway's national innovation system. *Science and Public Policy*, **36**(6), 431–44.

Feldman, M. (2003). The locational dynamics of the U.S. biotech industry: Knowledge externalities and the anchor hypothesis. *Industry and Innovation*, **10**(3), 311–29.

Feldman, M., Francis, J. and Bercovitz, J. (2005). Creating a cluster while building a firm: Entrepreneurs and the formation of industrial clusters. *Regional Studies*, **39**(1), 129–41.

Fitjar, R.D. and Timmermans, B. (2018). Knowledge bases and relatedness: A study of labour mobility in Norwegian regions. In: Isaksen, A., Martin, R. and Trippl, M. (eds), *New Avenues for Regional Innovation Systems: Theoretical Advances, Empirical Cases and Policy Lessons*. New York: Springer, pp. 149–71.

Fornahl, D. and Hassink, R. (eds) (2017). *The Life Cycle of Clusters: A Policy Perspective*. Cheltenham, UK and Northampton, MA, USA: Edward Elgar Publishing.

Gestrelius, S., Sandström, A. and Dolk, T. (2008). *National and Regional Cluster Profiles: Companies in Biotechnology, Pharmaceuticals and Medical Technology in Denmark in Comparison with Sweden*. Stockholm: VINNOVA – Swedish Governmental Agency for Innovation Systems.

Government of Norway (1985). St.meld. nr. 66 (1984—85) *Om høyere utdanning*. Oslo: Kultur- og vitenskapsdepartementet.

Government of Norway (2005). *Lov om Statens pensjonsfond*. Oslo: Finansdepartementet.

Government of Norway (2010). *Mandat for forvaltningen av Statens pensjonsfond*. Oslo: Finansdepartementet.

Government of Norway (2018). *Kapital i omstillingens tid: Næringslivets tilgang til kapital (NOU No. 2018:5)*. Oslo: Nærings- og fiskeridepartementet.

Grønning, T. (2009). Biotechnology in Norway: A marginal sector or future core activity? In: Fagerberg, J., Mowery, David C. and Verspagen, Bart (eds), *Innovation, Path Dependency and Policy: The Norwegian Case*. Oxford: Oxford University Press, pp. 235–62.

Grønning, T., Moen, S.E. and Olsen, D.S. (2008). Low innovation intensity. High growth and specialized trajectories: Norway. In: Edquist, C. and Hommen, L. (eds), *Small-Country Innovation Systems: Globalisation, Change and Policy in Asia and Europe*, Cheltenham, UK and Northampton, MA, USA: Edward Elgar Publishing, pp. 281–318.

Heitkøtter, V. (2016). Utrygt på Lesja etter Zymtech-konkurs. *Gudbrandsdølen Dagningen*, 29 May.

Innovation Norway and the Research Council of Norway (2007). *Naturally Inspired: Life Sciences in Norway 2007*. Oslo: Innovation Norway.

Innovation Norway and the Research Council of Norway (2010). *Naturally Inspired: Life Sciences in Norway 2010*. Oslo: Innovation Norway.

Innovation Policy Platform (2013). *Technological trajectories*. Accessed 23 September 2017 at: https://www.innovationpolicyplatform.org/content/technological-trajec tories.

IRIS Group (2017). *Dansk Life Science under Mikroskop: En Forskningsbaseret Styrkeposition der Forgrener Sig*. Copenhagen: IRIS Group.

Isaksen, A. and Trippl, M. (2014). *Regional Industrial Path Development in Different Regional Innovation Systems: A Conceptual Analysis*. Lund: Centre for Innovation, Research and Competence in the Learning Economy (CIRCLE).

Karlsen, J., Isaksen, A. and Spilling, O.R. (2011). The challenge of constructing regional advantages in peripheral areas: The case of marine biotechnology in Tromsø, Norway. *Entrepreneurship and Regional Development*, **23**(3–4), 235–57.

Kenney, M. and Patton, D. (2006). The coevolution of technologies and institutions: Silicon Valley as the iconic high-technology cluster. In: Braunerhjelm, P. and Feldman, M.P. (eds), *Cluster Genesis: Technology-Based Industrial Development*. Oxford: Oxford University Press, pp. 38–60.

Kreutzer, I. (2018). *An Integrated and Effective Nordic Ecosystem for Innovation and Green Growth: A Closer Look at Access to Risk Capital in the Nordic Countries*. Copenhagen: Nordic Council of Ministers.

Lall, S. (1992). Technological capabilities and industrialization. *World Development*, **20**(2), 165–86.

List, J.A. and Co, C.Y. (2000). The effects of environmental regulations on foreign direct investment. *Journal of Environmental Economics and Management*, **40**(1), 1–20.

Marvik, O.J. (2005). *Norwegian Life Science Industry: Overview and Status*. Oslo: Innovation Norway.

Menzel, M.-P. and Fornahl, D. (2009). Cluster life cycles: Dimensions and rationales of cluster evolution. *Industrial and Corporate Change*, **19**(1), 205–38.

Moodysson, J., Coenen, L. and Asheim, B. (2008). Explaining spatial patterns of innovation: Analytical and synthetic modes of knowledge creation in the Medicon Valley life-science cluster. *Environment and Planning A*, **40**(5), 1040–56.

Murmann, J.P. (2003). *Knowledge and Competitive Advantage: The Coevolution of Firms, Technology, and National Institutions*. Cambridge: Cambridge University Press.

Murray, F. (2002). Innovation as co-evolution of scientific and technological networks: Exploring tissue engineering. *Research Policy*, **31**(8–9), 1389–403.

Nelson, R.R. (1995). Co-evolution of industry structure, technology and supporting institutions, and the making of comparative advantage. *International Journal of the Economics of Business*, **2**(2), 171–84.

OECD (2003). *Biotechnology, Single Definition*. Paris: OECD.

OECD (2005). *A Framework for Biotechnology Statistics*. Paris: OECD.

OECD (2018). *OECD Economic Surveys: Norway. January, 2018*. Paris: OECD.

Oliver, A.L. (2009). *Networks for Learning and Knowledge Creation in Biotechnology*. Cambridge: Cambridge University Press.

Orkla (2008). *Orkla Annual report 2008*. Oslo: Orkla.

Owen-Smith, J. and Powell, W.W. (2006). Accounting for emergence and novelty in Boston and Bay Area biotechnology. In: Braunerhjelm, P. and Feldman, M. (eds), *Cluster Genesis: Technology-Based Industrial Development*. Oxford: Oxford University Press, pp. 61–86.

Pålsson, C.M. and Gregersen, B. (2011). Biotechnology in Denmark and Sweden. In: Göransson, B. and Pålsson, C.M. (eds), *Biotechnology and Innovation Systems: The Role of Public Policy*. Cheltenham, UK and Northampton, MA, USA: Edward Elgar Publishing, pp. 245–76.

Pavitt, K. (1984). Sectoral patterns of technical change: Towards a taxonomy and a theory. *Research Policy*, **13**(6), 343–73.

Powell, W.W., Koput, K.W. and Smith-Doerr, L. (1996). Interorganizational collaboration and the locus of innovation: Networks of learning in biotechnology. *Administrative Science Quarterly*, **41**(1), 116–45.

Riche, R.W., Hecker, D.E. and Burgan, J.U. (1983). High technology today and tomorrow: A small slice of the employment pie. *Monthly Labor Review*, **106**, 50–58.

Rosiello, A., Avnimelech, G. and Teubal, M. (2011). Towards a systemic and evolutionary framework for venture capital policy. *Journal of Evolutionary Economics*, **21**(1), 167–89.

Rosiello, A., Mastroeni, M., Teubal, M. and Avnimelech, G. (2013). Evolutionary policy targeting: Towards a conceptual framework for effective policy intervention. *Technology Analysis & Strategic Management*, **25**(7), 753–72.

Røtnes, R., Flatval, V.S. and Bjøru, E.C. (2017). *Virkemiddelanalyse av BIA*. Oslo: Samfunnsøkonomisk Analyse AS.

Sæther, B., Isaksen, A. and Karlsen, A. (2011). Innovation by co-evolution in natural resource industries: The Norwegian experience. *Geoforum*, **42**(3), 373–81.

Sandström, A. (2014). *Global trends with local effects: The Swedish Life Science Industry 1998–2012*. Stockholm: VINNOVA – Swedish Governmental Agency for Innovation Systems.

Sandström, A., Dolk, T. and Dolk, B. (2011). *Life Science Companies in Sweden including a Comparison with Denmark*. Stockholm: VINNOVA – Swedish Governmental Agency for Innovation Systems.

Sasson, A. (2011). *Knowledge Based Health*. Oslo: BI Norwegian Business School.

Secretariat of the Convention on Biological Diversity (2000). *Cartagena Protocol on Biosafety to the Convention on Biological Diversity: Text and Annexes*. Montreal: Secretariat of the Convention on Biological Diversity.

Souitaris, V. (2002). Technological trajectories as moderators of firm-level determinants of innovation. *Research Policy*, **31**(6), 877–98.

Suarez, F.F. (2004). Battles for technological dominance: An integrative framework. *Research Policy*, **33**(2), 271–86.

Trippl, M., Grillitsch, M., Isaksen, A. and Sinozic, T. (2015). Perspectives on cluster evolution: Critical review and future research issues. *European Planning Studies*, **23**(10), 2028–44.

UNCTAD (2019). *The State of Commodity Dependence 2019*. Geneva: United Nations.

United Nations (1993). *Convention on Biological Diversity*. Rio de Janeiro: United Nations.

Varis, M., Tohmo, T. and Littunen, H. (2014). Arriving at the dawn of the new economy: Is knowledge-based industrial renewal possible in a peripheral region? *European Planning Studies*, **22**(1), 101–25.

Vence, X., del Carmen Sánchez, M. and Rodil, Ó. (2013). Targeting biomed cluster from a mature pharma industry: The Medicon Valley experience. *Technology Analysis & Strategic Management*, **25**(7), 871–89.

Verspagen, B. (2007). Mapping technological trajectories as patent citation networks: A study on the history of fuel cell research. *Advances in Complex Systems*, **10**(01), 93–115.

Ville, S. and Wicken, O. (2012). The dynamics of resource-based economic development: Evidence from Australia and Norway. *Industrial and Corporate Change*, **22**(5), 1341–71.

Wadell, C. (2016). *Tillväxten i svensk life science-industri 2012–14: fortsatt nedgång eller nytändning?* Östersund: Myndigheten för tillväxtpolitiska utvärderingar och analyser.

Wadell, C. (2018). *Den Svenska Life Science-Industrins Utveckling – Statistik och Analys.* Östersund: Myndigheten för tillväxtpolitiska utvärderingar och analyser.

Waxell, A. and Malmberg, A. (2007). What is global and what is local in knowledge-generating interaction? The case of the biotech cluster in Uppsala, Sweden. *Entrepreneurship and Regional Development*, **19**(2), 137–59.

Wicken, O. (2009). Policies for path creation: The rise and fall of Norway's research-driven strategy for industrialization. In: Fagerberg, J., Mowery, D.C. and Verspagen, B. (eds), *Innovation, Path Dependency and Policy: The Norwegian Case.* Oxford: Oxford University Press, pp. 89–115.

3. Tentative indices for regional economic development: an exploratory study using Swedish municipal data

Tobias Arvemo and Urban Gråsjö

1. INTRODUCTION

In economic theory, it is acknowledged that there is a multifaceted relationship between economic growth and economic development. For instance, the directions of causality are not clear and have been debated for a long time. Some claim that the same elements that generate growth also bring progress in welfare and development. There are also obvious examples of causality in both directions. For developing countries, actions are often taken to improve welfare. This is expected to lead to an increase in income and growth, which in turn is expected to lead to further welfare improvements. In developed countries, however, policies are often geared towards efforts that will stimulate economic growth and, in turn, are expected to lead to economic development (Easterly, 2012). Of course, the conditions are different in developed and developed countries, but it is clear that the relationship between economic growth and economic development is more intricate than simply being summarized as a simple linear process. Furthermore, even when processes of economic growth and development seem fairly robust, there is usually an uneven geographical distribution of the benefits. Within a country, for instance, different neighborhoods, cities or regions may be at different stages of the process or even have contrasting processes (Feldman and Storper, 2018).

Consequently, it is not only about a set of contributing factors that enable either economic growth or economic development (or both). It is more about how these factors may interact in order to render benefits for society (Feldman and Storper, 2018). In order to put the interactions among contributing factors in focus and to highlight the differences between regions in a country, this chapter attempts to construct tentative composite indicators for economic development by using official Swedish municipal data from 2015 including variables such as gross pay per inhabitant, citizen satisfaction with the municipality, Gini coefficient, and population densities.

Composite indicators which compare country performance, for instance, are increasingly recognized as useful tools in policy analysis and public communication. They offer simplified comparisons of countries that can be used to illustrate complex and sometimes intangible issues in a variety of fields. However, composite indicators may send misleading policy messages if they are poorly constructed or misinterpreted and may invite users to draw simplistic analytical or policy conclusions. In fact, composite indicators must be seen as a means of initiating discussion and stimulating public interest. A composite indicator is designed when individual indicators are gathered into a single index on the basis of an underlying model. The composite indicator should ideally measure multidimensional concepts which cannot be captured by a single indicator (OECD, 2008).

Using variable selection methods this chapter examines variables potentially suitable as indicators for different dimensions of economic development as well as the relationships between the different dimensions in economic development. Since potential factors for measuring economic development typically will differ greatly over large geographical areas, we will study the indicators on municipality level to avoid large geographical units of analysis. In order to identify, and highlight, intra-municipal differences a higher geographical resolution would be preferable but due to data restraints this is not possible. In the next section a theoretical framework is presented, where the concept of economic development is defined. We then use the operationalization of this definition to find suitable variables to include in the variable selection process. Section 3 describes the method used to construct the composite indicators for economic development. In section 4, the results are presented. The final sections contain a discussion of the results and conclusions.

2.   THEORETICAL FRAMEWORK

2.1   Defining Economic Development

Economic development has no clear and agreed-upon definition. A list of definitions by different associations is stated in Haider (1986). These definitions include, among others, wealth creation – (i.e. producing goods and services that are valued in competitive society), improving the business climate or allowing free enterprise to work, the process of responding to change, and so on. In our attempt to construct regional composite indicators for economic development, this chapter will use the definition from Feldman et al. (2016, p. 10):

> Economic development is defined as the expansion of capacities that contribute to the advancement of society through the realization of individuals', firms', and communities' potential. Economic development is a sustained increase in prosperity and quality of life realized through innovation, lowered transactions costs, and the utilization of capabilities towards the responsible production and diffusion of goods and services.

The definition is inspired especially by the work of Sen (1999), who argues that to achieve economic development, focus has to be on individuals' capacities and potentials. Only if the individuals are allowed to develop these capacities can they contribute to the economy. Instead of only being regarded as an input in a production process, individuals become an important factor in the process of economic development.

2.2   Determining Sub-groups

Feldman et al. (2016) splits economic development into four main dimensions of capacities. An increase in each of the dimensions is assumed to indicate an increase in economic development *ceteris paribus*. These dimensions are:

1. *Community capacity*: The physical, social, and environmental assets that influence the context for economic development.
2. *Firm and industry capacity*: The assets relevant to firms and industry, including workforce, facilities and equipment, organization, and supply chain.
3. *Entrepreneurial capacity*: The potential for generating new small businesses, including a risk-taking culture, networks, and access to financial capital and a skilled workforce.
4. *Innovative infrastructure*: The capacity to support new products, processes, and organizations, in terms of facilities, support services, and willingness to take risks.

According to Feldman et al. (2016) economic development is about the development of capacities that expand economic actors' abilities. Stiglitz et al. (2009) argue that it is time to shift emphasis from measuring economic production to measuring people's well-being However, to capture economic development we do not need to dismiss, but we need to go beyond, the traditional factors usually used to explain economic growth. In order to measure and estimate economic development, these "hard" factors must be complemented by "softer" factors that take into account human development and quality of life. Feldman and Storper (2018) argue that instead of just looking at *produced output*, we need to proceed and include *personal per capita income*. The income may, however, be unevenly distributed, so *income distribution* should also be taken into account (Keefer and Knack, 2002). The income distribution is reflected by the quality of various employments, which require different skills, which in turn affects the *wages* for these jobs. To achieve the skills, *education* is a crucial necessity.

More and better education is a prerequisite for rapid economic development around the world (Gylfason, 2001). Education stimulates economic growth and improves people's lives through many channels, for instance by increasing the efficiency of the labor force, by fostering democracy (Barro, 1997) and thus creating better conditions for good governance, by improving health, by enhancing equality (Aghion et al., 1999), and so on. Obviously, it is not enough to include produced output, per capita income, income distribution, wages, education and so on to capture economic development.

Ideally, to incorporate the "softer" dimensions of economic development we need to include, as Feldman and Storper (2018, p. 49) suggest: "a humanistic vision of the economy as a source of human fulfillment, where people create, explore possibilities, earn self-respect, and create a good life for themselves through well-distributed opportunities for striving (Phelps, 2013)".

3. METHOD

The main strategy in this chapter is to use the theoretical work in section 2 to find possible indicators for economic development in a broad sense, to go through the seven-step process described below to construct indices, and then compare these indices with the theoretical work in section 2. This will enable us both to discuss the access to possible indicators and to compare the result of the data-driven process below to the theoretical framework in section 2.

In an effort to produce a tentative measure for economic development for Swedish municipalities we propose to use the following steps:

1. Find possible indicators;
2. impute data;
3. examine the dependency structure among possible indicators;

4. determine dimensions among the possible indicators and constructing indices using factor analysis (FA);
5. examine the internal reliability of the indices;
6. calculate final indices.

3.1   Find Possible Indicators

There are many possible indicators for economic development that could be used and to our knowledge no such list of indicators is currently agreed upon. In this study, we will try and gather indicators that have been used previously, for instance in growth studies, but not necessarily as indicators for economic development. To, as far as possible, ensure that we cover the area of economic development, we will perform an extensive search of official data repositories in Sweden such as Statistics Sweden (SCB), Growth analysis (Tillväxtanalys) and Kommun- och landstingsdatabasen.

3.2   Impute Data

There is a high probability that data will be missing for certain years and that an imputation procedure will be necessary, especially for survey data, since these data are not collected every year for all municipalities.

3.3   Examine the Dependency Structure among Possible Indicators

For further analysis to be plausible there needs to be sufficient correlation between the different indicators. This will be examined using Pearson correlation.

3.4   Determine Dimensions among the Possible Indicators and Construct Indices Using Factor Analysis (FA)

Factor analysis (FA) aims to describe a large set of variables in terms of a smaller number of factors and to highlight the relationship between these variables. The FA is based on a model that assumes that the data variance can be decomposed into that accounted for by common and unique factors. The decision on when to stop extracting factors basically depends on when there is only very little "random" variability left, and is rather arbitrary.

After choosing the number of factors to keep, it is standard practice to perform rotation so as to enhance the interpretability of the results. Various rotational strategies have been proposed. The goal of all of these strategies is to obtain a clear pattern of loadings.

In this study a FA using varimax rotation will be performed to analyze the underlying structure of the indicators. All factors with an eigenvalue over 1 will be considered (the Kaiser Rule: OECD, 2008).

3.5   Examine the Internal Reliability of the Indices

A reliability analysis using Cronbach's alpha will be used on the constructed indices. Cronbach's alpha is the most common estimate of internal consistency of items in a model or survey. It measures the share of total variability of the sample of individual indicators due to the correlation of indicators. If no correlation exists and individual indicators are independent, then Cronbach's alpha is equal to zero, while if individual indicators are perfectly correlated, it is equal to 1. Thus, a high Cronbach's alpha indicates that the individual indicators measure the latent phenomenon (i.e. economic development) well. A Cronbach's alpha exceeding 0.7 will be considered sufficient (Nunnaly, 1978).

3.6   Calculate Final Indices

The final indices will be calculated ensuring a sufficient internal reliability. This might exclude some indicators. The indices will be calculated as the average of the indicators for each index. Using other weights in the indices is possible but would require either theoretical knowledge of the importance of indicators in each index or matching empirical knowledge. Since both are lacking, using unweighted averages will be more robust.

4.   RESULTS

4.1   Find Possible Indicators

A number of possible indicators were gathered from official data repositories in Sweden. In Table 3.1 a list of the possible indicators is given with a short description. All data are from 2015.

4.2   Impute Data

The data was complete for all variables except the survey data. For the municipalities that participated in 2014 and 2016 but not 2015 the average between 2014 and 2016 was used. If the municipalities had data for either 2014 or 2016 but not for 2015, the data from the closest year was used. The

Table 3.1   Possible indicators

Variable	Description
Citizens' municipal satisfaction	Index revealing satisfaction with living in the municipality from the Citizen Satisfaction Survey (Statistics Sweden)*.
Recommendation index	Index revealing how likely it is for an inhabitant to recommend others to move to the municipality from the Citizen Satisfaction Survey (Statistics Sweden)*.
Labor possibilities	Index revealing accessibility to employment within a reasonable distance in the municipality from the Citizen Satisfaction Survey (Statistics Sweden)*.
Education possibilities	Index revealing accessibility to higher education within a reasonable distance in the municipality from the Citizen Satisfaction Survey (Statistics Sweden)*.
Housing possibilities	Index revealing access to and diversity in housing as well as quality of housing in the municipality from the Citizen Satisfaction Survey (Statistics Sweden)*.
Communication possibilities	Index revealing access to bicycle lanes, public transportation, both local and inter-regional, and by car in the municipality from the Citizen Satisfaction Survey (Statistics Sweden)*.
Shopping possibilities	Index revealing the supply of services, stores and restaurants within a reasonable distance in the municipality from the Citizen Satisfaction Survey (Statistics Sweden)*.
Leisure possibilities	Index revealing access to parks, recreation areas, nature, sport facilities, and culture in the municipality from the Citizen Satisfaction Survey (Statistics Sweden)*.
Safeness index	Index revealing the feeling of being safe from crime, violence, and burglary in the municipality from the Citizen Satisfaction Survey (Statistics Sweden)*.
Median income	The median income in thousands of SEK in the municipality 2015.
Municipal tax	The municipal tax in percentage 2015.
Population growth	The population growth in 2015 in percent.
Gini	Measure of income distribution. Values between 0 and 1, where 0 = totally equal distribution and 1 = totally unequal distribution.
Population density	Population density 2015 in persons per square km.
Sick days	Number of sick days per employed 2015.
Primary sector	Proportion of gainfully employed (16+ years) in primary sector (agriculture, forestry, hunting and fishing) by region of residence
Age dependency ratio	Number of persons 0–19 years old and 65 years old divided by the number of persons 20–64 years old.

Table 3.1   (continued)

Variable	Description
National election participation	Participation rate in national election 2014.
Expected lifespan	Expected remaining lifetime for a newborn 2011–2015. Based on death data.
New companies	Newly established companies per 1000 inhabitants
Employment rate	Percentage employed aged 16–64.
Gross pay per employed	Gross wages and other taxable reimbursements in thousands of SEK per employed by region of residence.
Higher education	Percentage of the population with post-secondary education (3 years or more).
Violent crimes	Number of reported violent crimes per 1000 inhabitants.
GMP per inhabitant	Gross Municipal Production. The value added (wages and enterprises' operating surplus) per inhabitant by region of residence.

Note: *The survey is performed twice a year and normally includes roughly 140 municipalities out of the 290 municipalities in Sweden. The number of randomly selected individuals per municipality is usually 600 in smaller municipalities and 1200 in larger municipalities. Altogether we have included 228 municipalities from this survey. The questions in each of the abovementioned dimensions are then weighted and aggregated to an index, ranging from 0 to 100.

fluctuation in the index between years in the same municipality is fairly stable and hence this imputation scheme will have a small influence.

4.3   Examine the Dependency Structure among Possible Indicators

The correlation between all possible indicators was calculated. A large majority of the indicators had significant correlations.

4.4   Constructing Indices based on Factor Analysis

To examine latent structures among the indicators a factor analysis was performed using a varimax rotation. Five factors had an eigenvalue larger than 1 and these five factors account for 74.9 percent of the variation in the data (see Table 3.2).

All factors except factor 5 among the rotated factors account for at least 10 percent of the variance among the indicators. The rotated factor loadings are given in Table 3.3.

Table 3.2   Variance extraction in factor analysis

Component	Initial Eigenvalues			Rotation Sums of Squared Loadings		
	Total	% of Variance	Cumulative %	Total	% of Variance	Cumulative %
1	10.544	42.175	42.175	4.531	18.126	18.126
2	3.065	12.259	54.434	4.525	18.102	36.227
3	2.138	8.552	62.986	4.300	17.200	53.427
4	1.576	6.303	69.289	3.300	13.199	66.626
5	1.393	5.573	74.863	2.059	8.237	74.863

4.5   Examine the Internal Reliability of the Indices

All variables were standardized to have mean 0 and standard deviation 1. All of the indicators marked in factor 1, all in factor 2 and so on were examined using Cronbach's alpha to evaluate internal reliability. The indicators for factors 1 to 4 all had a Cronbach's alpha exceeding 0.7. The marked indicators in the fifth factor only scored a Cronbach's alpha of 0.54, which is too low. In this case it was decided to keep the GMP per inhabitant since this is an economic measure of some interest, and to discard the other marked indicators.

4.6   Calculating Final Indices

The final indices were calculated after the internal reliability was checked. The first index was calculated using standardized variables as:

$$Index1 = \frac{Satisfaction + Recommendation + Education + Shopping + Leisure}{5}.$$

Index 1 seems to represent the "Quality of Living" for the municipality. For the second index:

$$Index2 = \frac{-Tax + GINI + Population\ dendity + New\ companies + Gross\ pay + Higher\ education}{6}.$$

Index 2 seems to represent the "Economic Capacity" in the municipality. For the third index:

Table 3.3   Rotated factor loadings

	Component				
	1	2	3	4	5
Citizens' municipal satisfaction	.747	.317	.497	−.044	−.143
Recommendation index	.698	.326	.564	−.032	−.059
Education possibilities	.633	.128	.239	.522	.121
Shopping possibilities	.843	.125	−.022	.069	.105
Leisure possibilities	.865	.175	.047	.136	.105
Municipal tax in percentage	−.237	−.653	−.141	−.348	.108
Gini-coefficient	.125	.878	.030	.033	−.070
Population density, persons/km²	.166	.644	.033	.173	.318
New companies	.070	.790	.242	−.003	.153
Gross pay per employed	.248	.609	.422	.406	.055
Higher education	.445	.618	.390	.218	.232
Median income	.155	.420	.739	.362	.096
National election participation	.218	.172	.676	.178	-.340
Employment rate	.069	.226	.791	.244	.261
Violent crimes	−.017	.021	−.673	.293	.306
Communication possibilities	.609	.171	.097	.629	−.006
Safeness index	.039	.129	.607	−.659	−.051
Population growth	−.051	.278	.077	.653	−.109
Primary sector	−.308	−.233	−.221	−.740	−.207
Housing possibilities	.472	.129	.083	.052	−.624
Age dependency ratio	−.288	−.062	−.071	−.499	−.678
GMP per inhabitant	.219	.255	-.104	-.062	.741
Labor possibilities	.507	.272	.478	.426	.160
Sick-days	−.220	−.597	−.540	−.266	−.113
Expected lifespan	.238	.560	.455	.128	−.144

Note: The largest factor loading greater than 0.6 or smaller than −0.6 are marked for each indicator.

$$Index3 = \frac{Median\ income + Election + Employment + Crimes}{4}.$$

Index 3 appears to represent "Wealth and Stability" for the municipality. For the fourth index:

$$Index4 = \frac{Communications - Safeness + Population\ growth - Primary\ sector}{4}.$$

The fourth index seems to represent "Growing Worries" in the municipality. The fifth index is just the standardized GMP per inhabitant.

Table 3.4　Correlations

	Quality of Living	Economic Capacity	Wealth and Stability	Growing Worries	GMP per inhabitant
Quality of Living	1				
Economic Capacity	.587***	1			
Wealth and Stability	.499***	.547***	1		
Growing Worries	.420***	.429***	.159*	1	
GMP per inhabitant	.070	.192**	−.074	.244***	1

Notes:
***. Correlation is significant at the 0.001 level (2-tailed).
**. Correlation is significant at the 0.01 level (2-tailed).
*. Correlation is significant at the 0.05 level (2-tailed).

4.7　Correlation between Indices

To examine the relationships between the indices, the correlation between all dimensions was calculated; see Table 3.4.

Interestingly, GMP per inhabitant correlates only with "Economic Capacity" and "Growing Worries", and has no significant, and close to zero, correlations with "Quality of Living" and "Wealth and Stability".

5.　DISCUSSION AND TENTATIVE CONCLUSIONS

The goal of this chapter was to try and construct indices for economic development. An extensive search yielded a number of prospect indicators to use even though the official data gathered in Sweden are not particularly suitable for investigating the softer dimensions of economic development.

When constructing an index it is important not to unknowingly mix input and output indicators; see OECD (2008). If we want to measure performance we should exclusively use output indicators in the index. The dimensions mentioned in section 2 are focused on capacities and hence do not measure performance. The survey indicators, that is, the first nine indicators in Table 3.1, are outputs and hence measure performance, while the more firm indicators are more of input character, for instance municipal tax. However, the difference between input and output becomes unclear since the causality is unclear in many cases involving economic development. It would be advisable to have more outputs in the index since having the means for development does not necessarily lead to development, which calls for more research on causality. It should also be noted that some of the indices might counteract each other (see Arvemo and Gråsjö, 2018).

The two first dimensions from Feldman et al. (2016) (see section 2) coincide fairly well with the first two dimensions presented in this study. The first dimension in Feldman et al. (2016) is *Community capacity*, whereas Index 1 contains self-estimated assets to good living conditions in the municipality. Feldman and Storper (2018) note that Human Development Index and per capita income have a high correlation at national level. Index 5 is the standardized GMP which is also a measure of productivity, as is per capita income, but on a municipal level we have no noticeable correlation between Index 5 and Index 1. Two possible explanations for this could be either that the link between productivity and quality of living disappears in a finer geographical resolution or that the definition of GMP obscures the link. This indicates that development and growth might not be as interrelated as one thinks.

The second dimension is *Firm and industry capacity* and Index 2 contains population density, human capital, tax and new companies, which are factors that traditionally are considered to be driving forces for company development. The presence of the Gini coefficient indicates that these driving forces for company development also have a concentrating effect on income distribution. Index 2 seems also to include indicators for entrepreneurship. One could also note that the indicators used are also commonly used in innovation studies and hence at least partly cover dimensions 3 and 4.

The other three dimensions presented in this study are not so easily compared to dimensions 3 and 4. It should be noted that for these dimensions many of the indicators that are included are not, at present date, available as measures, for instance risk-taking culture, network capacities and so on.

Index 3 is an index for wealth, democratic and political interest as well as employment and low crime rates. All these indicators are, to us, indicators of a good and stable community and therefore it is interesting to note that this index is not correlated to Index 5, GMP (see Table 3.4).

If Index 3, in some sense, indicates a stable and prosperous municipality, Index 4 indicates a growing municipality with its challenges. The structure of the index indicates a municipality with a high influx of inhabitants, good communications to other cities, a high crime rate and a low primary sector, which indicates a suburban municipality.

As noted in Feldman and Storper (2018), geography has a crucial role in economic development and agglomeration of both firms and people is a natural part of modern capitalism. In this study we have not been able to include any such explicit measures of geography or infrastructure in our work except the communications indicator. We do, however, use data on a municipal level, which should capture the geographical differences between the municipalities.

In conclusion: measuring development is a challenging task! Official data is not gathered with these types of measurements in mind, and the causality, both within the different aspects of development and in relation to growth, is unclear.

REFERENCES

Acemoglu, D., Garcia-Jimeno, C. and Robinson, J.A. (2015), State capacity and economic development: A network approach, *American Economic Review* **105**(8), 2364–409.

Aghion, P., Caroli, E. and Garcia-Penalosa, C. (1999), Inequality and economic growth: The perspective of the new growth theories, *Journal of Economic Literature* **37**, 1615–60.

Arvemo, T. and Gråsjö, U. (2018), Indicators of economic development – An exploratory study using Swedish municipal data contrasting economic development and growth, in Gråsjö, U., Karlsson, C. and Bernhard, I. (eds), *Geography, Open Innovation and Entrepreneurship*, Cheltenham, UK and Northampton, MA, USA: Edward Elgar Publishing.

Barro, R.J. (1997), *The Determinants of Economic Growth*, Cambridge, MA: MIT Press.

Easterly, W. (2012), *White Man's Burden: Why the West's Efforts to Aid the Rest Have Done so Much Ill and so Little Good*, New York: Oxford University Press.

Feldman, M. and Storper, M. (2018), Economic growth and economic development: Geographic dimensions, definition and disparities, in Clark, G.L., Feldman, M.P., Gertler, M.S. and Wójcik, D. (eds), *The New Oxford Handbook of Economic Geography*, Oxford: Oxford University Press, pp. 143–58.

Feldman, M., Hadjimichael, T. and Lanahan, L. (2016), The logic of economic development: A definition and model for investment, *Environment and Planning C: Government and Policy* **34**, 5–21.

Gylfason, T. (2001), Natural resources, education, and economic development, *European Economic Review* **45**, 847–59.

Haider, D. (1986), Economic development: Changing practices in a changing US economy, *Environment and Planning C: Government and Policy* **4**(4), 451–69.

Keefer, P. and Knack, S. (2002), Polarization, politics and property rights: Links between inequality and growth, *Public Choice* **111**(1), 127–54.

Nunnaly, J. (1978), *Psychometric Theory*, New York: McGraw-Hill.

OECD (2008), *Handbook on Constructing Composite Indicators: Methodology and User Guide*, Paris: OECD.

Phelps, E.S. (2013), *Mass Flourishing: How Grassroots Innovation Created Jobs, Challenge, and Change*, Princeton, MA: Princeton University Press.

Sen, A. (1999), *Commodities and Capabilities*, Oxford: Oxford University Press.

Stiglitz, J., Sen, A. and Fitoussi, J.-P. (2009), Report of the Commission on the Measurement of Economic Performance and Social Progress. Paris. Available online from the Commission on the Measurement of Economic Performance and Social Progress: http://www.stiglitz-sen-fitoussi.fr/en/index.htm.

4. Inclusive place innovation as a means for local community regeneration

Iréne Bernhard, Anna Karin Olsson and Ulrika Lundh Snis

1. INTRODUCTION

Innovative forms of collaboration can be a fundamental driver of local and regional economic development that leads to transformation of contemporary cities. Such initiatives have been studied by various scholars with different approaches, such as urban development (Book et al., 2010; Yang, 2014); urban regeneration (Mommaas, 2004); urban partnerships (Le Feuvre et al., 2016); destination development (Bornhorst et al., 2010; Bernhard and Olsson, 2015); city branding and place branding (Houghton and Stevens, 2011; Lucarelli and Brorström, 2013); place reinvention (Nyseth and Viken, 2009); place development (Healey, 2009; Olsson et al., 2018) and place innovation (Lindberg et al., 2015).

Research shows that "place innovation" is highly relevant as an overall concept to facilitate engagement in local and regional development (Lindberg et al., 2015; 2017). Place innovation combines renewal and innovation processes in shaping a place integrated with perspectives from community, local residents and industry. Collaborative place innovation is argued to be suitable in local regeneration (Lindberg et al., 2017; Knox and Mayer, 2013; Aas et al., 2005; Al-hagla, 2010; Yang, 2014; Le Feuvre et al., 2016; Olsson et al., 2016). The need for regeneration is often driven by structural changes such as deindustrialization, high unemployment or depopulation. This is especially crucial for smaller cities that often struggle with their adaption capacity (Mayer and Knox, 2010; Bell and Jayne, 2006; Richards and Duif, 2018), while still offering an attractive local community for the three main types of stakeholders: business, visitors and local residents (Vareide and Nygaard, 2015). There is hence a need for cities to act in creative and innovative ways when designing and implementing development strategies for local communities, especially smaller cities, since they often bridge larger urban centers with rural areas (Hamdouch et al., 2016). Earlier research has mainly focused on the regeneration and transformation of large cities, although there is an emerging interest in studies of smaller cities (e.g. Mayer and Knox, 2010; Bell and Jayne, 2006; Richards and Duif, 2018). For smaller cities place innovation can be based on tangible and intangible resources, that is, existing or potential resources that belong and give meaning to a place. The meanings attached to a place are often linked to ties such as belonging, ownership, identity and heritage (Richards and Duif, 2018). The smaller city needs to grow in quality and authenticity and therefore should rely on its own local needs and resources (Mayer and Knox, 2010). As cities are contexts for interactions of multiple stakeholders from public, private and nonprofit sectors, the inclusion of stakeholders brings further challenges to place innovation and local community regeneration such as mixed visions, conflicting interests, divergent views of development, preservation and sustainability (Jamal and Stronza, 2009).

Recent studies of stakeholder inclusion have focused on tourist attractions (Garrod et al., 2012), events (Getz et al., 2006) and cultural heritage (Aas et al., 2005). Al-hagla (2010) argues for the importance of applying a bottom-up perspective, particularly in city development of historical areas, in order to balance issues of conservation, rehabilitation, and interpretation, that is, revealing the meaning of places and the links between people and places, and local economic development. Other challenges identified in previous research are fear of stagnation, fear of Disneyfication (Hamelink, 2008; Olsson, 2016), and varying degrees of information, engagement or influence. Antagonism, prejudice and conflicts among stakeholders (Robinson, 2005) may also be problematic. Various approaches for stakeholder involvement and inclusive networks are used as a means to gather different groups of interests (Le Feuvre et al., 2016; Olsson et al., 2018). Calls are made for further research to reach a deeper insight into the nature of partnerships and challenges of stakeholder interactions within local regeneration (Le Feuvre et al., 2016), hence also with special focus on local residents as stakeholders in innovation processes (Snaith and Haley, 1999; Presenza et al., 2013).

This chapter thus aims to contribute knowledge on stakeholder involvement in order to identify challenges and innovative processes at work in local community regeneration of smaller cities. From our viewpoint we apply place innovation perspectives to address issues of diversity in the renewal of a small city center or district. In order to explore the aim, the following research questions were formulated:

RQ 1: What are the stakeholder challenges in place innovation and local regeneration?

RQ 2: How can these challenges be integrated in collaborative approaches for place innovation and local regeneration?

The arguments of this study are based on case studies of development in two smaller coastal cities, one in Norway and one in Sweden. Both have a declining city center and struggle with lack of a common vision, strategic planning and governance and are thus in search of local collaborative approaches. These are linked to unique values based on different cultural heritages, in these cases seaside resort and fortress city. As this study takes its points of departure from a local community perspective, an "inside view" (Bartunek and Louis, 1996; Islind et al., 2016), the views of tourists and visitors are not in focus. The stakeholders that are studied represent local community, local residents and industry, by including a mix of merchants, residents, property owners, craftsmen, nonprofit associations, educational institutions, government and municipal organizations, and elected officials. Many of these individuals represent several categories.

2. THEORETICAL CONCEPTS

For our study the inclusion of diverse stakeholders' perspectives as well as the issues of identity and uniqueness are of crucial importance. Hence, for a city's place innovation activities we will consider aspects that will facilitate and integrate new participative forms of interaction and unique features to be promoted as service attractions.

2.1 Involving Stakeholders' Perspectives

Research shows that more and more emphasis is being put on developing innovative solutions to societal challenges through inclusive innovation processes, compared with the previously dominant focus on expert-driven innovation (Lindberg et al., 2015). Target group thinking is a prime issue parallel to user-driven innovation, such as Living Labs (Bergvall-Kareborn and Stahlbrost, 2009). In such processes of innovation development and implementation, trust is an important parameter (Bernhard and Wihlborg, 2014). Stakeholders are here defined as "any group or individual who can affect, or is affected by, the achievement of the organization's objectives" (Freeman, 1984: 46). The traditional stakeholder model is based on the idea of the organization/firm as a central node in stakeholder collaboration (Freeman, 1984), while in urban collaboration the focus is on the partnership itself, with multiple and competitive perspectives, goals and visions (Le Feuvre et al., 2016). There are many different categorizations of stakeholders, often based on sectors such as public, private and volunteer in urban development (Yang, 2014). The author emphasizes the essential need to obtain the full picture of stakeholders, and identify context-specific groups and their concerns by applying stakeholder analysis methods, such as a two-stage process of stakeholder analysis: (1) to identify stakeholder groups and their interests, followed by (2) stakeholder prioritization, that is, "to analyzing stakeholders' influence on urban development, and decisions about which stakeholders' interests should be addressed preferentially" (Yang, 2014: 839) and then to make appropriate decisions.

Evans (1997) instead suggests a categorization of stakeholders that are shaping urban centers as those who produce the place, that is, property owners, retailers and developers, those who use the place, that is, residents, employees and visitors, and those who mediate the place, that is, local and national government, the municipality.

Furthermore, Getz et al. (2006) suggest more detailed stakeholder roles and identify the following stakeholder categories in event tourism: investors, directors, employees, volunteers and advisors; co-producers, referring to stakeholders from local trade and industry as well as independent organizations and individuals who participate voluntarily for their own reasons and take on roles other than sponsor, supplier or venue, for example restaurant tents. Municipalities that provide streets and parks, or firms and organizations taking part in markets, often participate by co-producing the total event offering. Facilitators as non-participating resource providers make the event possible, as for example state, municipalities and different grants or gifts. The media may also take on the role of facilitator when covering the event. Suppliers and venues represent the costs of the event and include for example performers (paid musicians and actors) and the arenas for the events. The roles of allies and collaborators refer to inter-event collaboration and sharing of experiences. Regulators refer to the need for approval and cooperation required, such as local authorities, police and fire department concerning the number of visitors and their safety.

Accordingly, there is a lack of insight into the dynamics of how different stakeholders, perspectives and resources are bound together. Hence, many studies show the need to form different partnerships while there have been limited studies on interaction and stakeholders' views of collaboration and their behavior towards co-stakeholders in the local community (see Le Feuvre et al., 2016).

2.2 Place Innovation, Identity and Unique Features

Place innovation means an open innovation approach that mostly follows the line of economic value or technical products. In Lindberg et al. (2015), place innovation is viewed as a coherent perspective on innovative thinking about place design. They further argue that social, cultural, economic and technological aspects to increase place attractiveness are integrated into a place innovation perspective among existing and potential visitors, residents and investors.

It is important to pay attention not only to the resources vital for the place (such as infrastructure, physical facilities and resources) but also to the factors that encapsulate more emotive aspects of a place, such as its appearance and image, or intangibles, such as the perceptions and values derived from cultural heritage, services and collaborative partnerships.

The local cultural heritage of a place is often drawn on as an important and unique resource in development processes (Ahmad, 2006; Al-hagla, 2010). Cultural heritage is a broad concept used in various ways and may include tangible and intangible aspects such as the place, buildings, historical areas, towns, geographic landscapes, and human environments (Ahmad, 2006). In urban regeneration this thus enhances the importance of local residents, as pointed out by Al-hagla (2010): "For tourism, local people, as an integral part of the 'heritage locus,' can contribute vitality to an area and thereby assist in the maintenance of an atmosphere conducive to tourism. For local people, tourism can promote the rehabilitation of historic areas, thus improving the lives of the residents" (p. 236). Gospodini (2004) studies the ways specific aspects of urban regeneration such as built heritage and "the innovative design of space" may contribute to place identity in European cities. This study shows that innovative place development can be effectively supported by landmarks and promotion of tourism and economic development and may also generate new social solidarities among local residents grounded on civic pride and economic prospects. Hence, as argued by Mommaas (2004), "it is necessary to develop a more sophisticated understanding of the complex dynamics involved" (p. 507). Central to this is a locally specific appreciation of the changing interaction between culture (place) and commerce (market). This implies both a critique and advancement of existing theories concerning the role of culture and identity in local regeneration and the development of a more detailed comparative perspective on place innovation as such. Notable is the uniqueness of coastal cities, where especially the seaside heritage tends to be viewed nostalgically (Walton, 2000). Jarratt and Gammon (2016) argue that nostalgia-fueled heritage tourism offers a valuable lifeline for some resorts in transformation. This is also in line with the fact that innovation processes are extended to the attribution of new, highly cultural and emotional meanings embedded in the place (Fanzini et al., 2013). Thanks to people's perceptions and beliefs about innovation, emotions and meanings may enhance the value of identity and uniqueness. The place will be the environment that is valued as the same social dynamics that support quality of life. The regenerative power of such cultural dynamics tends to extend to smaller urban settlements, particularly where the cultural heritage is widespread (Fanzini et al., 2013).

Another issue vital for city center regeneration is safety and a sense of security (MacLeod, 2011). Recent contributions, acknowledging that safety is important, uncover how city regeneration is focused around an implicit consensus to preserve the circumspect city and prompting non-trivial questions about the precise manner in which political representation, democracy and substantive citizenship are being negotiated (MacLeod, 2011). However, in general, other studies show that higher rates of violent crime positively correlate with higher average incomes and larger population (Bettencourt et al., 2010).

In sum, the mix of unique features and different stakeholders in urban regeneration processes is complex and, as Ashworth (2017) emphasizes, linked to past, present and future: "heritage is the medium through which senses of place are created from senses of time" and thus also includes "the process of identification of people with places and the role of heritage as a contemporary use of the pasts" (Ashworth, 2017: Introduction). Accordingly, the communication between heritage and tourism stakeholders is of major importance, as is the inclusion of the local community (Aas et al., 2005), hence affecting the image, identity and marketing of the city. Snaith and Haley (1999) argue that "understanding the perceptions and truly incorporating the opinions of resident populations within the management and promotion of their city may prove to be the most creative method of re-positioning the historic city as an authentic tourist and living experience" (p. 603). Al-hagla (2010) suggests the heritage trail as an integrative and capacity-building bottom-up tool for local community development based on heritage. Al-hagla (2010) focuses on the interaction between three components: the place, locals and tourists, hence also addressing the overall theme of sustainability and subthemes of conservation, interpretation of the historic city, and local economic development. There is a continuous interaction or balancing act between place, local residents and tourists. Lindberg et al. (2015) argue that the hub in this balancing act is the identity of a place, which needs to be identified, negotiated, formulated and communicated in order to increase the attractiveness of a place for local residents as well as for visitors and investors (p. 12). The place identity should be based on the uniqueness of the tangible and intangible resources of a place, that is, what distinguishes it from other places.

3. RESEARCH APPROACH

In order to capture diverse stakeholders' opinions of challenges in local community innovation processes we have applied a qualitative, inclusive and inside research approach (Bartunek and Louis, 1996; Islind et al., 2016).

3.1 Research Method and Material

Case studies as research method allow for "the study of a contemporary phenomenon, which is difficult to separate from its context, but necessary to study within it to understand the dynamics involved in the setting" (Halinen and Törnroos, 2005: 1285). A multiple case study of two cases was conducted to study two different cultural heritage cases and stakeholder collaboration related to place innovation in the two cases' unique contexts over time 2016–2018 (Yin, 2018). Thus, the two cases representing the empirical setting of the present study are the Old Town District in the Norwegian city of Fredrikstad (throughout the chapter referred to as the "Old Town") and Lysekil, a small Swedish seaside resort city (referred to as the "Seaside Resort"). Both cities are involved in development and regeneration to increase the competitiveness and innovation capacity mainly in trade and tourism in close collaboration with local actors. In the last decade, these cities have participated together in several cross-border development projects in order to learn and inspire each other. Both cases include several partly overlapping formal and informal networks that have had varying levels of influence on the local development over time. There were existing conflicting interests and mistrust among networks in both cases.

The Norwegian context, Old Town, is a preserved fortified city with small shops, galleries, craft studios, cafés and restaurants. Around 340 residents live in Old Town. The approximate number of visitors is 100 000 a year, mainly during summer season. The Old Town is an arena for several different cultural events such as music festivals, military history events, and book festivals. There are many vacant premises in the Old Town and several small entrepreneurs struggle to survive year-round (see pilot study Bernhard et al., 2017).

The Swedish context, Seaside Resort, is a small harbor town that has been characterized by fishing and shipping industries since the 16th century. During the 19th century the town established an attractive seaside resort on the Swedish west coast. Tourism is still important today although the seasonal variations are a challenge for the local trade. Around 7500 residents live in the town center. The seaside resort also has strong links with refineries and manufacturing industries as well as maritime research.

Our study employs qualitative methods as this approach seeks to investigate a phenomenon from the perspective of those involved in the context (see Alvesson and Kärreman, 2011). In the present study we explore the stakeholder perceptions of challenges and visions for collaboration. We aimed for in-depth insights and thoughts of stakeholders, that is, people who were in some sense connected to the Old Town or the Seaside Resort. In-depth interviews with stakeholders gave nuanced descriptions and answers to open questions about what, why and how different perceptions are represented and developed. The semi-structured interviews followed an interview guide as an instrument of a low level of control, but at the same time they were supportive in giving thematic guidance for the interview situation (see Kvale and Brinkmann, 2009). In addition to questions regarding the stakeholder's background and role, present and future views of place innovation and local regeneration, the guide was designed to focus on personal experiences and current perceptions of collaboration, information exchange and vision thinking in order to reveal challenges and ideas.

The data collection was conducted from November 2016 to May 2018.[1] Before these interviews the authors visited Old Town and Seaside Resort several times during the autumn of 2016 and spring of 2017 where observations were carried out on walks and guided tours as well as meetings with local elected officials and public administrators. Furthermore, local documents and websites were studied. To sum up, data collection included in-depth interviews, documents, visits and observations on site. Documents included websites, local and regional analysis and earlier studies of visitors and residents.

Our primary data includes 36 one-hour interviews with a total of 40 respondents and many of them had multiple roles as business owners, residents and local politicians. The selection of this study represented both new and established actors in and around Old Town and Seaside Resort. The mix included socially active respondents involved in several associations and networks as well as more "invisible" and not very active respondents still with an interest in the area. The selection of respondents was based on a snowball sample to capture different stakeholder groups in order to avoid a certain bias. Snowball sampling is based on referral sampling where one respondent recommends the second, who refers to the third and so on. Snowball sampling is a particularly valuable method to reach and locate a target group or hidden groups within the studied population, giving access to social circles and encouraging involvement in the study, since it is often based on trust. This method is furthermore suitable in trying to reach the street level or insiders in conflict environments in order to uncover social experiences, lifestyles and perspectives of various groups.

In order to enhance the validity mixed methods were applied (see Atkinson and Flint, 2001; Cohen and Arieli, 2011). The 40 respondents were represented as follows: in the Old Town the 21 stakeholders were: merchants (3), restaurants (3), hotel (1), tourist firms (3), property owners (2), arts and craftsmen (2), nonprofit associations (2), educational institution (1), museum (1), government and municipal organization (1), and elected officials (2). Nine of these were also residents in the Old Town. The 19 stakeholders from Seaside Resort were: merchants/outdoor activity firms (5), restaurants (2), hotels (4), property owners (2), arts and craftsmen (1), media (2), museum (1) and government and municipal organizations (2). A majority of these were also residents in the Seaside Resort.

The interviews, with the permission of the respondents, were recorded and then transcribed. The material has been anonymized and handled with informed consent. Analysis of the material has taken place both in research pairs and in collaboration with the entire research group. Illustrative quotations were chosen based on recurring themes.

Analysis and compilation of results were based on our interpretation of the challenges experienced by the stakeholders, their visions and ideas for increased collaboration. The quotes were translated from Swedish and Norwegian into English.

Since this study aimed to create "robust" knowledge, the process and results are validated through continuous respondent validations in which the results and drafts of reports were presented and discussed with local community stakeholders at open meetings in both cities (see Torrance, 2012), as well as follow-up participatory observations during 2017 and 2018. Furthermore, the findings from the two cases have been presented for local municipal directories, local politicians and public administrators.

4.   FINDINGS

Below, the interview material is analyzed according to categories and key concepts related to the aim about challenges of stakeholder involvement and collaboration in place innovation in local community regeneration of smaller cities. The guiding themes for structuring and presenting the findings are: diverse interests, lack of communication and information, place identity, place innovation initiatives, coordination and communication, inclusion of stakeholders and bottom-up perspectives. Each finding has excerpts and stories from both the Norwegian (Old Town) and Swedish (Seaside Resort) cases.

4.1 Stakeholder Perceptions on Challenges in Collaboration

4.1.1 Diverse perspectives, conflicts and attitudes

In Old Town as well as in Seaside Resort there are many different stakeholder groups from different sectors and from different levels, both local and regional, and in the case of Old Town, national as well. In Old Town there are many associations that meet often and whose members are deeply committed to the place. Several of the respondents of this study belong to multiple stakeholder groups and thus represent different associations, or have multiple roles as local resident, property owner and/or business entrepreneur. This gives rise to a diversity of interest areas, which in many cases collide. There are many stakeholders who want to achieve a lot in Old Town but several respondents to this study think that everyone wants to develop Old Town in their own way and do not collaborate with others. There are many different things going on in many different arenas. Respondents think that conflicts between groups as well as individuals have hampered the development of Old Town over time. There are issues about preservation of the environment and facilities, and issues about development and contemporary use of cultural heritage in creating new experiences and structures. The following quotes illustrate the complexity:

> So it's a mix of state, municipal, and to some extent private ownership, which in itself makes management, governance and coordination complicated.

> And of course there are different interests here, as it is said, a cultural heritage that is to be preserved, it's a residential area, most of them live there, about 300 people live there and they own their properties, and of course they want a good living environment and then there are a number of entrepreneurs who have their business or other activities that primarily should have this as a business area.

> But there are so many of the old guard who were allowed to govern in the past, who just sit and protect the old things and when something's going to happen, it's on their premises, hence there will often be conflicts with the older generation.

> It is the case that the conflicts of interest in Old Town cover everyone from those who do not want to do anything in Old Town to those who want to do a lot. And then all those who are in between.

Some also believe that the reported conflicts are exaggerated and that, although there are contradictions, these are not as serious as often described.

> First of all, I've probably never experienced the conflict level or the oppositions as strongly as they are described in the media.

The stakeholders in Old Town do not experience the conflicts as serious, but what seems most disturbing is that conflicts do hamper development. This disturbs those who do not have a purely conservative agenda. They are not afraid of conflict and many respondents express a wish that someone would step in and point out the direction for the future, not so much to resolve the conflict but to initiate action.

In the Seaside Resort there are many stakeholders who feel that a major problem for development of the place is a decades-old prevailing local attitude. This is described as a tone used by residents who are born in the municipality. Many actors believe that these attitudes are primarily problem-oriented and can counteract positive development and that they may impede their personal activities.

> Those of us who were not born here usually say that it takes seven generations to enter the community in the Seaside Resort. It's a slight exaggeration, but there is something to it.

> My experience of this place is that you are very problem-oriented, and you do not see opportunities. And do not pick out what we can be proud of, only looking for mistakes.

> It's a little different attitude here in the Seaside Resort that I feel needs to be changed. . . it's almost like. . . take care of yourself and shame on the rest.

4.1.2 Lack of communication and information
Respondents in both cases clearly state that there is limited coordination and communication both internally among the stakeholders and between the cases and the respective municipal city centers. There are issues such as lack of common store hours, planning of events and shared communication to external stakeholders such as visitors and municipality. There is limited and fragmented communication within networks, although not inclusive. Observations of stakeholders' websites show a variety of information and offers related to the place that indicate a lack of collaboration and common place identity. There is furthermore no common communication channel so that updated and complete information can be spread within the area and within all stakeholder groups. These quotes are from respondents in the Old Town:

> We need a shared platform to meet and discuss how we can benefit from each other.

> Missing a common communication – no overview – a lot happens but no one knows – Exclusive email groups. . . Information is fragmented.

In the Seaside Resort many respondents consider communication and information between actors to be very valuable and that this must be strengthened to get an attractive city center. It is important to get information about what other actors do.

> There is poor communication between the various activities at the city center, I do not know what the others are doing.

The external communication and joint marketing of the place need to be developed in different channels. The lack of a single communication channel between the municipality and the stakeholders in the Seaside Resort is stressed.

> The business unit [of the municipality] exists but there's a lot of redirection before you get an answer. It would be great for someone with knowledge that can help me to the right person. . . there should be one window to look in [to the municipality] and not a hundred. . . Calling the reception desk is useless. . ..

4.1.3   Indistinct place identity

Many of the stakeholders express challenges related to place identity, viewing places as unique and genuine environments. In Old Town most of the stakeholders consider that the environment and cultural heritage need to be preserved, maintained and to some extent developed without endangering the uniqueness.

> You have to sell what is genuine. That's what people want! They think it's pleasing to cross the streets and look at the houses and the amazing authenticity. . . so do not change things, show it [Old Town] as it actually is.

> What I want is that Old Town should be an authentic cultural heritage, that we should be experienced as authentic.

There is still some disagreement about Old Town's identity. Many respondents emphasize its distinctive profile and location and want the collaboration to strive for more consensus.

> My impression is that there are many things to disagree about. One does not wish the Old Town to be the same as the city center, most people anyway, maybe there are some who want this, those with more modern companies, but most people understand and wish that Old Town should develop towards an even more unique profile, the special thing about Old Town, namely that it is old and different than the modern city, and I think that most people agree that this is the effort to make and to build on.

The stakeholders express that Old Town has a high market value, as confirmed in local studies of visitors, and that they are amazed by the lack of recognition and development of Old Town as a major tourist attraction in the municipality and the region. Respondents representing the local residents strongly state that Old Town should not merely be seen as a picturesque scenic backdrop or stage set but as a real, living city that includes local residents, businesses and visitors. Other respondents representing businesses express a wish to preserve the past, the cultural heritage, by using it in the present time, for example by filling it with people, events, cafés and restaurants so that everyone has a chance to enter Old Town and for a few hours experience this unique place, and hopefully pass on something to the future.

> The Old Town is good at craft traditions, stories, preserving the fortress town, there is no need to create a circus to bring life to the Old Town without developing what's there. There are shops and cafés that fit in, we do not want anything flashy and carousels but the ones that fit in Old Town.

Furthermore, an attractive city must have several social spatial attributes that indicate a living and active city.

> For a city to work, the social space must be. . . you have to have a square where there should be chairs exposed saying that inside the walls there is a café, you have to have a bookshelf of books outside on the street that says there are more books and a bookstore inside. And there must be a transition from outer to inner social space. Not ten stairs up but on the same level. Outdoor social spaces are crucial for a city to work.

In the Seaside Resort many of the stakeholders also express pride in living and working in a beautiful setting, and several stakeholders highlight the quality of life they perceive through living in the Seaside Resort with its authenticity and beautiful nearby coastal landscape. However, many stakeholders express a nostalgic longing for what has been in the past and for a more vibrant city center. This view is also confirmed in earlier local visitors' and residents' studies. Respondents describe a time that seems to be a few decades ago when the Seaside Resort was crowded with people during the summer with many events in the city, unlike today where there has been a declining development with fewer people in the streets, not only in the off-peak season but also in the summer season.

> Now I have been running the business for several years, I think if you go back to the first summer, there were always a lot of people out in the city center. . . But today on a Sunday there are almost no people in the streets.

Also, in the Seaside Resort many respondents express a sense of resignation with the place development as illustrated in the following quotes:

Another problem is that there is also a kind of fatigue, resignation among the stakeholders in the city center . . . like: we've done this before . . . nothing will be better.

There has been information sent [from the municipality] by e-mail to information meetings, but it has been a bit of time-wasting for us businessmen, since many have considered that nothing has happened in the local development. Therefore, I have not attended the meetings.

Furthermore, today many storefronts are empty and some respondents in the Seaside Resort stress the fear of rising crime in the city center.

I have quite a lot of problems in terms of drugs and crime. . . we may need a police officer stationed outside or something.

4.2   Stakeholders' Visions and Ideas for Addressing the Challenges

4.2.1   Inclusion of stakeholders and bottom-up perspectives

A future understanding and acceptance of each other's perspectives and interests is called for as a necessity in order to start work on resolving conflicts and developing shared visions for Old Town as well as for Seaside Resort. Information and clarity about the regulatory framework and external framework for all actors is therefore a fundamental requirement for starting work on vision development in both cases. In Seaside Resort the importance of working together and not merely in informal overlapping networks is emphasized.

It should not be us and them, but we should all be here to complement each other and never see each other as enemies.

There are groups high and low and if you speak out, everyone runs their own race. One can do so much more with collaboration, though everyone is eager to take care of their own business of course.

In Seaside Resort respondents also express a need to clarify the roles of stakeholders but also to include those who are not involved in local regeneration, that is, property owners and those businesses that are located outside or on the outskirts of the city center.

In both cases the property owners are a group of stakeholders that other stakeholders want to get more involved in the collaboration and development processes. The property owners state that they are interested in having a good living environment, and in many cases they are also business owners and rent out homes and commercial space. It is up to every property owner to choose whom to rent to, but there is a wish that property owners should have a long-term perspective when renting housing, to rent in a way that allows residents to stay for a long time.

Some stakeholders in Old Town think that their task is to preserve a unique historical environment for future generations, and that this implies a responsibility towards those living in Old Town. Although these actors also realize that entrepreneurs are important to Old Town and that they need to have a fair chance to survive, they consider the long-term perspective to take precedence over the short-term.

The importance of filling the empty premises in the city center is also strongly argued by the respondents in the Seaside Resort.

> The most important thing is to establish firms in the empty premises in the city center – but how do we attract them? That's the hard part!

The seasonal variation is perceived as a problem in both cases, while also providing a basis for an expanded range. In order to achieve a more even flow of visitors throughout the year in Old Town, it is proposed that municipal services, such as health centers, should be moved to the Old Town. In addition to the number of stores, which some argue is fitting and others consider inadequate, several actors discuss that the supply must fit into the Old Town's environment and character, both in terms of content and appearance, and that coordination regarding hours of operation is necessary.

> The Old Town has the same problems that many other centers have, but one must define what one wants. . . you have to figure out why it's important to have year-round shops and visitors all year and find arguments for that.

New establishments of firms and other city center stakeholders are hence sought out in both cases. There is a need and place for a wider range of year-round shops, restaurants, activities, and so on. The local development and offerings should be adapted for those who live there and for visitors, not the other way around, that is, a bottom-up approach is required. However, in Seaside Resort the difficulties of being a new entrepreneur in the city are mentioned, referring to the business climate as well as attitude towards new actors. It takes time to be accepted and to build reliable business relationships.

> When we came here, we said that we planned to work with the local actors. Thus we had some difficulties to get into the networks . . . and to find partners we really could rely on.

Furthermore, respondents in Old Town commented on the range of shops and other offerings year-round and on weekdays, not just during summer season or at weekends. Safety is referred to as a need for better lighting in the streets during winter.

> So I think, having things that people need every day is important. Grocery store, florist, bakery, post office, more ferry times, lighting, cleaning, parking and traffic. . . Better offerings for children.

4.2.2 Coordination and communication

Local collaboration and communication requires a coordinating daily leader, for example in the form of a center developer, provided that this role has local anchoring according to respondents in both cases. In Old Town this role should also include being Old Town's collective voice in collaboration with major actors such as the municipality, county and defense building.

> I think the municipality should play a greater role in future business ventures, and I think it is necessary. People are a little tired and wondering how the municipality will get involved and that something is happening now and not just talk.

> The initiatives need to be with the business community. Ownership is important. The municipality needs to show greater responsibility for what we want with Old Town, but not take ownership.

In Seaside Resort respondents also call for someone who can work strategically and coordinate stakeholders.

> If that person has a strategic mission and resources to get facts and background data. . . and is able to coach people and businesses. But not to hire an event coordinator!

Overall, respondents express the need for collaboration and a coordinating force. A digital platform for continuous meetings and dialogue where all different actors can meet and learn from each other is also of importance.

> What's unique about Old Town is that it's a whole city [an old town district], not just a few streets. It is completely unique. There is no other city in Norway that has such conditions as Old Town, but here they really are a lot of trouble. . . What's needed is an old-fashioned mayor who could see and make decisions.

> A center developer would be fine, provided that this person has the right contacts and mandate to decide and who works for development of Old Town year-round.

> Old Town lacks wireless networks – Develop information via the internet. Wireless is good when you want to make the story more accessible and with

the crafts tradition, live the story. . . We need a common platform to meet and discuss how we can benefit from each other in the development of Old Town. Important to learn from each other.

All respondents express a need for improved communication among stakeholders as well as with residents and visitors. In Seaside Resort several stakeholders mention digital marketing and improving the skills of social media.

When we have our customers on Facebook we are building relations – we know many of them very well.

We have the ordinary social media platforms such as Facebook, Instagram and Twitter and a website and blog of our own of course. . . we build relationships with customers this way. . . here we have a need for younger skilled employees to be able to develop this.

Several of the respondents in Seaside Resort furthermore have established, or plan to establish, e-commerce to complement their stores and to level out seasonal variations.

4.2.3 Internal and external relationships based on shared visions
The need of a common vision in place innovation and local regeneration is emphasized in both cases. In Old Town the perceived lack of common conceptual visions and municipal passivity results in difficulty in reaching consensus on what Old Town is and should be, which creates uncertainty and frustration about the future according to the respondents.

The municipality must be more active towards the Old Town. . . go in and resolve conflicts and do not just leave us who are in conflict to resolve it.

The respondents mention that there are difficulties in integrating Old Town into the municipal development strategy, in order to increase attractiveness and entrepreneurship, housing and visitors for the whole municipality. Even though the policy is to take formal decisions based on the entire municipality's development strategy, Old Town has been granted a relatively large degree of independence within the municipality, which has formed informal decision-making structures regarding the development of Old Town. The municipality is seen as a passive stakeholder.

The municipality has in no way taken hold or ownership in the Old Town!

Respondents emphasize that it is necessary to clarify the framework of who makes decisions in Old Town. In the city center of the municipality a developer has been co-employed by the municipality and the city center's retailers in order to enhance collaboration and attractiveness, which has left Old Town in a culture of divisions and conflicts.

Respondents in the two cases discuss the role of the municipalities in place innovation and local regeneration. In Old Town there was a clear wish that the municipality's responsibility and presence in Old Town needs to increase, hence that the development processes should be performed in close collaboration with the stakeholders of Old Town. There is a need to clarify and anchor responsibilities, roles and functions due to the committed cross-sector diversity of stakeholders.

> I think that's important, first of all, one has to accept that there are different interests, so that you have to accept that all these different interests are legitimate.

> All the things that are done, are done by committed private individuals. I think committed private individuals are absolutely necessary; many arrangements could not be implemented without them.

> The municipality should be in charge of the development of Old Town but in consultation with the actors of Old Town. This is because there are several different ownership interests in Old Town.

However, different stakeholders may have different time perspectives related to their specific interests in Old Town. The following quotes illustrate this:

> I think you have some unrealistic expectations about what Old Town should be. I think you should be a little realistic. And let things build up slowly.

> For a city to work, there must be past, present and future, not just history. . . we will develop Old Town so that it can meet the million [visitors] that come in five years.

In Seaside Resort respondents also mention the need of a shared vision, hence also that communication among the city stakeholders as well as communication with the municipality needs to be strengthened to increase collaboration.

> There is poor communication between the different actors in the city. . . one must work together to get to a development, to understand what others do and you must see the big picture.

4.2.4   Place innovation initiatives

In Old Town and Seaside Resort there is ongoing collaboration, including successful innovative, almost symbiotic collaboration, although within limited groups. New initiatives for collaboration have recently been launched through the tourism destination organization in Old Town. The initiative is based on collecting common funds and having a common voice both inside and outside Old Town. All of them point out, however, that this is a temporary solution.

> Important to learn from each other by meeting. Collaboration at all levels is important. Important to gather all actors regularly and have dialogue once per month or quarter.

In Seaside Resort there are initiatives and collaboration around the newly established city laboratory where the municipality aims to work in a more open and integrated way with stakeholders and the community, for example meetings, workshops, and living labs. Furthermore, symbiotic collaboration can be illustrated as when different stakeholders helped each other with temporary premises and co-created new concepts during renovation of real estate in the city. In Old Town a similar innovative living lab collaboration was launched in 2018 to act as a meeting point for local stakeholders and students.

In addition to the above, respondents state that a common starting point is needed that is considered neutral and interesting to all actors. Working together in projects is mentioned as it brings inspiration, development and hope for the future, according to respondents in Seaside Resort.

> We get inspiration from the project. The composition of people is great. Everyone can be heard and if you are male or female does not matter. We all work for the same thing!

> Projects are good in many respects. I develop my business in collaboration with other businesses and the municipality.

Several respondents view projects as a lever to get things done with some extra resources, although the projects should not serve as an excuse not to work continuously with these issues in the municipality.

In Seaside Resort many respondents express visions of a future city that is vibrant with small city charm and nostalgia with a street life including a wide range of small shops, restaurants and coffee shops for residents as well as visitors. According to respondents, Seaside Resort should be characterized by increased services, improved personal relations and safety.

5. TOWARDS AN INCLUSIVE PLACE INNOVATION APPROACH

In this chapter we present and discuss how place innovation perspectives can be used to address issues of diversity and stakeholder collaboration in the renewal of a small city center. The unique resources of a place, in this case cultural heritage, with tangible and intangible values, offer a rich potential for the local community while at the same time contributing complex prioritization of decisions in place innovation and regeneration processes (see Aas et al., 2005; Ashworth, 2017; Yang, 2014). Both cases include diverse stakeholder interests and sectors (see Yang, 2014). Stakeholders show a lack of insight into and understanding of the needs and motives of other stakeholder groups. Pride and authenticity based on cultural heritage are prominent in the two cases. Conflicting interests towards place innovation and lasting conflicts characterize Old Town (see Hamelink, 2008; Cohen and Arieli, 2011), whereas nostalgia, a parochial attitude and a sense of resignation, as well as lack of a common vision dominate Seaside Resort (see Fanzini et al., 2013). Several challenges were identified related to diverse perspectives, conflicts and attitudes; limited inclusion of stakeholders; lack of communication and information; and indistinct place identity. These were mainly due to the diverse mix of stakeholder interests, among those stakeholders who produce, use and intermediate Old Town and Seaside Resort (see Aas et al., 2005; Al-hagla, 2010; Evans, 1997; Knox and Mayer, 2013; Lindberg et al., 2017; Richards and Duif, 2018). An urgent challenge that is mentioned only in Seaside Resort is fear of increased crime and loss of safety in the city center (see Bettencourt et al., 2010; MacLeod, 2011).

Regarding prioritization, the elements of place, residents, businesses and visitors need to be balanced since they are mutually dependent (see Lindberg et al., 2015; Al-hagla, 2010). The following guiding principles address how to meet the identified challenges towards inclusive place innovation as a means for local community regeneration:

1. To identify and include diverse perspectives.
2. To build community on transparent communication and common physical and digital platforms.
3. To cultivate the place identity.
4. To apply a step-by-step regeneration process.

Respondents wish to be included and suggest doing this step by step to build community inclusion and trust (see Al-hagla, 2010). Yang's (2014) suggested steps in stakeholder analysis in urban regeneration (identification of stakeholders and interests, prioritization and decisions) may be a first step in meeting the challenges of inclusion. The different time frames of respondents should be taken into consideration in regeneration processes since some of the small businesses struggle to survive year round and hence have a shorter time perspective compared to stakeholders from a public organization, an association or property owners. In both cases there are obvious flaws in communication and information because the information currently available is fragmented and rarely reaches beyond its own grouping. The studied organizational structure, or lack of it, implies a need for trust and an organizing body that coordinates activities and flow of information among all stakeholders (see Bernhard and Wihlborg, 2014; Getz et al., 2006), hence a bottom-up perspective is suggested to increase inclusion. Stakeholders call for continuous information and a common communication platform (physical and digital) that includes all stakeholders involved in regeneration processes.

In order to find innovative, inclusive bottom-up approaches for collaboration and urban regeneration, findings clearly show that physical meetings and discussions at neutral arenas are needed, such as city center laboratories, workshops and other similar living lab initiatives that both cases now have established (see Bergvall-Kareborn and Stahlbrost, 2009; Olsson et al., 2018). Furthermore, digital communication, especially social media platforms, is vital and applicable in local innovation and regeneration processes for internal as well as external communication. The place identities of Old Town and Seaside Resort are not fully discussed, communicated, negotiated or anchored among stakeholders and/or related to the municipality and the city center (see Lindberg et al., 2015; Mommaas, 2004). There is then a need for a place innovation process, as a holistic local community design process that develops visions, strategies and action plans related to the specific place identity.

The present study contributes by responding to calls for further research to deepen the insights into stakeholder identification and dynamics of stakeholder interaction in place innovation and regeneration processes (see Yang, 2014; Le Feuvre et al., 2016; Lindberg et al., 2015) by discussing practical as well as policy implications.

Collaborative approaches suggested by the stakeholders should focus on integration and inclusion of all stakeholders; a cumulative step-by-step process to build local community and place identity; trust and learning from each other; producing visions and strategies that enable prioritizing among interests; and a shared communication platform for internal and external communication (see Al-hagla, 2010; Aas et al., 2005; Lindberg et al., 2015; 2017; Yang, 2014; Bernhard and Wihlborg, 2014). Accordingly, there are multiple stakeholder challenges in place innovation and regeneration processes related to cultural heritage, and this needs to be further researched.

NOTE

1. Apart from the authors of this chapter, the data collection was performed together with two colleagues at University West.

REFERENCES

Aas, C., Ladkin, A. and Fletcher, J. (2005). Stakeholder collaboration and heritage management. *Annals of Tourism Research*, **32**(1), 28–48.

Ahmad, Y. (2006). The scope and definitions of heritage: From tangible to intangible. *International Journal of Heritage Studies*, **12**(3), 292–300.

Al-hagla, K.S. (2010). Sustainable urban development in historical areas using the tourist trail approach: A case study of the Cultural Heritage and Urban Development (CHUD) project in Saida, Lebanon. *Cities*, **27**(4), 234–48.

Alvesson, M. and Kärreman, D. (2011). *Qualitative Research and Theory Development, Mystery as Method*. London: Sage Publications.

Ashworth, G.J. (2017). *Senses of Place: Senses of Time*. Abingdon: Routledge.

Atkinson, R. and Flint, J. (2001). Accessing hidden and hard-to-reach populations: Snowball research strategies. *Social Research Update*, **33**(1), 1–4.

Bartunek, J.M. and Louis, M.R. (1996). *Insider/Outsider Team Research*. Vol. 40. London: Sage Publications.

Bell, D. and Jayne, M. (2006). *Small Cities: Urban Experience beyond the Metropolis*. Abingdon: Routledge.

Bergvall-Kareborn, B. and Stahlbrost, A. (2009). Living lab: An open and citizen-centric approach for innovation. *International Journal of Innovation and Regional Development*, **1**(4), 356–70.

Bernhard, I. and Olsson, A.K. (2015). *A Nordic Perspective on Co-operation for Sustainable Regional and Destination Development*, Report no. 2015:3. Trollhättan: University College West.

Bernhard, I. and Wihlborg, E. (2014). Policy entrepreneurs in networks: Implementation of two Swedish municipal contact centres from an actor perspective. *International Journal of Entrepreneurship and Small Business*, **21**(3), 288–302.

Bernhard, I., Lundh Snis, U. and Olsson, A.K. (2017). The Old Town district: Not just a scenic backdrop – stakeholders' perspectives in urban re-generation. In Iréne Bernhard (ed.), *Uddevalla Symposium 2017: Innovation, Entrepreneurship and Industrial Dynamics in Internationalized Regional Economies: Revised papers first presented at the 20th Uddevalla Symposium 15–17 June, 2017* (pp. 111–27), Trollhättan: University West.

Bettencourt, L.M.A., Lobo, J., Strumsky, D. and West, G.B. (2010). Urban scaling and its deviations: Revealing the structure of wealth, innovation and crime across cities. *PLoS ONE* **5**(11), e13541.

Book, K., Eskilsson, L. and Khan, J. (2010). Governing the balance between sustainability and competitiveness in urban planning: The case of the Orestad model. *Environmental Policy and Governance*, **20**(6), 382–96.

Bornhorst, T., Ritchie, J.B. and Sheehan, L. (2010). Determinants of tourism success for DMOs and destinations: An empirical examination of stakeholders' perspectives. *Tourism Management*, **31**(5), 572–89.

Cohen, N. and Arieli, T. (2011). Field research in conflict environments: Methodological challenges and snowball sampling. *Journal of Peace Research*, **48**(4), 423–35.

Evans, R. (1997). *Regenerating Town Centres*. Manchester: Manchester University Press.

Fanzini, D., Bergamini, I. and Rotaru, I. (2013). Sustainability, culture and urban regeneration: New dimensions for the technological project. TECHNE. *Journal of Technology for Architecture and Environment* [S.l.], 60–65, May.

Freeman, R.E. (1984). *Strategic Management: A Stakeholder Approach*. New York: Cambridge University Press.

Garrod, B., Fyall, A., Leask, A. and Reid, E. (2012). Engaging residents as stakeholders of the visitor attraction. *Tourism Management*, **33**(5), 1159–73.

Getz, D., Andersson, T. and Larson, M. (2006). Festival stakeholder roles: Concepts and case studies. *Event Management*, **10**, 103–22.

Gospodini, A. (2004). Urban morphology and place identity in European cities: Built heritage and innovative design. *Journal of Urban Design*, **9**(2), 225–48.

Halinen, A. and Törnroos, J.Å. (2005). Using case methods in the study of contemporary business networks. *Journal of Business Research*, **58**(9), 1285–97.

Hamdouch, A., Nyseth, T., Demaziere, C., Førde, A., Serrano, J. and Aarsæther, N. (eds) (2016). *Creative Approaches to Planning and Local Development: Insights from Small and Medium-Sized Towns in Europe*. Abingdon: Routledge.

Hamelink, C.J. (2008). Urban conflict and communication. *International Communication Gazette*, **70**(3–4), 291–301.

Healey, P. (2009). City regions and place development. *Regional Studies*, **43**(6), 831–43.

Houghton, J.P. and Stevens, A. (2011). *City Branding and Stakeholder Engagement*. In Dinnie, K. (ed.), *City Branding*. Basingstoke: Palgrave Macmillan, pp. 45–53.

Islind, A.S., Lindroth, T., Lundh Snis, U. and Sørensen, C. (2016). Co-creation and fine-tuning of boundary resources in small-scale platformization. In Lundh Snis, U. (ed.), *Nordic Contributions in IS Research: 7th Scandinavian Conference on Information Systems, SCIS 2016 and IFIP8.6 2016*, Ljungskile, Sweden, 7–10 August (pp. 149–62). Springer International Publishing.

Jamal, T. and Stronza, A. (2009). Collaboration theory and tourism practice in protected areas: Stakeholders, structuring and sustainability. *Journal of Sustainable Tourism*, **17**(2), 169–89.

Jarratt, D. and Gammon, S. (2016). 'We had the most wonderful times': Seaside nostalgia at a British resort. *Tourism Recreation Research*, **41**(2), 123–33.

Knox, P. and Mayer, H. (2013). *Small Town Sustainability: Economic, Social, and Environmental Innovation*. Walter de Gruyter.

Kvale, S. and Brinkmann, S. (2009). *Interviews. Learning the Craft of Qualitative Research Interviewing*. Los Angeles, USA, London, UK, New Delhi, India and Singapore: Sage Publications.

Le Feuvre, M., Medway, D., Warnaby, G., Ward, K. and Goatman, A. (2016). Understanding stakeholder interactions in urban partnerships. *Cities*, **52**, 55–65.

Lindberg, M., Karlberg, H. and Gelter, J. (2017). Tourism networking for regional place innovation in Swedish Lapland. *International Journal of Innovation and Regional Development*, **7**(4), 257–72.

Lindberg, M., Ericson, Å., Gelter, J. and Karlberg, H. (2015). Samhällsdesign genom platsinnovation. *Design Research Journal*, no. 1, 9–13.

Lucarelli, A. and Brorström, S. (2013). Problematising place branding research: A meta-theoretical analysis of the literature. *The Marketing Review*, **13**(1), 65–81.

MacLeod, M. (2011). Urban politics reconsidered: Growth machine to post-democratic city? *Urban Studies*, **48**(12), 2629–60.

Mayer, H. and Knox, P. (2010). Small-town sustainability: Prospects in the second modernity. *European Planning Studies*, **18**(10), 1545–65.

Mommaas, H. (2004). Cultural clusters and the post-industrial city: Towards the remapping of urban cultural policy. *Urban Studies*, **41**(3), 507–32.

Nyseth, T. and Viken, A. (eds) (2009). *Place Reinvention: Northern Perspectives*. Abingdon: Ashgate Publishing.

Olsson, A.K. (2016). Canals, rivers and lakes as experiencescapes: Destination development based on strategic use of inland water. *International Journal of Entrepreneurship and Small Business*, **29**(2), 217–43.

Olsson, A.K., Bernhard, I. and von Friedrich, Y. (2018). Approaches to inclusive networking in place development: An illustration from six smaller Scandinavian cities, *International Journal of Innovation and Regional Development*, **8**(3), 259–80.

Olsson, A.K., Therkelsen, A. and Mossberg, L. (2016). Making an effort for free: Volunteers' roles in destination-based storytelling. *Current Issues in Tourism*, **19**(7), 659–79.

Presenza, A., Del Chiappa, G. and Sheehan, L. (2013). Residents' engagement and local tourism governance in maturing beach destinations. Evidence from an Italian case study. *Journal of Destination Marketing & Management*, **2**(1), 22–30.

Richards, G. and Duif, L. (2018). *Small Cities with Big Dreams: Creative Placemaking and Branding Strategies*. New York: Routledge.

Robinson, D. (2005). The search for community cohesion: Key themes and dominant concepts of the public policy agenda. *Urban Studies*, **42**(8), 1411–27.

Snaith, T. and Haley, A. (1999). Residents' opinions of tourism development in the historic city of York, England. *Tourism Management*, **20**(5), 595–603.

Torrance, H. (2012). Triangulation, respondent validation, and democratic participation in mixed methods research. *Journal of Mixed Methods Research*, **6**(2), 111–23.

Vareide, K. and Nygaard, M. (2015). *Regional analyse for Fredrikstad 2014 – Attraktivitetsanalyse: Befolkningsutvikling, næringsutvikling og scenarier:* TF-notat nr. 8/2015, Telemarksforskning.

Walton, J.K. (2000). *The British Seaside: Holidays and Resorts in the Twentieth Century.* Manchester: Manchester University Press.

Yang, R.J. (2014). An investigation of stakeholder analysis in urban development projects: Empirical or rationalistic perspectives. *International Journal of Project Management*, **32**(5), 838–49.

Yin, R.K. (2018). *Case Study Research and Applications: Design and Methods.* 6th edn. Los Angeles, CA: Sage.

5. Patent generation in US metropolitan areas

Gordon F. Mulligan

1. INTRODUCTION

In recent times social scientists have become increasingly interested in both the features and implications of metropolitan creativity. Particular attention has focused on identifying those factors that help transform this creativity into inventions, which in turn lead to the innovation (and eventual diffusion) of new products and processes. These inventions are manifestations of new technical or scientific knowledge, often called *useful knowledge*, and therefore must be protected by patents (Mokyr 2009). In regional science and economic geography, the main contributors to this stream of research have included: Jane Jacobs (1969) and Edward Glaeser (2011) on spatial externalities, Richard Florida (2002, 2005) on the creative class, and Michael Porter (1979) on business strategy. This ever-widening research stream has also led to a growing appreciation of the complexities of useful knowledge and has shown how the processes of innovation and diffusion can both be affected by the forms assumed by this knowledge (Scott 2007).

During the rise of the so-called knowledge-based industries the US's 380 metropolitan economies have begun separating into two broad groups of leaders and laggards. The cities in the first group have become significantly wealthier, richer in human capital, more productive, and more innovative, while those in the second group continue to fall farther and farther behind. Moretti (2012), for one, believes that a permanent gap—based largely on region or location—has taken place in the life prospects for the nation's tens of millions of metropolitan inhabitants. In any case many theorists and policymakers have become very concerned about the widening rift in social welfare that now characterizes metropolitan America.

A Schumpeterian perspective, emphasizing both enterprise and creative destruction, has become popular for understanding why American metropolitan areas are now growing at such different rates (Schumpeter 1934). Here long-term prosperity can only be assured when enforceable property rights are put in place to protect the fruits of that enterprise (North 1990). Rights for (utility) patents are especially important because they ensure that entrepreneurs are rewarded for their efforts once they have created new products or processes. The current chapter follows in this tradition by studying the geographic aspects of metropolitan patenting, which is now recognized to be a key ingredient of innovation-driven growth. But patents only become important drivers of sustained regional prosperity when they are of high quality, and then some observers have equated the positive benefits of generating patents to those of having a high-quality workforce (Rothwell et al. 2013). Later in the chapter, unambiguous evidence is given that patenting activity became increasingly concentrated in America's very largest metropolitan economies during the 25-year period of 1990–2015. This trend is likely to reflect ongoing improvements in the national efficiency of patenting but also indicates widening disparities in the different regional levels of patenting.

This chapter estimates both patent *volumes* and per capita patent volumes, often called patent *densities*, at 5-year intervals over that same period. Given various data limitations, the analysis for 2000–2015 is more extensive than that for 1990–2000. Here a series of cross-sectional linear regressions endorses, and then extends, Ó hUallacháin's (1999) claim that population size largely accounts for the current variation in metropolitan patenting volumes. These new regressions also indicate that the roles of Economic Size, Location, and Industrial Specialization have become more important during the past fifteen years, while the roles of Human Capital and Prime Working Age have become less important.

2.   LITERATURE

A wide body of literature is devoted to the role of patents in economic development. This short review is designed to highlight those parts of this literature that are most relevant to metropolitan patenting activity.

2.1   Patents

A patent or trademark is designed to confer an intellectual property right on an owner, usually for a period of 20 years. The patent is meant to protect the way in which an expected invention will work or be used, whether that invention constitutes a machine, process, or method; in other cases, however, the patent is meant to protect an entirely new item that can be manufactured. Utility patents are usually differentiated from design patents, which instead protect the aesthetic or ornamental attributes of an item. The patent data used in this chapter refer to utility patents, which are the most common kind of patent issued by the US Patent and Trademark Office (2018). In the US, patent data are annually provided at several geographic scales and are assigned to regions or locations according to the place of residence of the primary inventor. This can lead to assignment problems when patents involve more than a single inventor or when multi-location firms apply for the property right. The early work on patent generation was often carried out at the state level but the metropolitan level is more appropriate because the boundaries of these urban regions define the nation's various labor markets (Mulligan et al. 2014). Patents do not confer obligations on owners even though the expected result, the so-called invention, might be entirely viable. This incentive system can sometimes lead to excessive patenting, especially in areas like biotechnology, and over-patenting can prove to be a barrier to the creation of new products or processes. So-called patent mills are more likely to be found in large metropolitan areas and in other places that specialize in the knowledge-based industries just mentioned.

Even before the influential work of Griliches (1990), patents were widely regarded as being reliable and objective indicators of inventive activity. Among other things, these inventions create new information that can be used by other agents, so the issue of knowledge appropriability invariably arises. Following Schumpeter (1934), patents have also been adopted as proxies for the different rates of innovative activity that are seen across regions, where innovations are the commercial outcomes of those inventions. However, the strict linear or sequential perspective has fallen into disfavor because it is now recognized that innovative processes will always be tempered by other conditions in the region, including the quality of institutions, the age and skills of the workforce, and the availability of credit.

2.2 Regional Knowledge Production

Utility patents have been used for some time in the US to measure the volume of useful (technical and scientific) knowledge. Not so long ago, in fact, such knowledge was estimated from invention citations in trade periodicals because no national agency issued annual patent counts. However, after Jaffe (1989) and Feldman (1994), attempts were made to differentiate areas—states or metropolitan labor markets—according to their regional knowledge production functions (RKPFs). These studies have shown that metropolitan patent production is tied to volumes of both university and private research, where strong distance decay occurs in the local (within-region) knowledge transfers of both types of research

(Anselin et al. 1997). Presumably the unexplained variation in these models was due to local particularities like specialization in the economic base or the quality of the local infrastructure. More recent research, much of it international, has addressed the role of various institutional factors in knowledge production, including the facilitating role of local social capital and the importance of linkages between local research agencies (Capello 2002; Balconi et al. 2004; Fritsch 2004). Clearly the presence of research and development agencies in cities appears to be a common ingredient for advancing new technical knowledge.

Despite this extensive research very little is really known about the variation of patenting activity across the *entire* US metropolitan system. Some of the early studies of RKPFs only examined patents generated in the nation's very largest cities, much like those targeted by the Brookings Institution today, and the methodologies were never intended to apply to smaller cities. Moreover, most studies of patenting activity fail to account for the effects of important contextual factors like age of the workforce or productivity of the local economy. As matters now stand, it is difficult to assess the stability of those effects over time or to distinguish those factors that are becoming more important from those that are becoming less important.

2.3   City Size

A more general approach was outlined by Ó hUallacháin (1999), who investigated US metropolitan patent generation during a single year. He contended that the widespread advantages conferred by city size—arising from scale economies, corporate headquarter locations, and early business spinoffs—would be likely to overwhelm the narrow advantages conferred by research agencies and, as a result, population size should be considered the prime contributor to patenting activity. To back up this claim he developed a linear regression model with five explanatory variables, where population size alone accounted for nearly 80 percent of the patenting activity across some 270-plus metropolitan areas. The other variables of his model included: the proportion of employment found in a few key manufacturing industries; the proportion of the city's adult population with a university degree; a location in the Manufacturing Belt; and an indicator of the importance of Research One universities and funded R&D laboratories. The five variables together accounted for nearly 90 percent of the variation in patents across the nation's metropolitan areas. Surprisingly, the effect of research facilities was found to be the least significant factor of all, probably because so many small cities simply lacked these knowledge-generating facilities.

Given Ó hUallacháin's favorable results for this one year, 1996, more studies of metropolitan patenting activity are needed that recognize the importance of city population size. Furthermore, these studies should be undertaken for different years if only to clarify the stability of the estimates, especially when drawn from cross-sectional regressions. But the original approach needs further modification for a handful of reasons. First, dividing up the metropolitan areas into two groups according to their locations—inside versus outside the Manufacturing Belt—now seems highly tenuous because, among other matters, this groups together the many stagnant places of the Southeast with the notable "high fliers" of the West and Pacific Northwest. Second, there are other key variables like wages and amenities that must be included in the analysis. Omission of these variables might distort the regression estimates and provide a false picture of the underlying bases for the different growth trajectories seen in these metropolitan areas. And, third, the estimation would be more accurate if both the levels of variables, as well as the relationships between those variables, could somehow be considered in the regressions. This should be done to reflect, or even expose, the very different innovation ecosystems that now exist across the nation's metropolitan areas.

2.4 New Issues and Perspectives

The upcoming analysis considers these and other changes to Ó hUallacháin's methodology. Instead of dividing the observations according to the boundary of the Manufacturing Belt, heating and cooling degree days are now used to recognize the different locations of the hundreds of metropolitan areas. These variables also have some instrumental merit because various studies have shown that American households exhibit a willingness to accept lower wages when they reside in places having milder climates. Second, instead of using only five variables, the upcoming analysis adopts more than 20 variables for the estimation (see below). These variables cover a wider array of human activities and address the remarkable variety that now exists in metropolitan amenities. And, third, instead of estimating patent volumes (or densities) using this array of variables, the current chapter reduces those variables down to six independent factors (clusters of interrelated variables) and then uses the factor loadings in the estimation. This approach not only captures some aspects of the nation's metropolitan innovation ecosystems, where relationships and linkages are key features, but also partly addresses the endogeneity problem that plagues most cross-sectional estimations. Once these clusters have been identified by multivariate techniques, linear regression is applied in the usual way to a set of orthogonal factors, and changes to the coefficients on each of those factors can be traced over time.

3. DATA

This section addresses the variables that were used in the analysis. Special attention is given to the sources for those variables as numerous agencies, websites and almanacs were consulted in order to assemble the required data.

3.1 Observations

Patent data were collected annually over a 25-year span for those metropolitan areas that are currently being monitored by the Bureau of Economic Analysis (BEA) (2018). In fact, these data were assembled from two separate tables that are available at the same website: (1) annual grants for county and metropolitan areas in 1990–1999; and (2) annual grants for micropolitan and metropolitan areas in 2000–2015 (US Patent and Trademark Office 2018). The patent data in (2) were adopted as a base and then the data in (1) were adjusted, if required, and then merged. In fact, two different types of adjustments were made before the data in the two tables could be matched. First, the 1990–1999 patent counts for individual counties were used to estimate earlier counts for those micropolitan areas that only reached metropolitan status after 2000; this was required because micropolitan areas were not even recognized prior to the 2000 national census. Second, any changes made to the composition of the metropolitan statistical areas—especially the very largest ones—over the entire study period were accounted for. The hybrid patent table was then modified slightly to include only those 380 metropolitan areas that are now being monitored by the BEA, all of which are recognized by the US Census Bureau.

3.2 Patent Measures

The upcoming analysis makes use of two somewhat different indicators of patenting activity. The first measure, *PATVL*, is the annual volume of utility patents while the second measure, *PATDN*, is the annual density of those patents. The density figure, calculated as *PATVL/POPUL* (times 1000), standardizes patent generation by that year's metropolitan population and is preferred by some as a measure of patenting activity. The data for patent volumes have been taken from the US Patent and Trademark Office (2018) website.

3.3 Contextual Variables

A grand total of 24 variables were considered for the estimations carried out at 5-year intervals between 2000 and 2015. These variables covered a wide range of metropolitan attributes including population size, location, industrial specialization, human capital, recent growth, and amenities.

Four variables were chosen to capture the very different demographic and economic characteristics of the metropolitan economies. Population size, *POPUL*, was adopted because, as Ó hUallacháin and others have pointed out, the nation's largest cities, like New York and Chicago, have production ecosystems—with highly beneficial internal and external scale economies—that are very different from those of the nation's smallest cities like Yuma, AZ and Dothan, AL. A second variable, *WAGES*, was chosen because average wages and salaries are known to vary a lot across the metropolitan landscape, in part because substantial qualitative differences exist in the workforces of those places. Greater patent production, as well as more active entrepreneurship, should occur in those areas enjoying higher wages and salaries. A third variable, *LABFP*, was chosen to capture the (gross) labor force participation rate, which is measured here as the ratio between total employment and population; and a fourth variable, *GDPPC*, was chosen to capture the different levels of per capita productivity seen across the many metropolitan economies. Two other variables were constructed to capture recent trends in the labor markets of those places. The percentage population growth, *POPGR*, and the percentage wage growth, *WAGGR*, were calculated for the three years prior to each estimation year, thereby conforming to the same time interval chosen by several agencies that monitor US metropolitan growth. Data for these variables were taken from the US Bureau of Economic Analysis (2018) website or were manufactured from those BEA data.

Other data provided by the US Census Bureau (2018) were used to address some of the qualitative differences that existed across those numerous metropolitan workforces. *PRIME* was constructed to represent the volume of workers in the youthful (prime) cohort (aged 15–44) while *BACDG* and *ADVDG* were chosen to represent the number of people (aged 25 or over) having bachelor's degrees and advanced degrees, respectively, in those metropolitan populations. Each of these raw figures was in turn changed into a percentage format, where the corresponding variables *PRPRI*, *PRBDG* and *PRADV* represent the relative share of a youthful population or the relative incidence of a university-educated workforce, respectively. So, in all, six variables were adopted to capture key age-related features of the metropolitan labor markets.

Data for two key employment variables were chosen to indicate the very different industrial specializations of the various metropolitan areas. Using the BEA website, overall jobs in the manufacturing sector, *MANEM*, classified as NAICS 31–33, were chosen to highlight those economies that were still highly engaged in activities of the prior industrial era. On the other hand, jobs in the professional, scientific, and technical services, *PROEM*, classified as NAICS 54, were chosen to highlight those economies engaged more in the knowledge-based industries of the post-industrial era. These two volumes were then divided by total employment to estimate *PRMAN* and *PRPRO*, respectively, which measure the varying percentage importance of both types of jobs across those metropolitan economies. So, in total, four variables were adopted to reflect the (changing) economic bases of the metropolitan economies.

Other data for several contextual variables were taken from the *Places Rated Almanac* (Savageau 2000). Location, reflecting both site and situation characteristics, was addressed by adopting two separate climate-based variables: heating degree days, *HEDAY*, and cooling degree days, *CLDAY*. These two variables were preferred over a single variable, total degree days, because of the extreme regional variation that exists across the continental US in both temperature and humidity. Ranked scores for six other variables were taken from the *Almanac* to capture a variety of local conditions that might influence the decisions of either firms or households: ambience (*AMBIE*), recreation (*RECRE*), health (*HEALT*), education (*EDUCA*), transportation (*TRANS*), and housing costs (*HOUSE*). The values for many of these attributes are known to vary positively with city population size but each still proves to be useful in providing contextual information about the different metropolitan areas. In each of these six cases the metropolitan scores remained constant during the period of 2000–2015.

The various contextual variables were all transformed into logarithmic form. This operation reduced the skewness of some variables and meant that extremely high or low factor scores were rarely generated in the multivariate analysis. Also, this meant that in the subsequent regression analysis the various factor loadings could be effectively interpreted as elasticities. So, by eliminating the scales of the contextual variables in the different cross-sectional regressions, the estimates of one year could more easily be compared to the estimates of another year.

4.   PATENT CONCENTRATION

Various reports by the Brookings Institution examine historic trends in US patenting activity and reveal how these trends have followed long-term

Table 5.1 *Analysis of patent volumes PATVL, 1990–2015*

	1990	1995	2000	2005	2010	2015
			Annual Count			
Nation	47482	55813	85068	74632	107788	140928
All Metro	43845	51722	79824	70459	102391	134474
% Nation	92.34	92.67	93.83	94.41	94.99	95.42
Top 100	36302	43051	66501	58469	86174	114567
% Nation	76.45	77.13	78.17	78.34	79.95	81.29
% Metro	82.79	83.23	83.31	82.98	84.16	85.19
			Herfindahl Index			
All Metro	0.0238	0.0233	0.0254	0.0276	0.0306	0.0339
Top 100	0.0342	0.0330	0.0355	0.0388	0.0420	0.0458
% Metro	45.64	47.92	48.66	46.31	49.86	54.21
Other 280	0.0102	0.0088	0.0093	0.0107	0.0119	0.0128
% Metro	54.36	52.08	51.34	53.69	50.14	45.79

Note: All Metro refers to the *n* = 380 places monitored by the BEA; Top 100 refers to the 100 largest metropolitan economies monitored by the Brookings Institution.

structural changes in the national economy (Rothwell et al. 2013). One such report traces nation-wide patenting rates, per 1000 persons, all the way back to 1790 and shows how these rates steadily rose up through a golden age until the years of the Great Depression, then declined precipitously for twenty years, bounced back again during the post-War era, fell back between 1974 and 1984, and then rose steadily again during the subsequent post-industrial era. In recent times annual fluctuations have reflected events like the post-2000 setback of the IT industry and the Great Recession of 2007–2009. While it is known that patenting activity is now heavily concentrated in the nation's largest metropolitan areas, where some 63 percent of all US (utility) patents are currently accounted for by only 20 metropolitan areas, little is known about how concentration has changed in recent decades.

The patent counts addressed above were used along with the national counts to analyze the changing nature of metropolitan patent concentration during 1990–2015. As the top half of Table 5.1 shows, the national counts showed a rise from 47 482 in 1990 to 140 928 in 2015, an increase of nearly 197 percent over the 25-year study period. During the same period the metropolitan counts *PATVL* rose some 207 percent from 43 845 to 134 474. In 1990 the nation's metropolitan areas accounted for 92.3 percent of the nation's patent volume but in 2015 this figure had grown to 95.4 percent. Table 5.1 also indicates how many of these patents were generated by the nation's 100 largest metropolitan areas, a group of key labor markets that are regularly monitored by the Brookings Institution (Shearer et al. 2018). These top-100 economies, whose populations all surpassed 0.55 million in 2018, generated a remarkable proportion, 76.4 percent, of the *national* patent total in 1990 and an even higher proportion, 81.3 percent, in 2015, where the steady rise seen from year to year was very similar to that seen for all metropolitan areas. As Table 5.1 also reveals, the proportion of all *metropolitan* patent counts attributable to these top-100 economies grew steadily over the study period, climbing from 82.8 percent in 1990 to 85.2 percent in 2015. In this case, however, there was a slight pre-Recession drop in 2005 and then a strong reversal back upwards afterward. So, in summary, during recent times patenting activity has not only become increasingly concentrated in the nation's array of metropolitan areas but it has become especially concentrated in the nation's 100 largest metropolitan areas.

The Herfindahl–Hirschman index is widely used to gauge the amount of concentration or degree of inequality in a chosen size distribution. In large part it is popular because the index is both easy to compute and simple to understand. In general, the index H is calculated as the sum of the squared relative shares (in employment, income, etc.), where the observation units can be firms, households, regions, and so on. The index ranges between a (theoretical) minimum of 0, indicating no concentration, and a maximum of 1, indicating absolute concentration. The Herfindahl index is usually used in studies having few observations, like industrial oligopolies, so the index values are generally high. However, there is no reason why the index cannot be adopted for analyzing concentration levels when there are numerous observations involved.

The bottom half of Table 5.1 uses these indices to reveal further aspects of the changing concentration in US metropolitan patent volumes *PATVL* during recent times. Across all 380 metropolitan areas, the degree of concentration rose steadily from $H = 0.0238$ in 1990 to $H = 0.0339$ in 2015. But among the top-100 labor markets monitored by the Brookings Institution the index climbed from $H = 0.0342$ to $H = 0.0458$ in 2015, indicating that patent volumes became even more concentrated within the upper tier of metropolitan areas than across the full array of such places. The same table indicates that patent volumes remained stable across the Other 280 smaller metropolitan economies, climbing only slightly (after an initial dip) from $H = 0.0102$ in 1990 to $H = 0.0128$ in 2015. It is a straightforward exercise to decompose the Herfindahl index in order to indicate the percentage of the overall H value that is due to each of the two metropolitan groups. This decomposition indicates that the top-100 economies accounted for 45.6 percent of the H value in 1990 but a remarkable 54.2 percent of the H value in 2015. This finding simply reinforces the observation made earlier that patent volumes in the US have become increasingly concentrated in the nation's very largest metropolitan areas.

A somewhat different perspective on these trends arises when looking at patent densities *PATDN*, which many analysts believe to be a better measure of patenting intensity across the array of metropolitan places. Here the patent volumes *PATVL* were standardized by the metropolitan populations in the appropriate year, and the subsequent figures were then multiplied by 1000. In 1990 the highest patent density, 1.78, occurred in Midland, MI while in 2015 the highest density, 7.43, occurred in San Jose, CA. Table 5.2 shows various descriptive statistics for these patent densities and a few of the longitudinal trends are worthy of note. The coefficient of variation, *CV*, an especially revealing descriptive statistic, indicates that per capita patent variation not only increased across all metropolitan places (by 54 percent) but that this variation increased most rapidly (by 129 percent) across the top-100 metropolitan places. In other words, during 1990–2015 the nation's largest metropolitan areas evidently were sorting themselves out between two camps: low patenting areas on the one hand and high patenting areas on the other.

Table 5.2   Descriptive statistics for patent densities PATDN, 1990–2015

	1990	1995	2000	2005	2010	2015
			All Metro			
Mean	0.1570	0.1685	0.2471	0.2066	0.2627	0.3180
St Dev	0.1803	0.1903	0.3422	0.3549	0.4598	0.5623
CV	1.148	1.129	1.385	1.718	1.750	1.768
			Top 100			
Mean	0.2007	0.2265	0.3489	0.2928	0.3841	0.4708
St Dev	0.1481	0.2070	0.4633	0.4640	0.6012	0.7943
CV	0.737	0.913	1.327	1.586	1.565	1.687

Note: $n = 380$ for All Metro and $n = 100$ for Top 100.

5. MULTIVARIATE RESULTS

Before moving on to the multivariate analysis a comparison should be made with the initial regression results for *PATVL* provided by Ó hUallacháin (1999, Table 4), where population size *POPUL* was used as the sole explanatory variable. Using the newer data, with $n = 380$ places, the estimates of the population-size elasticities rose steadily from 1.16 in 1990 to 1.29 in 2015; here it is notable that the estimates were all lower than 1.31, the figure computed for $n = 273$ places by Ó hUallacháin. His coefficient of determination, 0.78, was also much higher than any arising from the newer data set, where the six adjusted R-squares ranged between 0.63 and 0.67. Clearly, population size explains somewhat less of the metropolitan variation in patenting volumes for the newer and larger data set. Furthermore, once that data set was divided into two groups—Top-100 and Other 280—the year-specific elasticity estimates for the smaller metropolitan places always exceeded those for the larger places; for example, those two estimates were 1.08 and 1.38 in 2015. This result endorses Ó hUallacháin's observation that smaller places have higher population-size elasticities than larger places.

As already mentioned, the multivariate analysis could only be undertaken at four points in time: 2000, 2005, 2010 and 2015. In each case the same 24 variables were adopted for a standard factor analysis, applying normalization after a Varimax rotation, and the most important orthogonal dimensions were identified and labeled. After some experimentation, six factors were chosen in each case. When the analysis was restricted to this number, stability took place in the composition of those factors, although the importance (indicated by the variance explained) of each factor changed over the 15-year study period. An examination of the various loadings and scores led to the following general labels for each of those six factors: F_1, Economic Size; F_2, Human Capital; F_3, Economic Productivity; F_4, Location; F_5, Industrial Specialization; and F_6, Prime Working Age. Together these six independent factors accounted for 78.4 percent of the overall variance in 2000 and 77.9 percent in 2015, indicating substantial stability in the overall coverage.

The most significant factor loadings, whose absolute values exceeded 0.20, are shown in Table 5.3 for the latest year, 2015. Besides reflecting population and wage levels, the dimension of Economic Size (26.7 percent of the total variance in 2000 but 28.8 percent in 2015) captures the overall volumes of workers in manufacturing and the professional services, the

Table 5.3   Factor Loadings in 2015

Variable	F_1	F_2	F_3	F_4	F_5	F_6
POPUL	0.95					
POPGR		0.53		−0.21		
WAGES	0.63		0.62			
WAGGR		0.25	0.49	0.21		−0.29
LABFP		0.45	0.75			
GDPPC	0.38		0.82			
PRIME	0.95					
PRPRI						0.86
BACDG	0.93	0.23				
PRBAC	0.34	0.45	0.42	0.25	0.48	
ADVDG	0.91	0.26			0.25	
PRADV	0.26	0.43	0.31	0.26	0.55	
MANEM	0.90				−0.30	
PRMAN				0.35	−0.78	
PROEM	0.91	0.23			0.24	
PRPRO	0.56	0.26	0.27		0.57	
HEDAY				0.85		
CLDAY				−0.87		
AMBIE	0.36	0.66		0.27		
RECRE	0.45		−0.21		0.26	−0.51
HEALT		0.71	0.36			−0.28
EDUCA	0.40	0.70				
TRANS	0.32	0.66				
HOUSE	−0.35	0.24	−0.23		−0.62	0.25

Note: All variables are in logarithmic form; absolute value loadings > 0.20 are shown.

levels of highly educated people, and a few amenities. The next dimension, Human Capital (17.8 percent, 13.5 percent), represents those highly educated populations who prefer urban amenities and low housing prices, while the third dimension, Economic Productivity (10.7 percent, 11.0 percent), represents other well-educated populations who receive much higher wages and salaries but choose to face higher housing prices. The Location factor (8.2 percent, 9.8 percent) basically distinguishes between those metropolitan economies that are favorably located in the Northwestern states from those that are unfavorably located in the Southeastern states, so it does not represent a simple Snowbelt–Sunbelt dichotomy. The fifth factor, Industrial Specialization (8.0 percent, 8.7 percent), reflects a binary trade-off between those places that specialize in manufacturing versus those that specialize in professional, scientific, and technical services, while the last factor (7.0 percent, 6.1 percent), Prime Working Age, captures differences in the age composition of the workforce. In terms of accounting for the variance seen in each year's data matrix, the four factors of Economic Size, Economic Productivity, Location, and Industrial Specialization became more important during 2000–2015 while the two factors of Human Capital and Prime Working Age became less important during that same period.

The results of the multivariate analysis become much more transparent once the ranked factor scores are revealed. Table 5.4 identifies the top performers in three of the six distributions, showing those 10 metropolitan areas with the highest scores on Factors 1, 2 and 3, first in 2000 and then later in 2015. The lists for Factor 1 (Economic Size) indicate most of the nation's most populous and dominant metropolitan economies. The top performers on Factor 2 (Human Capital) include many small economies that are dominated by universities, while the top performers on Factor 3 (Economic Productivity) include many of the nation's wealthiest small- and mid-sized metropolitan economies. The top performers on Factor 4 (Location) are those places like Bellingham, WA and Corvallis, OR in the Pacific Northwest that have mild climates; on Factor 5 (Industrial Specialization) are those cities like Honolulu, HA and Barnstable, MA that have a surplus in professional services and a deficit in manufacturing; and on Factor 6 (Prime Work Age) are those places like Provo, UT and Athens, GA that are both youthful and fast-growing (the top-10 ranks are not shown).

The uneven shifting seen in the composition of these performance lists suggests that, over time, some of the six factors were more stable than the others and, in fact, this proved to be the case. For each of the underlying dimensions, Table 5.5 shows the degree of correlation between the scores estimated for the initial year 2000 and the scores estimated for the ensuing years 2005, 2010 and 2015. Clearly there was very little longitudinal vari-

Table 5.4   The ten highest ranked metropolitan areas: F_1, F_2, and F_3

Rank	F_1 2000	F_2 2000	F_3 2000
1	New York	Columbia	San Jose
2	Los Angeles	Ames	Boulder
3	Chicago	Iowa City	San Francisco
4	Austin	Champaign-Urbana	Bridgeport
5	Riverside	Lexington	Santa Cruz
6	Detroit	Ann Arbor	Napa
7	Philadelphia	Springfield, IL	Santa Rosa
8	Dallas	Madison	Boston
9	Houston	Lubbock	Trenton
10	Miami	Lincoln	Madera
	F_1 2015	F_2 2015	F_3 2015
1	New York	Columbia	San Jose
2	Los Angeles	Missoula	Midland
3	Austin	Lubbock	Elkhart
4	Chicago	Springfield, IL	Napa
5	Houston	Iowa City	Bridgeport
6	Dallas	Charlottesville	San Francisco
7	Detroit	Asheville	Trenton
8	Philadelphia	Lincoln	Bismarck
9	Atlanta	College Station	Boulder
10	San Francisco	Rapid City	Lake Charles

Table 5.5   Stability over time in the six factors

Factor	Label	2000–2005	2000–2010	2000–2015
F_1	Economic Size	0.967	0.938	0.955
F_2	Human Capital	0.930	0.930	0.832
F_3	Economic Productivity	0.814	0.666	0.713
F_4	Location	0.956	0.939	0.956
F_5	Industrial Specialization	0.938	0.874	0.902
F_6	Prime Working Age	0.809	0.473	0.298

Note: All figures are Pearson correlation coefficients.

ation in the pattern of scores for Economic Size, Location, and Industrial Specialization, where in all three cases the Pearson correlation coefficient between the distribution of 2000 scores and the distribution of 2015 scores exceeded 0.90. Moreover, the temporal change seen in the scores for

Human Capital and Economic Productivity were also remarkably low over the 15 years, although the association for the third factor weakened more quickly. Finally, the longitudinal change seen in Factor 6, Prime Working Age, as evidenced by the low correlation coefficients, was by far the most extreme of the six cases.

The performance rankings based on these six factor scores can be used to create a signature vector for each metropolitan area at each point in time. Based on prior expectations, those economies that are favorably positioned to be inventive should have low scores (high rankings) on several, if not most, of the six dimensions while those that are unfavorably positioned to be inventive should have high scores (low rankings) on many of those dimensions. Here it is useful to note that a score of 38 (19) or lower on any dimension places that city in the top 10 percent (5 percent) of all performers. To illustrate, the signature of Seattle, WA was (18, 160, 18, 10, 157, 139) in 2000 and then (15, 239, 22, 8, 113, 195) in 2015, while the signature of Dalton, GA was (241, 304, 22, 210, 329, 71) in 2000 and then (182, 306, 89, 215, 325, 178) in 2015. Obviously, the strong economic conditions and the favorable social attributes of Seattle should have made that city a far superior place for inventive activity at both points in time. Nevertheless, from a relative perspective, Seattle's strong initial positioning declined somewhat in Human Capital and Prime Working Age, while Dalton's weak initial positioning declined even further in Economic Productivity and Prime Working Age between 2000 and 2015.

However, more interesting results arise from a series of regressions that use *PATVL* and *PATDN* as log-transformed dependent variables. First, the R-squares indicate that Economic Size steadily becomes a much better predictor than population size during the period 2000–2015. From Table 5.3 it should be clear that Economic Size not only captures the level of metropolitan population (loading on *POPUL* = 0.97) but also reflects productivity (0.38), education (0.34, 0.26), and the incidence of scientific and technical workers (0.56). Second, the corresponding elasticities were estimated to be some 15 percent higher for Economic Size than for population size: in 2015 these elasticities were 1.46 and 1.26, respectively, for *PATVL*, and 0.38 and 0.28 for *PATDN*. So, there is both conceptual and empirical merit in performing the multivariate analysis prior to running the regressions because the "weighted" variables identified on the various orthogonal factors reflect some aspects of the different metropolitan innovation ecosystems.

But the findings using all six of the orthogonal factors as independent variables are even more revealing. In Tables 5.6 and 5.7 the various regression coefficients are interpreted as elasticities because all the input variables were expressed in logarithmic form. So, as Table 5.6 shows, in 2000 the patent volume *PATVL* increased by 1.27 percent for any 1 percent increase

Table 5.6   Regression estimates for patent volumes PATVL

	2000	2005	2010	2015
Constant	3.972 (116.6)	3.734 (101.2)	3.928 (102.3)	4.163 (110.2)
F_1	1.267 (37.2)	1.379 (37.5)	1.410 (36.8)	1.458 (38.3)
F_2	0.497 (14.6)	0.351 (9.6)	0.509 (12.9)	0.326 (8.4)
F_3	0.557 (16.3)	0.381 (10.2)	0.338 (8.8)	0.470 (12.4)
F_4	0.225 (6.6)	0.326 (8.9)	0.378 (9.9)	0.332 (8.9)
F_5	−0.009 (−0.3)	0.279 (7.5)	0.487 (12.6)	0.371 (9.9)
F_6	0.168 (4.9)	0.173 (4.7)	−0.093 (−2.4)	0.007 (0.2)
Ad Rsq	0.856	0.843	0.850	0.852

Note: $n = 326$; t-scores are in parentheses; all estimates based on logarithms.

Table 5.7   Regression Estimates for Patent Densities PATDN

	2000	2005	2010	2015
Constant	−1.780 (−50.3)	−2.038 (−56.6)	−1.884 (−46.9)	−1.680 (−42.1)
F_1	0.252 (7.1)	0.341 (8.8)	0.369 (9.2)	0.383 (9.5)
F_2	0.301 (8.5)	0.175 (4.6)	0.297 (7.2)	0.158 (3.8)
F_3	0.373 (10.5)	0.334 (8.5)	0.293 (7.3)	0.399 (10.0)
F_4	0.369 (10.5)	0.451 (11.7)	0.499 (12.5)	0.452 (11.4)
F_5	−0.009 (−0.3)	0.188 (4.8)	0.338 (8.4)	0.260 (6.6)
F_6	0.143 (4.0)	0.146 (3.7)	−0.062 (−1.5)	0.020 (0.5)
Ad Rsq	0.522	0.513	0.560	0.536

Note: $n = 326$; t-scores are in parentheses; all estimates based on logarithms.

in Economic Size but later, in 2015, this response was even higher—a 1.46 percent increase. The estimates for both Human Capital and Economic Productivity dipped substantially before the Great Recession but then mostly recovered, although some of the reversal seen in the two estimates between 2010 and 2015 could have been caused by compositional shifts in the factors themselves. Both Industrial Specialization and Location (climate) clearly became more important over time in the generation of patent volumes. So, in the first case, those places that attracted more professional and technical workers (or fewer manufacturing workers) patented a lot more over time while, in the second case, those places with mild or cool climates patented substantially more than those places with hot and humid climates. Finally, the factor Prime Working Age had an ever-diminishing impact on the geography of patents over the 15-year study period.

In most respects the shifts in the estimates for patent density *PATDN*, as seen in Table 5.7, mirror those trends already highlighted. But several of the new results are worthy of note. First, the effect of Economic Size on per capita patenting grew by half again over the study period, as the elasticity estimate for Factor 1 rose from 0.25 in 2000 to 0.38 in 2015. Second, the role of Human Capital appeared to diminish between 2000 and 2015 and this was an unexpected finding. If anything, the estimate for human capital was expected to rise, or at least hold constant, even though the effect on volumes fell as seen in Table 5.6 earlier. Finally, the role of Location (climate) in patenting intensity strengthened somewhat more than was expected. More research is needed to clarify whether these per capita results are statistical anomalies, perhaps created by the cross-sectional approach, or actual trends in the six orthogonal effects. By extending the data back in time, and adopting a panel approach, it might also be possible to uncover how the variation in these estimates is tied to events before and after the Recessionary years of 2007–2009.

So, overall, the paired sets of regression estimates indicate that three variables have especially strengthened their role in the generation of patents across US metropolitan areas. First, those large and dominant economies, like New York and Los Angeles, evidently widened and deepened their initial advantages during 2000–2015 as Economic Size became an even more important source of patenting activity. Second, those metropolitan economies having locations with mild winters and cool summers, like San Diego and Seattle, also strengthened their positions as sources of patenting activity. And, third, those economies that have attracted employment in technical and scientific activities, including many smaller university cities, have really benefited as well. But here it should be recognized that Location is really a surrogate for other matters, besides climate, including the fact that some Snowbelt cities continue to house many of the nation's finest research facilities and many of its most important corporate headquarters.

6. CONCLUSIONS

This chapter is part of a project focusing on the economic changes seen across the US system of metropolitan areas in recent decades. The chapter specifically addresses metropolitan patent generation between 1990 and 2015, with special attention being given to the 15-year period between 2000 and 2015. Utility patents are an accurate indicator of the production of useful knowledge, and it is widely believed that patent volumes designate those economies where innovation-driven growth will take place. The ongoing project will eventually examine two other indicators of metropolitan change: proprietor's (self) employment and the births and deaths of firms (Glaeser 2007).

The data unambiguously indicate that patents in the US are increasingly being generated in metropolitan areas as opposed to non-metropolitan areas. Moreover, more and more of these patents are being generated in the nation's very largest metropolitan areas. Patent creation has come to rely increasingly on technical and scientific expertise and the nation's largest metropolitan economies typically provide the required knowledge base and work skills for this expertise. In fact, these large economies benefit from entrepreneurial capitalism and, through the unfolding of the product cycle, big-firm capitalism (Baumol et al. 2007). There is also evidence that larger places are home to newer ideas, and these serve to stimulate even more patent generation (Packalen and Bhattacharya 2015). Although population size alone is an obvious contributor to (the levels and rates of) patenting activity, the differences in the quality of the hundreds of metropolitan innovation ecosystems are responsible for the significant patenting variation that is evident across the national system. Moreover, more effort should be made to understand how the structure, conduct and performance of local industries are tied to these different metropolitan ecosystems. While these place-specific ecosystems are inherently complex, and very difficult to identify with any precision at this scale, multivariate analysis does shed light on their most distinctive attributes (Tsvetkova 2015).

However, other factors must clearly be considered. A multivariate analysis designed to deconstruct the economies of all US metropolitan areas indicates that human capital, size-related productivity, industrial specialization, and location (climate) each have a key role to play in patent generation. During the recent period 2000–2015 it seems that location in the national system of cities has played an increasingly important role in this activity. Places with mild climates have simply been more productive in patenting than other places with more extreme climates.

Future research should focus on several issues. First, more effort should be made to differentiate patents according to their importance. Patent citation data, once made available for post-2000 years, should differentiate between the physical and technical barriers to knowledge spillovers (Mukherji and Silberman 2018). Second, an adjustment model should be estimated to see how patents interact with other key labor-market attributes—including population, employment, amenities and wages—to clarify the roles of those social and economic forces that have been unevenly driving metropolitan growth in recent times. Particular attention could be given to the role of natural and human-created amenities in attracting or maintaining workers involved in inventive and innovative activity. Third, more attention should be given to the multivariate analysis outlined earlier. Especially with the inclusion of more points in time, a panel estimation might generate more general results where, perhaps, spatial lags should be adopted. Clearly, too, other types of employment variables could be considered, perhaps even including occupation data, and manufacturing employment itself could be disaggregated. A more accurate portrayal of research capabilities could be given by measuring the expenditures, or employment, of those major public and private research agencies found in each metropolitan area. More importantly, perhaps, self-employment should be targeted as a separate category, so that the relationship between patenting and proprietor's employment can be better clarified. Attempts also could be made to adopt STEM data or to include, at least for the most recent years, other data addressing venture capital. Finally, data should be collected to reflect the varying taxation and expenditure measures adopted by these metropolitan economies as the differences in their fiscal practices have probably become increasingly important (and transparent) to households and investors in recent times, but especially since the Great Recession.

All in all, this is a very important topic for applied regional research to address in more detail. With an improved understanding of the nature of metropolitan growth, policymakers might make better decisions about improving the welfare of people living in (increasingly) lagging areas. In any case, analysts should eventually have a better idea about how these three key measures of metropolitan change—inventions, proprietor's employment, and firm dynamics—are working in tandem to sort out the largest US cities into various growth clubs.

REFERENCES

Anselin, L., Varga, A. and Acs, Z. (1997). "Local geographic spillovers between university research and high technology innovations", *Journal of Urban Economics*, **42**, 422–48.

Balconi, M., Breschi, S. and Lissoni, F. (2004). "Networks of inventors and the role of academia: an exploration of Italian patent data", *Research Policy*, **33**, 127–45.

Baumol, W., Litan, R. and Schramm, C. (2007). *Good Capitalism, Bad Capitalism, and the Economics of Growth and Prosperity*. New Haven, CT: Yale University Press.

Bureau of Economic Analysis (2018). *Interactive Tables: Personal Income and Employment*. Accessed 22 March 2018 at: www.bea.gov/regional/index.htm.

Capello, R. (2002). "Spatial and sectoral characteristics of relational capital in innovation activity", *European Planning Studies*, **10**, 177–200.

Feldman, M. (1994). *The Geography of Innovation*. Boston, MA: Kluwer Academic Publishers.

Florida, R. (2002). *The Rise of the Creative Class*. New York: Basic Books.

Florida, R. (2005). *Cities and the Creative Class*. New York: Routledge.

Fritsch, M. (2004). "Cooperation and the efficiency of regional R&D activities", *Cambridge Journal of Economics*, **8**, 829–46.

Glaeser, E. (2007). *Entrepreneurship and the City*. Discussion paper no. 2140. Cambridge, MA: Harvard Institute of Economic Research.

Glaeser, E. (2011). *Triumph of the City*. New York: Penguin Books.

Griliches, Z. (1990). "Patent statistics as economic indicators: a survey", *Journal of Economic Literature*, **28**, 661–1707.

Jacobs, J. (1969). *The Economy of Cities*. New York: Random House.

Jaffe, A. (1989). "Real effects of academic research", *American Economic Review*, **79**, 957–70.

Mokyr, J. (2009). *The Enlightened Economy*. London: Penguin Books.

Moretti, E. (2012). *The New Geography of Jobs*. New York: Houghton Mifflin Harcourt.

Mukherji, N. and Silberman, J. (2018). "Knowledge flow among U.S. metro areas: innovative activity, proximity, and the border effect", *The Review of Regional Studies*, **48**, 193–216.

Mulligan, G., Reid, N. and Moore, M. (2014). "A typology of metropolitan labor markets in the U.S.", *Cities*, **41**, S12–S29.

North, D. (1990). *Institutions, Institutional Change, and Economic Performance*. New York: Cambridge University Press.

Ó hUallacháin, B. (1999). "Patent places: size matters", *Journal of Regional Science*, **39**, 613–36.

Packalen, M. and Bhattacharya, J. (2015). *Cities and Ideas*. Working paper 20921. Cambridge, MA: National Bureau of Economic Research.

Porter, M. (1979). "How competitive forces shape strategy", *Harvard Business Review*, March–April, 137–45.

Rothwell, J., Lobo, J., Strumsky, D. and Muro, M. (2013). *Patenting Prosperity: Invention and Economic Performance in the United States and its Metropolitan Areas*. Washington, DC: Brookings Institution.

Savageau, D. (2000). *Places Rated Almanac*. Millennium edn. New York: Hungry Minds.

Schumpeter, J. (1934). *The Theory of Economic Development*. Cambridge, MA: Harvard University Press.

Scott, A. (2007). "Capitalism and urbanization in a new key? The cognitive-cultural dimension", *Social Forces*, **85**, 1465–82.

Shearer, C., Shaw, I., Friedhoff, A. and Berube, A. (2018). *Metro Monitor 2018*. Accessed 18 March 2018 at: www.brookings.edu/research/metro-monitor-2018.

Tsvetkova, A. (2015). "Innovation, entrepreneurship, and metropolitan economic performance: empirical test of recent theoretical propositions", *Economic Development Quarterly*, **29**, 299–316.

US Census Bureau (2018). *American FactFinder*. Accessed 19 March 2018 at: www. census.gov.

US Patent and Trademark Office (2018). *Calendar Year Patent Statistics: Listing of all U.S. Metropolitan and Micropolitan Areas, Total Patent Utility Counts, 2000–2015*. Accessed 20 March 2018 at: www.uspto.gov/web/offices/ac/ido/oeip/ta f/reports_cbsa.htm.

6. Theorizing transformative innovations: the role of agency in real critical junctures

Lilja Mósesdóttir and Ivar Jonsson

1. INTRODUCTION

According to Schwab (2015), the fourth industrial revolution (4IR) is already underway. It was triggered by the fusion of the new technologies blurring the lines between the physical, digital, and biological worlds, that generates transformation not only of production and management but also of governance. New forms of collaboration will have to be developed to make use of the opportunities created by the fusion of new technologies across the economic and social spheres. Governments and regulatory agencies need to collaborate closely with business and civil society. The governance required is the one preserving the interest of the consumers and the public at large while continuing to support innovation and technological development.

We would like to argue that a move from producer-orientated innovation systems to systems of transformative innovation plays a crucial role in the 4IR involving the development of future alternatives. A shift towards transformative innovation systems requires innovation policy to take into account the interests of a larger number of stakeholders than before and to engage users and end-consumers in policy formation processes. Moreover, climate change, demographic shift and technological development are posing a threat to socio-economic and environmental sustainability such that there is a need for new ways of determining (broadening the scope of) the objectives of innovation and technical change. Hence, innovation policy will need to be mission-orientated (Mazzucato 2018), giving direction to economic growth and innovation in order to tackle societal and technological challenges. It is a huge challenge to build successful collaboration around systems of transformative innovation as it involves a much larger number of actors than in the producer-orientated innovation system. At the same time digital technology has made it easier to integrate interests of more people (big data analytics) and to engage varieties of actors at digital platforms (see e.g. OECD 2018, p. 30).

We claim that the present era is a period in which societies are facing the challenge of a shift in societal and technological regimes. Periods of this kind are marked by 'real critical junctures' in which stakeholders and political actors struggle for different alternatives in societal development after long periods of relatively stable institutions and actor relations. The force behind the struggles is shifting power positions of various actors due to techno-socio-economic change. During critical junctures, actors attempt to build coalitions around a shared vision of how future society is to be constituted (Jonsson 2016a; Mósesdóttir 2001; Mósesdóttir and Ellingsæter 2017). Hence, analysis of the present 'real critical juncture' requires that political power relations and the balance of power between stakeholders and other political actors are taken into account.

Contemporary economic theories of technical change and industrial revolutions under-theorize political agency. Contributions by economists such as Schwab (2015; 2016) and neo-Schumpeterians (Freeman and Perez 1988; Mazzucato 2013) presume that the history of capitalism is character- ized by technical change that led to industrial revolutions. In periods of industrial revolution, technical change requires that societies adjust to the needs of the emerging new technologies. Moreover, these scholars claim that societies need to find ways to generate consensus and coalitions among economic and political actors in order to adjust societal develop- ment to the requirements of the new technology. Various actors, especially the state, are presumed to have the role of generating new technology. Although highlighting the importance of actors in this respect, economists such as, for example, Schwab and the neo-Schumpeterians do not explain adequately what actually takes place when actors interact and build their coalitions.

We claim that the neo-Schumpeterian school has developed the most advanced research program (RP) to explain the interplay between, on the one side, technical change that induces long economic waves and, on the other side, institutional change in society. However, the neo-Schumpeterian RP suffers from a 'Lakatosian stagnation'. According to Lakatos, a RP is stagnating if its theoretical growth lags behind its empirical growth, that is, as long as it gives only post-hoc explanations either of chance discoveries or of facts anticipated by, and discovered in, a rival programme ('degen- erating problemshift') (Lakatos 1970, p. 100). Following Lakatos' train of thought, it appears that the neo-Schumpeterian RP needs a 'progressive problemshift' for it to progress further. Hence, its theoretical growth must generate empirical growth in terms of predicting novel facts with some success. Moreover, the neo-Schumpeterian RP will only be successful as long as it can progressively explain more chance discoveries or facts than rival RPs, and 'supersede' them. We argue that a 'progressive problemshift' in the neo-Schumpeterian RP requires that the role of agency and a theory of 'real critical junctures' will be integrated into it. Theoretical integration of this kind enables the neo-Schumpeterian RP to consider how contextual specificity affects the interaction between actors. This shift would generate substantial empirical growth as part of the theoretical basis of the neo-Schumpeterian RP.

In this chapter we attempt to contribute to a progressive problemshift by providing a theoretical framework that deepens our understanding of the role of agency in periods of 'real critical junctures'. Before we do that, we need to highlight what characterizes the present critical juncture in terms of the shift from 'producer-orientated innovation systems' to 'systems of transformative innovation'.

2. SYSTEMS OF TRANSFORMATIVE INNOVATION (STI)

The present technological revolution is a challenge to stakeholders and politicians as it requires economic and innovation policies that are very different from the traditional policies of the post-World War II era. The escalating political and economic polarization and environmental crisis calls for new framing of innovation systems that broadens the socio-economic objectives of innovation activity compared to the traditional producer-orientated innovation systems (TISs) of today. At the same time, it requires closer and widened collaboration of stakeholders concerning common policy formation.

The TISs developed in two phases that accommodated the development of capitalist societies from Fordism to post-Fordism.[1] A common feature of the TISs is that producers of goods and governments predominantly define their goals. The participation of users and consumers of goods and services in defining the goals of innovation is minimized. Concerns for social and environmental consequences, pollution and climate change are not emphasized as a necessary part of the goals of innovation.

The TISs of Fordism and post-Fordism differ in terms of the roles that the nation state plays and in terms of globalization. The Fordist phase emphasized national economic growth (import-substitution) and presumed that science and technology policy (STP) should aim at increasing economic welfare via a Fordist socio-technical system based on mass production and consumption controlled by Keynesian economic policies. The state's STP was influenced by the Cold War and limited to a particular field of innovation activities such as agriculture, defence, telecommunications, medical research, geological surveys, and civil engineering works.

The post-Fordist version of producer-orientated TISs took shape in the neo-liberal era in the 1980s. It emphasizes international competitiveness (export promotion) and globalization. STP aims at increasing economic welfare via a post-Fordist socio-technical system based on international specialization, corporate networks and alliances, innovation, partnerships, flexible specialization of production and market niches. National systems of innovation (NSI) that cover the items above become essential part of the STP.

In recent years, TISs have faced severe criticism from various stakeholders that point at its narrow anthropocentric worldview, undemocratic elitism and corporate social irresponsibility. The critique concerns TISs' lack of broader stakeholder collaboration in terms of framing technological options and directions. This framing is missing in the operation of innovation networks, although established through government intervention. Technocratic politics that reduce the aims of innovation policies to maximize economic growth continue to dominate innovation policy framing. The critiques' alternative or counter-framing to the TISs explicitly request participatory and democratic processes when goals of STPs are decided upon. This kind of restructuring of the formation of STPs presumes the importance of empowering users and end-consumers of goods and services to participate in identifying socio-environmental sustainable alternatives and to influence or take decisions regarding these alternatives (Schot and Steinmueller 2016).

It appears that the alternative framing of STI requires closer and widened collaboration of stakeholders concerning common policy formation. The collaboration on innovation between corporations, research institutions and public authorities was the main thrust of the TISs. The list of collaborating actors of the new STI will be much larger and include actors such as research institutions, actors in civil society (e.g. non-profit societies and/or firms, interest and issue organizations, NGOs and end-consumers/ users), corporations and public authorities. In short, it requires intensified collaboration and coalition building on stakeholders' activities of 'collective innovation and entrepreneurship'. It presumes collaboration between individuals within firms and institutions, as well as between firms and/or institutions on a national as well as international level. Such collaboration produces constellations of groups or social units which become relatively autonomous and who collectively form their aims and strategies despite contested views. Hence, collective innovation is a process of collaboration evolving on the grounds of interaction and purposeful formation of common goals of the participants of the coalitions in question (see Jonsson 1994; 2016a, pp. 177–87).

The Main Features of the Advancing Systems of Transformative Innovation

The scope of framing STIs reflects a worldview that is quite different from its traditional producer-orientated counterpart, the TIS. Unlike the anthropocentric exploitative worldview of the TIS, STI emphasizes biocentric and socially responsible use of natural and human resources. Moreover, the scope of transformative innovation is societal; it aims at restructuring future societies so that human society can improve human well-being in terms of social and environmental sustainability and moral justice. STIs' view of agency supersedes the utilitarian view of the egoistic and rational 'homo economicus' that aims at maximizing economic welfare presuming conditions of perfect market competition. The idea of the sovereignty of the individual and market competition as a point of departure is replaced by democratic decision-making in which stakeholders interact and generate collective aims and means to realize social justice and environmental sustainability. Consequently, public intervention, citizen grassroots participation and social experiments are institutionalized as part of the transformative systems. Table 6.1 highlights the main characteristics of the scope and policy of the STI.

An increasing number of national and international political actors appear to jump on the STI bandwagon. Examples at hand are the European Commission's report *Mission-Oriented Research & Innovation in the European Union* (Mazzucato 2018). The government of Finland has introduced experiments with citizen wages (Kangas 2016) and Danish municipalities have implemented transformative welfare policies in which local citizens at grassroots level take part in searching for and defining needs for technological innovation in the field of social services (Lauritzen 2012). The Norwegian government emphasizes transformative innovation in its research and development (R&D) policy, which is financed and coordinated by the Norwegian Research Council's innovation strategy for the public sector 2018–23 (Norges forskningsråd 2018).

Western societies host varieties of capitalism that institutionalized and regulated markets in different ways. Their welfare states are also different in scope and scale. Hence, Western societies are based on different societal paradigms that are reflected in their different levels of state intervention in markets, various types of democracy, scope and scale of social services and ethical aims such as quality of life and attitudes towards preservation of nature. It appears from the discussion above that STIs will be impregnated with societal paradigms that emphasize increased public intervention in innovation activity and would emphasize societal objectives such as empowering of citizens, social and health well-being and environmental sustainability. At the same time, the implementation of STIs would depend

Table 6.1   *The system of transformative innovation of the 6th Kondratiev: innovation for biocentrism/sustainabilism 2020+?*

Scope of framing	Social and biocentric transformation (social and ecological sustainability promotion); STI aims at generating a better world in terms of social and environmental responsibility with democratic participation of stakeholders; Requires societal transformation and implementation of socio-technical systems (STS) that are sustainable and involves democratic participation of stakeholders, producers and consumers
Rationale/ Justification for policy intervention	The central focus is on the preconditions of **fundamental systemic change** in the interests of social, economic and environmental sustainability; Shortcomings of science, technology and innovation are highlighted and issues of sustainability and poverty or inequitable income distribution are addressed; **STI takes into account and critically evaluates who benefits from social and technical change**; Technologies are constructed by powerful actors in line with their worldviews and/or interests; Alternative innovations offer greater potential for social inclusion income equality; This requires a science and technology politics that opens up space for societal learning, public debate, deliberation and negotiation; Socio-technical transition research must build upon evolutionary economics and STS with a focus on how to achieve transformative change
Innovation model and actors	Mixture of supply and demand driven innovation model that aims at transformation of **socio-technical systems (STS)**; STS includes skills, infrastructures, industry structures, products, regulations and policies, user preferences, and cultural factors that co-evolve together in a socio-technical system; **System innovation** involves **social innovation**, since the focus is not only on the technological components, but on all the components including user preferences, policies and the perception of the value and culture by actors within the system; **Socio-technical experiments** are essential as there is no single best pathway to sustainability, income equity and other socially desirable goals awaiting discovery; Innovation is assumed to be a **search process**, guided by social and environmental objectives

Table 6.1   (continued)

Policy practices	Policy practices emphasize **collective experimentation** and learning, hence finding the means to facilitate and **empower those engaged** in these processes is essential; Reflecting on social and environmental needs is essential and the search process has to be guided by improvements in **anticipation** of collateral effects and consequences; Developing forums and processes through which anticipation might be feasible is a priority; Processes similar to foresight activities and technology assessment groups are feasible and should be developed further; The aim of anticipation is to identify areas for **experimentation** with socio-technical innovation
Alternative or counter framings (ACFs)	ACF would address the social and environmental challenges through the implementation of capital-intensive solutions (e.g. centralized energy production with big wind and solar farms, the expanded use of nuclear energy and further development of a global value chain of waste products; geo-engineering) and technologies that aim to mitigate ex-post the impacts of carbon-intensive development (e.g. carbon capture and storage); In this ACF, actors focus on the economic growth agenda, while distributional consequences (social and ecological costs) are of secondary importance

Source: Based on Schot and Steinmueller (2016).

on tradition for collaboration among central actors and the country-specific institutional framework. Hence, it would evolve in different forms and scope as well as speed of diffusion across Western societies.

We would expect that the Nordic countries with their sizable universalist welfare states and their tradition of neo-corporatist consensus making will have comparative advantage in implementing STIs. These countries have comparative advantage in terms of long traditions of citizens' empowering as well as public intervention and promotion of R&D in the field of health and social services as well as information and communications technology (ICT) and cybernetics. This last point brings us to the question of the role of the actors that define, decide and institutionalize research policies and the researchers who execute the actual R&D. Without the contribution of these actors, the transformation of the present TISs to STIs will not come about.

As mentioned in the introduction above, it is a huge challenge to build successful collaboration and concertation on shifting the existing producer-orientated innovation system towards systems of transformative innovation. Moreover, research into preconditions for such a shift appears to suffer from a lack of a substantial theoretical framework for further research. We will now discuss the state of the art of theories in this field of research and their shortcomings.

3. A SHIFT TOWARDS SYSTEMS OF TRANSFORMATIVE INNOVATION

Until now, research into technical change and shifts in technological regimes have predominantly been analysed with the economic theories of scholars in the field of business management studies and neo-Schumpeterians. While the former group concentrates on current transformation that they term industrial revolution, the latter group works within a Schumpeterian framework of long-waves in economic history: the so-called Kondratievs.

Insofar as scholars in the field of business management studies emphasize agency, they focus on actors' responses to challenges of technical change at the micro-level of individuals and corporations. Moreover, they tend to presume that actors' responses have the evolutionary function of adjusting individuals' and corporations' endowments and skills to the needs of technical change (Schwab 2016; Brynjolfsson and McAfee 2014). Compared to business management approaches, the neo-Schumpeterians, Freeman and Perez (1988), provide a more comprehensive approach of the role of cultural, social and political 'institutions' in technological revolutions and their necessary adjustment to the needs of new technological regimes. However, the business management and the neo-Schumpeterian approaches presume a techno-determinist view of institutional adjustment and actors' responses to technical change. They need more in-depth analysis of agency and actor–structure relations in societal development during the critical juncture.

A closer look at the neo-Schumpeterian approach is needed to develop a proper theoretical framework that takes into account agency when actors are engaged in collective coalition building. Freeman and Perez (1988) and Freeman and Louçã (2001) have tried to provide a holistic interpretation of the relationship between economic cycles and technological change, associating the upswing stage of long waves. In their analysis of the 5th Kondratiev, that is, the long economic wave based on ICT and rising biotechnology, Freeman and Perez (1988) used their framework of techno-economic paradigm to identify how the production and consumption spheres are fundamentally reconstructed to make better use of the opportunities created by ICT technology. According to Freeman and Perez

(1988, pp. 60–61), the restructuring of the production sphere to accompany ICT technology involves more integrated systems of management, production and marketing systems, demand for high and low skill profiles and extensive computer-based investment. The shift towards the IT paradigm creates a persistent shortage of the high-level skills and persistent surplus capacity in the older energy-intensive industries. New social and political solutions/institutions are needed to solve these structural problems. These solutions are flexibility in hours of work, re-education and retraining systems, regional policies, new financial systems, possible decentralization of management and government, and access to data banks and networks at all levels as well as new telecommunication systems.

Freeman and Perez (1988, p. 61) acknowledge that more radical changes need to take place in the social and political institutions that were created during World War II but discuss neither the forces behind these changes nor their outcomes. They posit that innovation and technological changes lead to long waves of economic growth and assume that existing institutional structures and social relations will adjust to the requirements of the new technology and consequent production systems. Although this adjustment will appear in increased social unrest, Freeman and Perez have not provided any sound theory of which actors do generate this adjustment and how they do it. Hence, an analysis of the relation between agency–structuration–structure is missing (Jonsson 2016a). Freeman and Perez leave us with a rather hollow idea that the increased productivity and the growth of GDP during a long wave will outweigh by a large margin the cost of social unrest due to growing unemployment created by skill mismatches.

Because of their positive and acritical view of capitalism and markets, the neo-Schumpeterian economists have largely ignored the problems of unequal income distribution and social unrest that technical change fosters in uncontrolled markets. Following Pagano and Rossi (2011), Evangelista (2018) summarizes the main shortcomings of neo-Schumpeterians:

> This technology-based perspective of economic growth reveals all its limits in interpreting what might be regarded as one of the major macroeconomic paradoxes materialized over the last decades: the mismatch between, on one hand, the strong opportunities offered by the technological achievements reached in the last few decades and, on the other hand, the parallel increase of economic and social inequalities, the permanence of a large amount of unsatisfied social and human needs, the unsustainable pressure that our economic model puts on natural resources and on the natural environment. (2018, p. 145).

The consequence of the paradox between the large economic benefits of technical change and lack of social progress is that the macroeconomic demand will not be able to absorb the increased productivity levels or the new commodities (Evangelista 2018, p.144). Freeman and Perez (1988, pp. 59–60) assume that competition in capitalist societies can adjust demand to supply when socio-institutional systems (e.g. public re-skilling programmes) resolve 'market failures' (e.g. skill-mismatch). Evangelista (2018, p. 146) claims that this line of argument has been losing its explanatory power due to the amount of time that has passed since ICT first appeared and its widespread application.

Unlike neo-Schumpeterians, Schwab (2015; 2016) acknowledges that inequality represents the greatest societal concern associated with the 4IR. The largest beneficiaries of innovation tend to be the innovators, shareholders and investors, which explains the rising gap in wealth between those dependent on capital versus labour. Moreover, machines will also displace many low-skilled workers while the diffusion of new technologies may result in a net increase in jobs for the highly skilled. According to Schwab (2015), growing polarization in income and wealth will in turn lead to an increase in social tensions. However, Schwab's analysis suffers from the same shortcoming as that of the neo-Schumpeterians. Both approaches lack an account of how social and political actors resist and/or seek to shape how the diffusion of new technologies proceeds. Instead they are preoccupied with taxonomical categorization of the main features of technical change. This critique of the neo-Schumpeterian and 4IR applies also to Evangelista's criticism of neo-Schumpeterians' legacy as they do not problematize the question of 'structuration' and the dynamic role of agency.

Kuhlmann and Rip's (2018) analysis of the next generation of innovation policies addressing Grand Challenges in transformative ways provides useful insights into the role of agency. According to Kuhlmann and Rip (2018, p.451), agency is no longer central but distributed across different groups of actors and driven by institutional entrepreneurs such as civil society organizations. Hence, there is a need for horizontal coordination of constellations of actors in the form of concerted action or by mutually considering actions of others and proactively adjusting. Moreover, intermediary organizations such as funding agencies and spaces for interaction are important to enable and improve concerted action when there is no master strategy. Apart from being a part of the concertation, the government's role could be to provide reflection on the nature of the Grand Challenges, offer legitimation by, for example, creating platforms for collaboration, and to provide a link with democratic decision-making. Following Ornston and Schulze-Cleven (2015, p. 575), Kuhlmann and Rip (2018, p. 452) claim that concertation in practice will look like a patchwork that can result in broader, more diverse 'varieties of cooperation' in advanced capitalist economies. Hence, next generation innovation policies will be 'tentative' in addressing political and organizational complexities and uncertainties with explorative strategies (Kuhlmann et al. 2019; Kuhlmann and Rip 2018).

Surprisingly, Kuhlmann and Rip do not consider what actors other than the government can take on vertical coordination of distributed groups of actors. We claim that distributed agency and the need for mission-orientated and experimental ways of addressing complex challenges open up opportunities for actors other than the government (national level) to become multi-level coordinators. As Hanssen et al. (2013, p. 883) argue, counties in a country like Norway can be a suitable actor to take on the role of multi-level coordinator as they are able to combine network and consensually based coordination with some form of hierarchical authority. Hence, the pressure may mount on regional authorities (meso-level) to allocate more resources to the coordination of constellations of actors at, on the one hand, the micro- and meso-levels and, on the other hand, governmental strategies at the macro-level. The growing importance of regional coordination means that coordination of institutions and entities at different levels does not necessarily occur at a higher level (cf. vertical coordination).

Power relations within and across constellations of actors are also missing in Kuhlmann and Rip's analysis of agency. The concept of 'power' is fundamental to the analysis of political science. However, different scholars define this concept differently. A frequently used definition of power in mainstream political science refers to the decision-making process (Poulantzas 1975, p. 104). Implicit in this definition is a similar thought as in the democratic theories of the 1950s and 1960s (Macpherson 1979); individuals or groups enter the abstracted and distinct political system or decision-making process and act rationally and in a goal-orientated way. Power defined in this way is too narrow and misleading. As Poulantzas (1975) has observed:

> (i) it succumbs to a voluntarist conception of the decision-making process, through disregarding the effectiveness of the structures, and it is not able exactly to locate beneath the appearances the effective centres of decision inside which the distribution of power works; and (ii) it takes as a principle the 'integration-ist' conception of society, from which the concept of 'participation' in decision-making is derived. (1975, p. 104).

We acknowledge that the concept of power has to take into account that political decisions are affected by the nature and form of the political structures in which such decisions are taken. Moreover, political decisions are determined by the 'balance of power' between the stakeholders and actors who interact in the particular contexts of decision-making and policy formation. By 'balance of power' we mean the relative power and capacity of the different actors to use political resources to organize support or opposition against state policy, institutions and forms of regulation and for or against each other's strategies.

In the present era, societies are facing the challenge of a shift in societal and technological regimes. Forces behind the shift are techno-socio-economic changes such as digital technologies, growing inequality, crumbling trust in existing political institutions and financialization that are altering the balance of power between stakeholders and actors. Periods of this kind are marked by real critical junctures in which stakeholders and political actors struggle for different alternatives in societal development after long periods of self-reinforcing 'path dependency' characterized by relatively stable institutions and actor relations. During critical junctures, the actors attempt, despite their conflicting interests and visions, to build coalitions around a shared vision of how future society is to be constituted (Jonsson 2016b). Moreover, the actors proceed and begin to restructure society according to future visions in a process we highlight as 'process of structuration' and we will discuss below in the next section.[2] In cases when changes are far reaching and touch upon all spheres of society and related societal paradigms,[3] the struggle of actors may lead to changes on a societal scale that we would coin as an 'industrial revolution' or 'post-industrial revolution'.

Transformative change to an alternative path requires transformative innovation involving cooperation of various actors operating in various constellations of balance of power between the actors at the micro-, meso- and macro-levels. In the following section, we will focus on the main characteristics of a transformative shift in terms of the concept of 'process of structuration' that is constituted by the interplay between agency and structures in real critical junctures.

4. TRANSFORMATIVE INNOVATION AND AGENCY

For decades, innovation systems have been organized on the regional, national and international level. They have played an important role in generating growth and social well-being. Due to technological progress, demographic development and climate changes, various stakeholders and actors have started to focus their efforts/struggles on shaping how to organize innovation systems of the future. The challenge they face is how to decide the aims of future innovation, what stakeholders and actors should take part in deciding the objectives of innovation activities and whose interests should be prioritized. In this period of real critical juncture, the

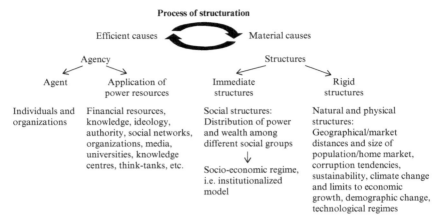

Figure 6.1   Agency and structuration

struggles of actors and stakeholders for different future alternatives call for 'processes of structuration'. Figure 6.1 highlights the main elements of a process of structuration.

The figure highlights that the process of structuration involves actors using power resources to mould social structures and regimes. Moreover, existing structures form the actors and their power resources. As power resources are unevenly distributed among actors, the outcome of the processes of structuration is likely to be skewed and in favour of those actors who have more power than the other actors, that is, those with a 'hegemonic position'. Hence, structuration is not 'voluntary'; it is contextually determined by the real critical juncture at hand.

Interest in studying 'critical junctures' and 'regime change' has increased in recent years among scholars of comparative politics. The concept of critical juncture is fundamental to historical institutionalism and its dualistic view of societal development. The main idea is that institutional development is characterized by, on the one hand, long periods of self-reinforcing 'path dependency' in which institutions are stable and reproduced and, on the other hand, short periods in which new forms of institutions will be decided and a new period of long-term self-reinforcing path dependency prevails.

This general dualist view of institutional change is often preoccupied with the mechanisms of 'institutional equilibria' but pay too little attention to critical junctures. When they do, they tend to explain the divergence during critical junctures in terms of structural, antecedent conditions rather than actions and decisions taken during the critical junctures themselves. This train of thought underestimates the role of actors in transformative processes of development. It tends to reduce explanations to correlations between abstract structural variables such as economic, cultural, ideological and organizational relations. It presumes a 'successionist' view of causation that characterizes 'closed systems' approaches that natural sciences adhere to by means of laboratory experiments (Sayer, 2000). An alternative approach would be to focus on contingency, that is, the role that powerful political actors play under conditions of critical juncture when decisions are taken concerning an alternative future institutional arrangement. This approach suffers from a shortcoming that characterizes much mainstream political research that tends to reduce the analysis to political decision-making processes, participants in such processes and their political resources. Moreover, this approach presumes that structures and their constraints have somehow temporarily moved from the scene so that the existing social and power relations are not effective in critical junctures. The result is that actors' decisions are presumed to be voluntarist.

Rather than treating contingency as 'voluntarist contingency', we would adhere to the idea that critical contingency is better seen as 'real contingency', as constraints of structures have temporarily diminished, but not disappeared. A 'real critical contingency' approach is rooted in an ontological view of causality which assumes that when actors or 'agents' transform societal institutions in concrete contexts, their actions, aims and choices are partly limited by the inertia of institutions, social structures and power relations that constitute the context they attempt to change. It presumes a view of causation that characterizes 'open systems' approaches predominant in social sciences. In the social world, 'open systems' prevail and they are characterized by causality in which the same causal factor can produce different outcomes and alternative developmental opportunities. Hence, different contexts with different actors and their relations would tend to lead to different outcomes. Outcomes are neither teleological nor predetermined (Sayer 2000). Frequently, the concept of critical juncture is used in *post-festum* analyses that deduce what is 'critical' in a juncture from events that take place after the critical instance. Unlike this, we define the 'critical' aspect of a juncture with reference to actions taking place in the context prior to path dependency. Agency presumes that collective and individual agents reflect on the opportunities for transforming structural hindrances in the existing material context and consequently organize necessary resources for change. Opportunities for transforming the material context in question are identified and the ideologically preferred state of affairs is realized. Moreover, the efficiency of agency, as an 'efficient cause'[4] of change, depends on the emergent properties allowed by existing social structures. Consequently, causality can neither be reduced to agents' intentions, voluntary actions and/or discourse nor to determination of their actions by structures. Let us not forget that structures of social relations usually contain properties that can lead to different results in terms of transformed social relations.

The process of structuration takes place in particular periods that are part of long-term structural change, referred to as material causes in Figure 6.1 above. This must be kept in mind as the contexts of real critical junctures are historically different and the balance of power between actors is qualitatively different in different real critical junctures. Today, it is possible to identify at least two developments affecting the balance of power that have more or less prevailed since World War II: the growing dominance of the financial sector and digital technologies, while the post-World War II era was characterized by dominance of the industrial corporate sector and assembly line technologies of mass-production.

In recent decades, financial capital has gradually gained a stronger power position due to the process of 'financialization' of societies and economies (Foster and Magdoff 2008). According to Deutschmann 2011 (cited in Hahn 2019, p. 924), financialization of the economy involves two areas of change related to firms and their institutional environment. First, the increasing importance of investment banks and private pension funds as traditional banks have moved towards promising investment activities and the ageing challenge has led to a growth in pension savings. Secondly, institutional investors have become important players not only in financial markets but also in firms as public shareholders. This process of financialization has swung the power balance from cooperation in the production sector towards the financial sector (Berghoff 2016; Deutschmann 2011).

According to a recent study by Battiston et al. (2018), financialization in the EU has had a negative effect on economic growth, innovation and inequality. Economic growth is depressed as financialization implies that a larger fraction of credit is directed towards unfruitful investment projects (higher housing prices), possibly generating economic crises. Financialization also has a negative impact on innovation as the separation between actors taking risks from innovation and actors extracting rents from innovation entails a lower share of reinvested profits (short-termism). Finally, financialization contributes to inequality by strengthening top earners' bargaining power in terms of higher wages and lower taxation, as well as by burdening public budgets with fiscal assistance to financial institutions in times of crisis. Hence, financialization may hamper innovation activities as they seek to broaden their scope of priorities and the involvement of actors in order to achieve greater socio-economic sustainability.

Technological innovations are also putting pressure on the prevailing balance of power between different economic actors. Examples are e-commerce and digital platforms that are shifting the balance of power to digital giants (Google and Facebook) and customers. The enormity of scale in the digital economy has created digital giants/monopolies using intangible barriers (e.g. closed membership) to entry by crowding out competition. Hence, the phenomenon of 'winner-takes-all' or a situation where a product or business that is ahead, gets further ahead and one that loses advantage, loses further. Digitalization offers not only cost advantages through operational efficiency but also channels for greater customization (business analytics). With low or no costs for end users, digital monopolies seek to cut down supply costs (Amazon) and use the customer base to identify market trends and to implement customer-specific, personalized pricing, as, for example, Uber (Ghotgalkar et al. 2017; Schwab 2015).

In addition to the two trends discussed above, a demographic shift on a global scale has been taking place in recent decades. The shift involves a qualitative change in the world population in terms of its ageing, and a quantitative jump in the growth of the world population. These changes are unfolding in an increasing scale of migration and the foreseeable need for a rise in expenditure on health services is creating fiscal challenges for states (World Economic Forum 2019; OECD 2014). The demographic change is part of the material causes mentioned in Figure 6.1. Eventually, humanity is faced with challenges that require new policies of transformative innovation and coalitions on a national and international scale.

The process of structuration in real critical junctures has its 'efficient causes' in agency, that is, actors and their use of power resources (se Figure 6.1). In the present era, the process of structuration is in its early stages in which actors respond to deepening institutional crises of legitimation of the ailing regime of Fordism and post-Fordism. The current situation is similar to that of the economic and political turmoil of the 1930s. During that period, capitalist economies went through economic, social and political polarization that led to increasing mistrust in liberal democracy and growing violent clashes between social classes and the eventual threat of civil war. As Kregel (2018, p. 149) puts it:

> After . . . the stock market break and then the failure to stem rising unemployment over the following three years culminating in the collapse of the financial system created an aura of increasing helplessness and desperation; a failure of a liberal democratic solution. Citizens marching in support of what were considered to be successful policy responses to the crisis by Fascist and Communist countries made the failure of traditional policies to reverse the crisis and its culmination in the national closure of banks more debilitating.

It became the role of President F.D. Roosevelt to convince Congress and voters to accept the New-Deal policies that involved the creation of a concerted rejection of orthodox economic policies and acceptance of state interventionism (Kregel 2018, p. 164).

Following the collapse of the fascist regimes of Italy and Germany, the balance of power between capital and labour had shifted towards the trade unions in Europe. The success of Fordism required consensus on developing a tripartite collaboration of the main organized interests, that is, trade unions, employers' unions and the state (often called neo-corporatism). These three actors had in common a high level of hierarchical organization and centralization of power in the hands of the elites of the tripartite system.

In the late 1970s, Keynesian anti-cyclical policies proved ineffective and neo-liberalist policies and regimes spread their roots during the 1980s. Diffusion of ICT technology and automation, flexible specialization, deregulation, globalization, outward FDI and rising unemployment reduced membership of trade unions. All these factors undermined the institutionalized balance of power of neo-corporatism and accelerated the global power position of the financial sector in the new era of post-Fordism (Giorgi 2017).

Post-Fordism, with its neo-liberal policies, contributed to the development of intensified uneven income and wealth distribution. As Oxfam reports, increasing amounts of income and wealth go to those at the very top. At the same time, the middle classes are losing out just as much as the poorest people. In rich countries, the middle classes often see their incomes stagnate. A core reason for this inequality is that 'between 1980 and 2016, the poorest 50% of people only received 12 cents in every dollar of global income growth. By contrast, the richest 1% received 27 cents of every dollar' (Oxfam 2019, p. 11).

The key factors behind the growing inequalities as well as innovation, productivity gains and economic growth are globalization and technological progress involving, among others, outsourcing, increased competition from low-wage countries, and automation. The financial crisis of 2008 exacerbated these inequalities as many saw their homes, jobs and much of their wealth and retirement savings disappear. The aftermath of the crisis witnessed fast-spreading fear and anxiety in Western societies and rapidly increasing distrust in the established political system of liberal democracy and in the political elites of these societies. This situation resembles the political crisis that evolved following the financial crisis in the Great Depression of the 1930s. Indeed, research indicates that the aftermaths of the financial crisis in the 1930s and after 2008 follow a rather similar pattern in terms of how the voters and political actors respond.

In their study of the implications of the Great Recession for voting and general trust, using regional data across Europe, Algan et al. (2017) found that a rise in unemployment goes hand in hand with a fall in political trust and a rise in political extremism. These findings are in line with those of Funke et al. (2016), who studied 20 advanced economies over the years 1870–2014. They found that political polarization increases after financial crises and voters seem to be particularly attracted to the political rhetoric of the extreme Right after a crisis. These results correspond to those of a recent study by de Bromhead et al. (2012) focusing on the electoral consequences of crises in the 1920s and 1930s. Moreover, Funke et al. (2016) found that implementation of policies and reforms became more difficult after financial crises, irrespective of which parties are in power.

The aftermaths of the financial crisis in the late 1920s and 1930s generated a real critical juncture that gave birth to the post-World War II Fordism and subsequent path dependency. This real critical juncture developed in four main phases. In the first phase, polarization of capitalist economies and escalating severe social unrest urged political leaders and intellectuals to define and analyse the fundamental reasons for the situation. Consequently, a search period set in when feasible solutions to the problems were defined, new ways of thinking promoted and policies formulated. We call this first phase of a real critical juncture 'the search phase'. A second phase starts when actors and the public in general become increasingly disillusioned with policies created in the search phase that proved to be ineffective in solving the pressing socio-economic problems to the extent that they escalate. We term this second phase 'the phase of realism'. A third phase begins when actors and stakeholders are convinced that radical changes are necessary and they start to build coalitions for concerted strategies of societal transformation. We call this third phase 'the phase of consensus building'. A fourth and final phase is reached when radical strategies of transformative change have been implemented and the public accepts its advances and expects that it will generate general well-being. A move from one phase to another in the critical juncture is not necessarily linear as backlashes or lock-in situations may occur when regressive groups gain political capacities to stop or reverse transformative changes.

We can now analyse the main features of the present real critical juncture in terms of these phases. The financial crisis of 2008 has prolonged the first phase in the critical juncture as it temporarily reduced the political polarization as many voters turned from left-wing parties to right-wing parties. However, polarization in wealth and income continued to increase after the crisis, especially in the hardest hit countries, which in turn has enhanced the legitimization crisis of the current institutional regimes. The growing legitimization crisis has intensified the search of those in power for alternative solutions to the complex challenges of the techno-socio-economic changes. However, advanced capitalist societies have not yet reached the second phase in the critical juncture, the phase where actors have become disillusioned with the outcomes of experimental and often only incremental changes to institutional regimes that have repeatedly demonstrated an incapacity to provide sustainable socio-economic welfare for most people. The third phase will be reached when powerful constellations of actors are able to agree on, mobilize support for and implement transformative changes to the current social and political institutions or, in other words, what we term systems of transformative innovation. The final phase in the critical juncture occurs when various systems of transformative change have managed to produce relatively stable institutions and actor relations paving the way for a period of self-reinforcing 'path dependency'.

CONCLUSION

In this chapter we have attempted to contribute to further development of the neo-Schumpeterian research programme by theorizing the role of actors in real critical junctures. The aim is to achieve a 'progressive problemshift' in the neo-Schumpeterian research programme in order to generate substantial empirical growth as part of its revitalized theoretical basis.

The present cybernetic, bio-technological revolution is having widespread effects across different sectors, creating winners and losers, which puts pressure on the prevailing balance of power between different actors. Hence, we have entered a period marked by a real critical juncture in which a variety of stakeholders and political actors struggle for various alternatives in societal development.

We argue in this chapter that a transformative change to a more sustainable socio-economic development requires transformative innovation involving cooperation of different actors around mission-orientated and experimental policies in various constellations at the micro-, meso- and macro-levels. How the actors shape transformative change depends on the challenges and opportunities created by the context of the real critical juncture, balance of power and their capacity to collaborate on restructuring society as well on the form and extent to which their efforts in multi-level networks are coordinated.

Our improvement of the neo-Schumpeterian research programme involves connecting innovation activities to distributed agency, power relations, cooperation and contestation, multilevel coordination and real critical junctures. Hence, we provide a theoretical framework for future empirical analyses of the interaction between various stakeholders and political actors during different phases of critical juncture periods of transformation focusing on (conflicting) interests, shifts in power relations and the nature of coalition building as well as its (lack of) multilevel coordination. Based on our contribution, we presume further studies may tackle research questions such as: What groups of actors are searching for future alternatives and for what reasons? Are groups of actors at either the micro-, meso- or macro-level attempting to build coalitions around certain future developmental models and what barriers do they encounter and why? Who is participating in these coalitions and for what reasons? To what extent are innovation policies mission-orientated, experimental and transformative? To what extent are the phases in real critical junctures valid for different case studies and to what extent are our four phases able to generate empirical growth in terms of predicting novel facts?

NOTES

1. For further reading on the concepts of Fordism and post-Fordism see Aglietta (1979), Hirsch and Roth (1986) and Lipietz (1987).
2. See Giddens (1984) for a discussion of the concept of structuration.
3. For analysis of different 'institutional' contexts in terms of 'societal paradigms' for comparative studies, see Jonsson (2001). There are four types of societal paradigms. 'Techno-economic paradigms' refer to ideas about what constitutes the best practices and means of organizing production, services and consumption in general. Secondly, 'power-political paradigms' refer to ideas about how 'collective' decision-making is best organized and its enforcement institutionalized. Thirdly, 'reproduction-social paradigms' refer to ideas about the roles different social groups and institutions should play in regard to sexuality, biological reproduction, care of children, old persons and the disabled, and socialization. Fourthly, 'ethical-prescriptive paradigms' refer to worldviews and general ideas about right and wrong conducted in different situations, the aims and quality of life and attitudes towards preservation of nature.
4. See further discussion on efficient and material causes in Archer (1995, pp. 90 and 153) and Lewis (2000, pp. 260 and 264).

REFERENCES

Aglietta, M. 1979, *A Theory of Capitalist Regulation: The US Experience*, London: New Left Books.
Algan, Y., Guriev, S., Papaioannou, E. and Passari, E. 2017, 'The European trust crisis and the rise of populism', *Brookings Papers on Economic Activity* (Fall), pp. 309–82.

Archer, M. 1995, *Realist Social Theory: The Morphogenetic Approach*, Cambridge: Cambridge University Press.

Battiston, S., Guerini, M., Napoletano, M. and Stolbova, V. 2018, 'Financialization in EU and the effects on growth, inequality and financial stability', *ISIGrowth*, accessed 25 May 2019 at: http://www.isigrowth.eu/wp-content/uploads/2018/07/working_paper_2018_36.pdf.

Berghoff, H. 2016, 'Varieties of financialization? Evidence from German industry in the1990s', *Business Historical Review*, **90**(1), 81–108.

Brynjolfsson, E. and McAfee, A. 2014, *The Second Machine Age: Work, Progress, and Prosperity in a Time of Brilliant Technologies*, New York: W.W. Norton & Company.

De Bromhead, A., Eichengreen, B. and O'Rourke, K.H. 2012, 'Right wing political extremism in the Great Depression', Discussion Papers in Economic and Social History, no. 95, University of Oxford.

Deutschmann, C. 2011, 'Limits to financialization', *European Journal of Sociology*, **52**(3), 347–89.

Evangelista, R. 2018, 'Technology and economic development: the Schumpeterian legacy', *Review of Radical Political Economics*, **50**(1), 136–53.

Foster, J.B. and Magdoff, F. 2008, *The Great Financial Crisis: Causes and Consequences*, New York: Monthly Review Press.

Freeman, C. and Louçã, F. 2001, *As Time Goes By: From the Industrial Revolutions to the Information Revolution*, Oxford: Oxford University Press.

Freeman, C. and Perez, C. 1988, 'Structural crises of adjustment: business cycles and investment behaviour', in G. Dosi, C. Freeman, R. Nelson, G. Silverberg and L. Soete (eds), *Technical Change and Economic Theory*, London: Pinter Publishers.

Funke, M., Schularick, M. and Trebesch, C. 2016, 'Going to extremes: politics after financial crises, 1870–2014', *European Economic Review*, **88**, 227–60.

Ghotgalkar, V., Baltora, J., Rosenberg, M.K. and Riley, T. 2017, 'How the digital economy is changing corporate pricing and inflation', *Investment Research*, 22 August.

Giddens, A. 1984, *The Constitution of Society: Outline of the Theory of Structuration*, Cambridge: Polity Press.

Giorgi, A. 2017, *Re-thinking the Political Economy of Punishment: Perspectives on Post-Fordism and Penal Politics*, London: Routledge.

Hahn, K. 2019, 'Innovation in times of financialization: do future-oriented innovation strategies suffer? Examples from German industry', *Research Policy*, **48**(4), 923–35.

Hanssen, G.S., Mydske, P.K. and Dahle, E. 2013, 'Multi-level coordination of climate change adaptation: by national hierarchical steering or by regional network governance?', *Local Environment: The International Journal of Justice and Sustainability*, **18**(8), 869–87.

Hirsch, J. and Roth, R. 1986, *Das Neue Gesicht des Kapitalismus: Vom Fordismus zum Post-Fordismus*, Hamburg: VSA-Verlag.

Jonsson, I. 1994, 'Collective entrepreneurship and micro-economies', in T. Greifenberg (ed.), *Sustainability in the Arctic*, Aalborg: NARF/Aalborg University Press.

Jonsson, I. 2001, 'Societal paradigms and rural development – a theoretical framework for comparative studies', in L. Granberg, I. Kovach and T. Hilary (eds), *Europe's Green Ring,* Aldershot: Ashgate Publishing.

Jonsson, I. 2016a, 'Economic crisis and real critical junctures – on the decay of the political party system of Iceland', *The Polar Journal*, **6**(1), 131–51.

Jonsson, I. 2016b, *The Political Economy of Innovation and Entrepreneurship from Theories to Practice*, London: Routledge.

Kangas, O. 2016, *From Idea to Experiment: Report on Universal Basic Income Experiment in Finland*, Helsinki: Kela.

Kregel, J. 2018, 'What we could have learned from the New Deal in dealing with the recent global recession', *Review of Social Economy*, **76**(2), 147–66.

Kuhlmann, S. and Rip, A. 2018, 'Next generation innovation policy and grand challenges', *Science and Public Policy*, **45**(4), 448–54.

Kuhlmann, S., Konrad, K. and Stegmaier, P. 2019, 'Tentative governance in emerging science and technology – conceptual introduction and overview', *Research Policy*, **48**(5), 1091–7.

Lakatos, I. 1970, 'History of science and its rational reconstructions', *Boston Studies in the Philosophy of Science*, pp. 91–136.

Lauritzen, J.R.K. 2012, *Social Innovation in Local Government – Experiences from Denmark, Produced as Part of 'Next Practice – New Forms of Innovation'*, Danish Technological Institute, Centre for Policy and Business Analysis.

Lewis, P. 2000, 'Realism, causality and the problem of social structure', *Journal for the Theory of Social Behaviour*, **30**(3), 249–68.

Lipietz, A. 1987, *Mirages and Miracles: The Crisis of Global Fordism*, London: Verso.

Macpherson, C.B. 1979, *The Life and Times of Liberal Democracy*, Oxford: Oxford University Press.

Mazzucato, M. 2013, *The Entrepreneurial State*, London: Anthem Press.

Mazzucato, M. 2018, *Mission-oriented Research & Innovation in the European Union: a Problem-solving Approach to Fuel Innovation-led Growth*, Paris: European Union.

Mósesdóttir, L. 2001, *The Interplay Between Gender, Markets and the State in Sweden, Germany and the United States*, London: Routledge.

Mósesdóttir, L. and Ellingsæter, A.L. 2017, 'Ideational struggles over women's part-time work in Norway: destabilizing the gender contract', *Economic and Industrial Democracy*, 6 January, https://doi.org/10.1177/0143831X16681483.

Norges forskningsråd 2018, *Innovasjon i offentlig sector: forskningsrådets strategi 2018–2023*, Norges forskningsråd, Oslo, accessed 22 January 2020 at https://www.forskningsradet.no/siteassets/publikasjoner/1254032549913.pdf.

OECD 2014, 'Policy challenges for the next 50 years', OECD economic, policy paper, no. 9, Paris: OECD.

OECD 2018, *OECD Science, Technology and Innovation Outlook 2018*, Paris: OECD.

Ornston, D. and Schulze-Cleven, T. 2015, 'Conceptualizing cooperation coordination and concertation as two logics of collective action', *Comparative Political Studies*, **48**(5), 555–85.

Oxfam 2019, *Public Good or Private Wealth?*, Oxford: Oxfam.

Pagano, U. and Rossi, M.A. 2011, 'Property rights in the knowledge economy', in E. Brancaccio and R. Fontana (eds), *The Global Economic Crisis*, Abingdon: Routledge, pp. 284–97.

Poulantzas, N. 1975, *Political Power and Social Classes*, London: New Left Books.

Sayer, A. 2000, *Realism and Social Science*, London: SAGE Publications.

Schot, J. and Steinmueller, W.E. 2016, 'Framing innovation policy for transformative change: innovation policy 3.0', Brighton: Science Policy Research Unit (SPRU).

Schwab, K. 2015, 'The fourth industrial revolution: What it means and how to respond', *Foreign Affairs*, 12 December.

Schwab, K. 2016, *The Fourth Industrial Revolution*, Geneva: World Economic Forum.

World Economic Forum 2019, *The Global Risks, Report 2019*, 14th edn, Geneva: World Economic Forum.

7. Exploring industrial PhD students and perceptions of their impact on firm innovation

Karin Berg and Maureen McKelvey

1. INTRODUCTION

During the 20th-century expansion of universities and colleges, the two main roles of universities in society have been to produce new knowledge and educate students. More recently, universities have been asked to contribute more directly to society and economic growth. Gibbons et al. (1994) argued that the changing production of knowledge in society should involve a wider range of stakeholders, and universities have been seen as more entrepreneurial and competitive in terms of obtaining allocated resources (Etzkowitz 2004; McKelvey and Holmén 2009). Universities are expected to develop new knowledge, and to spread that knowledge across society and industry, increasing societal benefits and economic development (Salter and Martin 2001; Bozeman et al. 2015). Because universities have changed and taken on these new activities, they have needed to become more entrepreneurial and interact more with the external environment (Etzkowitz 2013). The extensive literature on university–industry interaction has explored various mechanisms for technology transfer and for conceptualizing these new roles and responsibilities of universities, including especially the view of the university and the incentives of academics to engage in such activities (Ambos et al. 2008; Laredo 2007; Ankrah and Al-Tabbaa 2015; Rosli and Rossi 2016). Less research has focused on how collaborative research between university and industry may affect firms, in terms of innovation.

Therefore, this chapter explores industrial PhD students, including their activities and their perceptions of the impact of their studies and of their role in university–firm interaction on firm innovation. The limited number of previous studies of industrial PhD students mainly focus on broader issues related to these students' educational experience and learning outcomes (Thune 2009), whereas studies of PhD students moving to industry generally focus not on their activities during education but rather on what happens after graduation (e.g., Cruz-Castro and Sanz-Menéndez 2005; Garcia-Quevedo et al. 2011; Roach and Sauermann 2010). Here, we consider a specific empirical phenomenon, namely, industrial PhD students during their education, when they are simultaneously involved in both the university and the firm.

Because little research considers our phenomenon, we address two questions through detailed qualitative research, within the empirical context of collaborative research in the field of engineering in Sweden. Given the lack of previous research on this topic, our first question is: How should an industrial PhD student be defined? To answer this, we consider the conditions for education and employment, their specific activities, and the frequency of activities bridging the university and firm. Then we seek to explore their perceived contribution to firm innovation during their education as PhD students, so our second question is: What is the perception of how their activities impact upon firm innovation? To conceptualize this, we first present an existing conceptual framework for academic engagement with industry, and further elaborate on underlying concepts in order to develop a detailed analysis of the micro-level activities of these PhD students. Our results identify several activities of these industrial PhD students that merit analysis in future research, and specifically in relation to the development of firm capabilities for innovation.

Section 2 presents an existing conceptual framework for understanding the similarities and differences between universities' impacts on society through commercialization versus academic engagement. This chapter is positioned within a broader body of literature on academic engagement with industry, leading to the insight that collaborative research should be an important way to stimulate the firm's capabilities to innovate. More specifically, we start our research based on an existing conceptual framework detailing how collaborative research can yield two outcomes, either directly or indirectly affecting firm innovation (McKelvey and Ljungberg 2016). We then explain the relevance of this model for collaborative research to the phenomenon of interest.

Section 3 addresses our qualitative research design, and explains why it is useful for exploring industrial PhD students. Empirically, the phenomenon of interest is relevant to larger issues concerning the changing role of universities in society, because industrial PhD students have the explicit aim of developing, sharing and diffusing new knowledge relevant to both academia and the corporate world.

Section 4 organizes and presents the empirical material in order to answer the two research questions. Section 4.1 empirically defines the phenomenon to answer the first research question. Section 4.2 presents empirical material which will enable us to address the second question, through the analysis in section 5.

Section 5 analyses the empirical material in relation to the existing conceptual framework presented in section 2. Based on our analysis, we propose an updated and revised conceptual framework specifically relevant to industrial PhD students. Section 6 completes the chapter by specifying the main findings and indicating areas for future research.

2. THEORETICAL BACKGROUND: FRAMING WHY AND HOW INDUSTRIAL PHD STUDENTS MATTER FOR FIRM INNOVATION

2.1 How to Define Industrial PhD Students Empirically and Conceptually?

Here we examine industrial PhD students. Conceptually, we propose that these individuals and their activities constitute a specific form of university–industry interaction. We study them, when they are already in place, and hence where the decision to collaborate in this form has already been made. According to Thune (2009), doctoral students can assume three roles in university–industry relationships: producing knowledge; serving as channels for knowledge transfer between universities and firms; and creating and maintaining network links between universities and firms. The limited existing research into industrial PhD students suggests that they represent a heterogeneous phenomenon (Thune 2009; Borrell-Damian et al. 2010), indicating a need to start this study by defining the phenomenon, asking more generally: 'What is an industrial PhD student?'

Industrial PhD students act within a context. More generally, we place the topic of industrial PhD students as related to the extensive literature on the entrepreneurial university and on university–industry interaction, much of which focuses on academic scientists and their interactions with society. However, more recent literature specifically addresses academic engagement with industry, and in a thorough review, Perkmann et al. (2013) proposed that universities can interact through either commercialization activities or academic engagement with industry. On one hand, commercialization refers to activities that academics undertake that are designed to commercialize academic knowledge in the marketplace while retaining the resulting monetary rewards. The most typical outcomes are patents and start-up firms, and where university scientists, technology transfer offices and similar units engage in related activities such as licensing academic patents, and creating academic start-up firms. On the other hand, academic engagement with industry refers to a range of activities related to knowledge networks and relationships (Perkmann et al. 2013). This concept thus incorporates a wide range of formally and informally defined activities, such as collaborative research, contract research, consulting, ad hoc advising, networking with practitioners, and other forms of knowledge exchange.

On the university side, Perkmann et al. (2013) identified three categories of factors that influence the likelihood of university scientists, and hence academics, engaging with industry: individual characteristics, organizational context, and institutional context. In terms of individual characteristics, certain demographic attributes are more common than others, specifically researchers' seniority and success rate with grants and publications (Perkmann et al. 2013). Researchers participate in external collaborations for different reasons, which are reflected in the type of collaboration (Perkmann and Walsh 2008; Ankrah and Al-Tabbaa 2015). Organizational context refers to attributes of the involved university or department. Previous research has found that higher-quality publications, universities or departments are associated with less academic interaction with industry partners (D'Este and Patel 2007; Ponomariov 2007; Ponomariov and Boardman 2007). Institutional context concerns differences between scientific disciplines, national regulations, and public policies. In applied fields of research such as engineering, collaboration is more likely. There is limited evidence regarding national setting, but in national innovation systems with higher competitive funding constraints, academics have a greater incentive to collaborate with industry (Perkmann et al. 2013). In the present research, we have chosen engineering and a national institutional context that supports the phenomenon studied here.

On the firm side, the studied phenomenon requires the initial theoretical understanding that firms have an interest in continuing to develop and absorb new technological knowledge relevant to their industry. There is an extensive body of literature on firms' capabilities for technology and innovation, and the key points concerning the limited case of when firms collaborate with universities can be summarized as follows: the concepts of 'absorptive capacity' and 'technology-based firm' focus attention on the notion that the ability to create, develop and absorb new technology is crucial for firms to survive and remain competitive (Granstrand 1998; Cohen and Levinthal 1990). Due to the vital role of technological development, firms interact with universities (and other organizations) to develop new knowledge and technology (Mansfield 1995) in what has recently been seen as part of an open innovation strategy (Chesbrough 2003). Firms have different ways of increasing their absorptive capacity, for example, by involving employees in advanced technical training and by conducting research and development (R&D) (Cohen and Levinthal 1990).

Of relevance to this chapter, Cohen and Levinthal (1990, p. 132) argued that 'the firms' absorptive capacity depends on the individuals who stand at the interface of either the firm and the external environment or at the interface between subunits within the firm'. In this early literature, such individuals were called 'boundary spanners' (Allen 1977; Tushman 1977), and were identified as playing an important role in ensuring the sufficient creation and assimilation of new knowledge within the firm (Cohen and Levinthal 1990). The reasons why firms interact with academia can vary, resulting in multiple types of outcomes and benefits for firms (Bishop et al. 2011; Broström 2010; Perkmann and Walsh 2008; McKelvey and Ljungberg 2016). This study examines industrial PhD students who are simultaneously PhD students and firm employees.

Therefore, we characterize the studied phenomenon of industrial PhD students in the following way: they represent one specific form of academic engagement with industry, meaning that their activities span the organizational boundaries of both the university and the firm. Given the notion of knowledge networks, we propose that industrial PhD students are at the university–firm interface, and that they can stimulate the absorptive capacity of the firm to develop new technologies. From this conceptualization, we infer that we need to better understand the empirical phenomenon through identification of activities in relation to firm innovation, and we will do so by examining the institutional, organizational and individual perspectives on academic engagement.

2.2 What are Industrial PhD Students' Activities and How are they Perceived to Affect Firm Innovation?

Here we address the second question. We explore the activities of industrial PhD students and how they are perceived to affect firm innovation by starting with an existing conceptual framework that fosters insight into these matters. More specifically, the outcome of academic engagement, in relation to innovation, can be either direct or indirect, with the former being innovation as such and the latter helping in developing firm capabilities (McKelvey and Ljungberg 2016). For the purposes of this chapter, we start from this framework, elaborating on the underlying factors relevant to the specific context of study.

McKelvey and Ljungberg (2016) have studied different routes by which public policy on university–industry collaboration can affect firms in traditional industries. In contrast to literature on the special conditions of innovation in low- and medium-tech industries, they demonstrated that firms in the food industry do engage in advanced collaborative research, and that public policy can indirectly affect firm capabilities.

Two dimensions – defining the type of innovation and the degree of radicalness – merit discussion before introducing the conceptual framework. An established definition of innovation used by the Organisation for Economic Co-operation and Development (OECD) identifies four types: product, process, market, and organizational innovations. Also important is the degree of novelty of innovation, which can range along a continuum extending from incremental to radical (Freeman 1974). Incremental innovation entails minor changes to existing processes or products, while a radical innovation entails ground-breaking changes that are new. Incremental innovation is about improving existing processes or products, while radical innovation could result in entirely new processes or products.

As shown in Figure 7.1, the McKelvey and Ljungberg (2016) conceptual model has two routes by which collaborative research influences firm innovation, corresponding to commercialization and academic engagement.

The two routes are as follows: The direct route, shown at the top of Figure 7.1, concerns direct activities that enable commercialization. In this way, collaborative research can lead firms to experience outcomes that

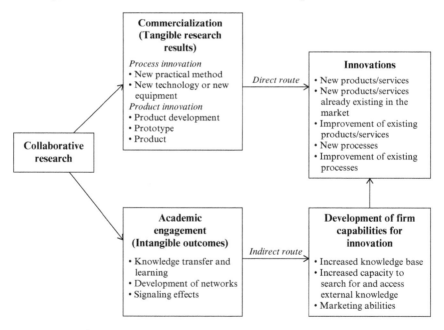

Source: McKelvey and Ljungberg (2016, p. 541).

Figure 7.1   *Conceptual framework for how collaborative research can affect firm innovation*

can be directly transferred to the firm and commercialized in the market. The second route, shown at the bottom of Figure 7.1, concerns indirect impact, conceptualized here as academic engagement. This indirect route may still be important in the long run for the development of new products, processes and services in firms, shown at the far right of the figure. However, meaningful innovation requires the middle step of developing firms' capabilities for innovation.

To elaborate on this conceptual framework for our case study, we briefly discuss the two routes with reference to the relevant literature.

Regarding the direct route, the university–industry interaction literature treats certain activities as relevant to direct innovation outcomes. For the purposes of this study, we categorize the following four activities as having direct impacts on commercialization and innovation: assisting in problem solving (Bishop et al. 2011); engaging in product and process development (Broström 2010; Gustavsson et al. 2016); identifying direct business opportunities (Broström 2010); and generating patents (Bishop et al. 2011). We believe that they qualify as direct innovation outcomes due to their direct and/or tangible nature.

Regarding the indirect route, the academic engagement literature stresses more intangible and indirect impacts such as knowledge networks and relationships. McKelvey and Ljungberg (2016) have specified the following three categories of such engagement: knowledge transfer and learning, network development, and signalling effects.

The first category, knowledge transfer and learning, includes general knowledge, specific technological developments, and how to execute new methods of analysis. The process of developing technology is likely to be facilitated by both labour mobility and active interaction between the parties involved in the collaborative research. Moreover, the university–industry literature presents us with a broader understanding of what this may entail, including activities involved in human capital management, such as recruiting young researchers, influencing undergraduate education, and securing research partners for firms (Broström 2010). Bishop et al. (2011) also discussed the recruitment and training of firm employees as potential outcomes. In addition, academics can serve as 'windows' on new technology (Perkmann and Walsh 2008). Some literature obliquely addresses industrial PhD students, namely, the literature treating transfer and learning, which specifically considers: accessing scientific knowledge (Thune 2009); developing technological competences (Thune and Børing 2014; Gustavsson et al. 2016); and developing internal R&D activities (Gustavsson et al. 2016). We consult this literature to enrich our empirical study.

The second category refers to network development within the collaborative research project, which serves as an important way to assess the knowledge of specialized experts. The key idea is that the firm obtains value by gaining access to networks. A broad body of literature shows that knowledge networks are important for innovation (Ahuja 2000a, 2000b; Lam 2007; Wang et al. 2014; Nerkar and Paruchuri 2005; Broekel and Boschma 2012). In the present context, we are interested in how industrial PhD students can create and be involved in knowledge networks.

Finally, McKelvey and Ljungberg (2016) recognized that signalling effects enable the supply of valuable information to third parties. Gustavsson et al. (2016) found that the increased legitimacy of a product or process (e.g., through coverage in scientific articles or dissertations) enabled firms to strengthen their ties to clients and business partners. Signalling firm quality, through financial intermediaries, has been noted to be especially important when information asymmetry is evident (Leland and Pyle 1977; Campbell and Kracaw 2012; Chemmanur and Fulghieri 2012; Chemmanur 2012; Nicholson et al. 2005). For example, previous research in biotechnology illustrates how 'star' scientists and the signals they send are important for securing funding in emerging industries (Higgins et al. 2011).

Based on this conceptualization – and especially the notion of the two routes by which collaborative research influences firm innovation – we wish to determine what activities of industrial PhD students need to be understood. Because the framework applies the distinction between commercialization and academic engagement with industry, we can use it to explore what activities and perceptions of industrial PhD students may affect these two routes.

3. RESEARCH DESIGN AND METHODS

We have chosen a qualitative research design for studying industrial PhD students and their interactions with connected parties, because these students occupy a unique position as boundary spanners undertaking advanced technical training. When investigating how academic engagement can influence innovation in firms, certain empirical environments merit more study than do others, given the many forms of university–industry collaboration (Ankrah and Al-Tabbaa 2015). In addition, previous literature reveals little about industrial PhD students. The research project is a qualitative single-case study (Yin 2014) whose aim is to obtain an in-depth understanding of industrial PhD students' perceptions and activities with regard to their contribution to firm innovation during their education. The case study focuses on the perspective of industrial PhD students in engineering at a Swedish technological university (hereafter, 'the University'). The engineering field was chosen due to its long tradition of collaborating with industry and hosting industrial PhD students.

3.1   Data Collection

Both primary and secondary data were collected. To answer the first research question, a combination of primary and secondary data was used. The secondary data were collected in order to define the criteria, conditions and other relevant quantitative information about industrial PhD students as a phenomenon. This overview was complemented with the analysis of primary data (see below) in relation to this question.

To answer the second research question, the primary data were gathered through semi-structured interviews. The total number of doctoral students in engineering at the University was 91; 17 of these were industrial PhD students, 8 of whom participated in semi-structured interviews. The interview guide used in the interviews was initially developed through a literature review concerning university–industry interaction, supplemented by a pilot interview with an industrial PhD student conducted in June 2017. The interviews were conducted in September 2017 and, based on their results, the interview guide was adapted and refined. Five of the interviews were transcribed and the remaining two were summarized; for each interview, a summary of the interview was sent to the informant to ensure respondent validation. An overview of the collection of primary data is presented in Table 7.1.

One informant, S.2.CH, was excluded from the sample as they did not fulfil the requirements for being an industrial PhD student as defined here. Therefore, only seven of the interviews will be included in the empirical

Table 7.1   Overview of the collection of primary data

ID number	Interview style (semi-structured)	Length of interview (recording)	Transcribed	Summary of interview reviewed by informant
S.1.CH	Face-to-face	01:02:02	No	Approved
S.2.CH	Face-to-face	00:53:41	Excluded from sample	
S.3. CH	Face-to-face	00:39:55	Yes	Approved
L.4.CH	Skype	01:01:29	Yes	Approved
S.5.CH	Face-to face	01:05:43	Yes	Adjusted and approved
S.6.CH	Face-to-face	31:49 + 30:25	Yes	No response
S.7.CH	Face-to-face	01:21:47	Yes	No response
S.8.CH	Face-to-face	00:46:59	No	Adjusted and approved

data and following analysis. In the following text, the ID numbers from Table 7.1 are used as identifiers.

3.2   Data Analysis of Interviews

To analyse the gathered data, the five interview transcripts and two interview summaries were imported into NVivo software. First, the individual interviews were analysed separately. Each interview was coded with first-order codes (e.g., 'presentations at firm', 'firm expectations of patents', 'matching own knowledge with firm challenges'), which were later grouped into second-order codes. The first-order codes are more detailed, specifying a specific experience of the industrial PhD student, while the second-order codes are on a more aggregated level. For example, the first-order codes 'firm expectations of patents', 'university expectations of patents', and 'filing for patents' all describe different perspectives and activities connected to the second-order code 'patents'. After coding the individual interviews with first- and second-order codes, the analysis of the data proceeded by combining all the information from all interviews (Eisenhardt 1989). In doing this, second-order codes can be grouped into third-order codes, or themes, raising the analysis to an even more aggregated level. The third-order codes are inspired by both theory and empirical findings.

4.   EXPLORING THE PHENOMENON OF INDUSTRIAL PHD STUDENTS

4.1   How to Define an Industrial PhD Student?

Above, we proposed conceptualizing industrial PhD students as individuals embodying a specific type of academic engagement with industry. Given the notion of knowledge networks, we have proposed that industrial PhD students are at the interface between the university and the firm, and that they may stimulate the absorptive capacity of the firm to develop new technologies.

This broad abstract conceptualization is useful for later research, but it provides insufficient detail to be useful in defining the phenomenon empirically. Moreover, industrial PhD students are heterogeneous, as noted by Thune (2009) and Borrell-Damian et al. (2010), potentially due to differences in organizational and institutional context, as noted by Perkmann et al. (2013). Therefore, we have used our explorative qualitative research to define the phenomenon of interest by discussing specific characteristics.

We did so by first differentiating industrial PhD students from academic PhD students and then by specifying the criteria for being considered an industrial PhD student as well as the specific characteristics of those studied here. This provided consistency in criteria, and was a necessary step because an empirically grounded definition generated through qualitative research serves as a foundation for later research into this under-examined topic. We propose that the phenomenon can be understood at the institutional, organizational and individual levels.

The first step was defining PhD students. In the Swedish context, most PhD students in general, and engineering students in particular, are both students and employees. They are enrolled in education programmes as PhD students, and required to take credit courses and write an independent thesis. In Sweden, 21 000 PhD students were enrolled across all universities in 2016 (Statistics Sweden 2017). On average, the numbers of male and female students are similar, though the balance may be skewed in specific disciplines. The universities and colleges employ 71 per cent of all doctoral students in Sweden (Statistics Sweden 2017), while another 23 per cent have various employment arrangements, such as stipends, medical residencies, or employment in organizations other than universities and firms. We define students employed by a university or on a stipend as academic PhD students. The remaining 6 per cent of doctoral students in Sweden are employed and financed by firms (Statistics Sweden 2017), fulfilling the following criteria for being considered industrial PhD students: (1) employed at a firm and (2) with more than 50 per cent of their salary financed by non-academic organizations.

In the Swedish context, industrial PhD students are most common in engineering disciplines, amounting to 14 per cent of all new PhD students in 2016 (Statistics Sweden 2017). We would also like to point out that entering into contracts and agreements to undertake joint PhD studies requires commitment from both the university and the firm. The involved parties must agree to interact and collaborate for a longer period, usually for the four to five years of the PhD studies.

The University is one of Sweden's largest technological universities, hosting close to 1200 PhD students in 2016, of whom 177 (15 per cent) were industrial PhD students, including 154 in technical fields. Of engineering PhD students, 17 (19 per cent) were industrial PhD students and 74 (81 per cent) academic PhD students.

As the University applies a finer-grained definition than does the national statistics office, we used its information to generate Table 7.2, which specifies the University's enrolment requirements for industrial PhD students.

Table 7.2   Enrolment requirements for an industrial PhD position at the University

Definition	Employment and financing	Study pace	Supervision	Teaching	Degree
1) A doctoral student employed by a firm (or corresponding organization) and pursuing graduate study at the University OR 2) A doctoral student who is part of a formalized co-operation agreement	1) Normally receives the whole salary from the firm as well as part of the cost of materials, instruments, supervision, etc., by agreement between the firm and the University OR 2) Doctoral student is entirely or partly on leave from his/her employment at the firm; the firm partly or entirely finances his/her salary	>50%	A supervisor group (two or more researchers) is responsible for the supervision. The main supervisor should be at the University while the assistant supervisor often is appointed at the firm.	Teaching time (20%) can be replaced with work at the firm and teaching qualifications of a different kind.	Licentiate or doctorate

Source: Authors' compilation.

Although the University has defined two types of industrial PhD student, we concentrate on the first type in Table 7.2, which is also the most common.

Let us now turn to the individual level, that is, the actual PhD students analysed here. The intention is to compare and contrast their industry conditions, financing, and actual tasks so as to better understand how they may perceive and act at the university–firm interface.

Industrial and work conditions differ between students, even though this study is limited to a subset involved in the engineering discipline. The details are as follows: five of the informants were collaborating with Firm A, which is a joint spin-off in the field of machine learning. Apart from S.8.CH, these informants had started their industrial PhD studies in other firms and had then been transferred to Firm A in recent years. The remaining informants represent collaborations with other firms. Firms C and D are both large global firms, the first in telecommunications and the second in the transportation and automotive industry.

In terms of financing, each of the seven students was employed at a firm that co-financed them jointly with an external organization, generally a research council or research foundation. Specifically, this meant that their salaries, supervisors' time, and doctoral education were financed both internally by the firms and by the external organizations co-financing their positions. Co-financing organizations support the firms with grants, partly covering the costs of the industrial PhD students. Co-financing organizations can dispense funds from either the government or foundations, and the firms (often with University support) apply for grants for each PhD student. The co-financing grants can be for different durations (usually three to four years in the present cases) and different amounts, but they are specifically designated to support the employment and education of industrial PhD students. In this study, two public initiatives (i.e., Public Co-financing A and B) and one foundation initiative (i.e., Foundation Co-financing A) supported the industrial PhD students' education. In the case of S.8.CH, it had not been decided exactly how the financing would be divided. Still, because all informants were employed at firms with individual employment contracts, this meant that all human resources (HR) matters, such as salaries and welfare benefits, were handled by the firms.

In terms of tasks, the students undertook many different tasks, divided between the 'academic work' and 'firm work' categories. What we call 'academic work' relates to the students' PhD studies and thesis research, defined as the time that the informants should spend on their education, research project, and teaching at the university. Five of the seven informants spent 100 per cent of their time on academic work, for example, 90 per cent PhD studies and 10 per cent teaching. The remaining two informants spent 90 per cent of their time on academic work. What we call 'firm work' refers to the amount of time that the informants were expected (by contract) to participate in firm-specific work. We have summarized our findings regarding financing and tasks in Table 7.3.

Firm work is often a way the students can apply their knowledge to benefit the firm. Not all informants were assigned firm work (see Table 7.3), but for those who were, the tasks usually concerned the informants' research projects in one way or another. S.7.CH cited an example: 'I became very involved in building servers for our group during the summer'. He also mentioned that he usually spent more time on firm work than was stipulated in his employment contract.

Table 7.3   Overview of financing and tasks

ID no.	Firm	Financing of PhD project			Division of labour of tasks		
					Academic work		Firm work
		Co-financing	Firm	The University	PhD studies	Teaching	
S.1.CH	Firm A	Yes, Public Co-financing A	Yes	0%	Yes	Yes	0%
S.3.CH	Firm A	50% Public Co-financing A	50%	0%	90%	10%	0%
L.4.CH	Firm C	50% Public Co-financing B	50%	0%	90%	10%	0%
S.5.CH	Firm D	50% Public Co-financing A	50%	0%	90%	10%	0%
S.6.CH	Firm A	50% Public Co-financing A	50%	0%	95%	5%	0%
S.7.CH	Firm A	50% Foundation Co-financing A	50%	0%	80%	10%	10%
S.8.CH	Firm A	To be determined			80%	10%	10%

The varied backgrounds of the individual PhD students comprise two components: previous competences and work experiences, and the competences acquired during their PhD studies. The students were diverse in terms of previous competences and experience. Two had worked in the same industry before starting their PhD studies, whereas one had switched industries. Informants S.3.CH, S.5.CH and S.6.CH all had five to six years of previous industry and work experience. S.3.CH was the only informant who had filed a patent, and he acknowledged that it was favourable to have filed for a patent before starting his PhD work. Building on his previous experience, S.5.CH was very much involved in identifying the knowledge gap in the firm that became his PhD project: 'So we identified this gap and that's why we created this project. I was involved pretty early in that phase. We found this gap to be significant and realized that we could work on it as a research topic as well'. Both S.3.CH and S.5.CH had previous experience in the same industry that their research projects addressed. In contrast, S.6.CH switched industries when he began his PhD studies. He thought that his previous industry experience was partly why he was hired as an industrial student at Firm A, for the following reasons: first, the technological knowledge from the previous industry is now also important in Firm A's industry and, second, the informant had experience of a specific work process (i.e., scrum) that Firm A intended to implement: 'These people are shifting from being a manufacturer that's basically dealing with hardware, and then they want to build a new company with software releases . . . I can surely help them, at least in terms of method I can help the company shift in that direction. That's partly why they hired me'. In terms of the competences acquired during the industrial PhD studies, L.4.CH stated: 'I think that, above all, it may be about training staff and that it could lead to something in the future, that I will be a good employee in the future'. L.4.CH also pointed out that he was learning things that might affect long-term strategic planning, and that the technological knowledge he acquired over time would be important for the firm's strategic choices. S.3.CH expressed it like this: 'The point is that I possess this knowledge and can be part of something . . . I should be able to stand for this knowledge . . . and I think that I have also built up intuition over time about what works and what doesn't'. In contrast, the other five students each have under six months of work experience, because they started their PhD work immediately after their Masters degrees.

Our findings help to define industrial PhD students and provide an overall understanding of them at the institutional, organizational and individual levels.

4.2 What are Industrial PhD Students' Activities and How are they Perceived to Affect Firm Innovation?

Given the above definition of industrial PhD students, one might expect them to be little involved in their firms during their PhD studies, given that 90–100 per cent of their time is dedicated to PhD studies. In view of this, we used this limited number of interviews to identify the industrial PhD students' various activities and to consider perceptions of how these students may affect firm innovation, including the issue of whether their activities can be seen as more direct or indirect ways of influencing innovation in their firms. From the empirical analysis, we have grouped their activities in three broad categories.

4.2.1 Directly working on products and processes

Directly working on new products and processes at the firm is the first and largest category of activities that we identified through our qualitative research. We asked about perceptions and activities that could explain whether, how and why the informants contributed to the development of their firms' new products and processes. They all clearly stated that industrial PhD students should be useful for commercialization. As one informant put it: 'They want to solve this problem and find an applicable industrial research solution, so that is their objective for part of my contribution to them'.

For product development, such direct involvement was uncommon because they were instead supposed to be engaged in research. Usually, industrial PhD students were not involved in the actual product development process, as illustrated by L.4.CH: 'I must admit, I'm not involved in product development at all'. However, they may be involved, depending on their past experience and the type of research they are conducting. Although they might not be directly involved in product development at the firm, some projects are more closely integrated with existing products in the market. As S.5.CH noted,

> It's very well connected to reality, and we use academic help to see and explore whether there are other possible control structures that we can use. But still, it's going to be practical because that's our objective, to provide an industrial solution, but with the research-based solution . . . it is easier for me to go from research to action, practical implementation.

One reason for this is the extended time between research and technical development. The informants explained that their contributions could lead to new products in the future, rather than immediately: 'Right now I'm working on problems that are not connected to any products in the near future . . . but maybe in the long term, within five to ten years'. Another informant explained that he took on the PhD position to move further away from the testing and robustness checks that need to be done when getting a product ready for commercialization. Yet another informant stated: 'It's not so far ahead, but I don't think the code I write will end up in a product. Rather, it is code based on what I have researched that might end up in a future product'.

Patents were uncommon and depended on the institutional context, and demands for patents differed between the firms and informants. Only Firm C stipulated in its contract with the informant that the goal was to file a certain number of patents during the student's education. Moreover, the informants reported that the specific research area could influence the need for patents in different ways. For example, in areas characterized by software development, it can be difficult to file patents due to open source code, and so on, while the telecommunications area seems to have more incentives to patent. Also, the firms' preferences for patents weigh in as well. So far, only one informant, S.3.CH, had filed patents during his education. This informant, with five years of previous industry experience and having filed a patent before beginning his PhD studies, said that his previous experience made it easier for him to file new patents during his PhD studies: 'The ones who come from industry are more used to it, if you have worked before and already been exposed to the patenting process'.

4.2.2   Discussing science and technology inside and outside the firm

Discussing science and technology inside and outside the firm is the second category of activities identified through our qualitative research. This discourse is likely to be facilitated by the individuals' moving back and forth between the two organizations, as all informants had office space at both the University and their firms. This space ranged from individual offices to open working environments. All informants attempted to visit their firms' offices at least once a week, some even spending all their time there except when teaching or engaging in other scheduled activities at the University. The informants regularly physically moved between the two organizations throughout their PhD studies.

Table 7.4 summarizes the various micro-level activities that we identified, giving an overview of how many of the seven informants mentioned specific activities when asked about them in a semi-structured interview.

Meetings with close colleagues at firms were reported to be a common activity by all informants. We found that these meetings could differ in intensity, frequency and purpose, and even involve different members of the firm. Technical meetings were described by S.5.CH as follows:

> We also have these group technical meetings at the firm . . . where you present all the technical advances within the local group. It's not even the full department or section, it's just this small group and still you get to present your results and conduct a discussion of what you are working on, even informally because this is more deeply and directly connected to the actual application.

Table 7.4   Firm activities (diffusing skills and knowledge) in which industrial PhD students participate

Firm activities	Number of industrial PhD students participating in the specific firm activity (7 = all industrial PhD students)
Technical meetings at firm	7
Presentations at firm	6
Written reports to firm	1
Firm-level coordination of industrial PhD students	2
Seminars and conferences	6
Papers and publications*	6

Note: *Publications include all kinds of publications, such as journal papers and papers in proceedings.

These technological meetings also occur one level up, at the section level of the firm. Industrial PhD students could also attend project meetings at which the new developments in a particular research area at the firm were presented. Another type of meeting was held with the supervisor, all informants except one (S.7.CH) having a clearly defined industrial supervisor at their firm. In addition, other people usually support the industrial PhD students as well, such as control group members, technical group managers, and other people from the particular work group to which the informant belongs at the firm. The informants have regular meetings with their supervisor, once a week or as needed. In S.7.CH's case, the original supervisor changed positions, and no other person assumed a complete supervisory role. However, the informant said that he got help from other people in the firm, for example, the technical manager. Finally, they described several other meetings at their firms in which industrial PhD students could participate, such as various group meetings and project meetings. Group meetings seemed to occur regularly according to the informants: 'Yes, so there are like routine meetings, like weekly meetings of the groups'.

Six informants reported regularly giving presentations at their firms, focusing on their research projects and sometimes involving personnel outside their closest circle of colleagues. Unlike a meeting, a presentation focuses on the contributions of the projects of the industrial students, who emphasize the results and implications of their own research. The industrial PhD students are expected to convey their knowledge during a presentation, which might not be the case during a meeting. For example, L.4.CH said that he presented several times a year at his firm: 'Several times a year I present my latest research results. It's fun as well – then you really get responses from the firm'. S.5.CH explained: 'I also present my research to the management team once a year'. In addition, S.5.CH also presented at the annual conference organized by the firm: 'And of course the . . . annual conference that we hold every year, and that's at the firm, open to all employees'.

Only one informant reported regularly submitting written reports. L.4.CH provided the firm with a written report every month to inform them of the progress of the research project:

> I always write monthly reports that go up in the hierarchy. Then, yes, somewhere in the organization a manager gets to know what I do, and then the next manager and the next. If I've done something good this month, it might be sent on to the next level of managers.

The implication is that his knowledge may diffuse further within the firm.

Firm-level coordination of industrial PhD students means that the firm has a specific and dedicated organization to bring together all its industrial

PhD students. We found that at Firms C and D, organizational structures were in place to organize industrial PhD students and their research at the firm level. Firm-wide gatherings were organized on a yearly basis for all industrial PhD students at these firms, so they could meet and share research developments and other experiences. This was also the case at one of the firms that hosted some of the informants before they were transferred to Firm A. As S.3.CH explained, 'Yes they have a programme for that, for [industrial] PhD students . . . It was quite fun because you learned what the other [industrial] PhD students were working on – there were all kinds of things'. No one was sure whether the new Firm A would also develop such organizational structures to facilitate meetings of industrial PhD students.

Similarly, regarding participating in seminars and conferences, the informants reported that the firms had a positive attitude towards their engaging in such activities. For example, the firms saw such participation as a good way to publicize research, as L.4.CH explained: 'Yes, absolutely [the University wants L.4.CH to attend conferences], and Firm C also wants that. I mean, it's a very good opportunity to make your research visible. So yes, I've already participated in number of conferences and also have a few more scheduled'.

Papers and publications are a normal part of research, including in PhD research in the field of interest here. As part of their academic work, the interviewed students were expected to attend conferences and publish papers, and six described this as beneficial for their firms. None of the firms had any specific requirement to publish papers, though the informants reported that the firms saw such publications as positive. Informant S.5.CH explained: 'I think they look at it as a prestige thing, if something is published by the section, because it brings more value to the company as well as the research area, so they favour publication'. In addition, S.6.CH stated that other employees at the firm also publish: 'I mean those people are also producing a lot of potential publications, at least they attend this academic conference every year'. Interaction about and via papers and publications was common at the firms.

4.2.3   Problem solving, articulating broader visions, and networking

Problem solving, articulating broader visions, and networking constitute the third category of activities that we identified.

In informal problem solving at the firms, the industrial PhD students were involved in both asking and answering questions through various discussions of technology. All seven informants indicated that they spent time in informal discussion with colleagues at their firms. In terms of asking questions or being questioned, it was mainly the informants who asked questions of firm employees. For example, S.6.CH stated: 'Normally, my work is, so to say, isolated from that of normal developers, so not much is related unless I have questions about tools or features and how to use their results. I mean, normally I will ask them'. However, the opposite could also occur, and the informants might be questioned by firm employees, as S.7.CH experienced:

> Usually it's questions about, not directly about my research project, but related to it. So, for example, if they wanted to install measurement equipment on the vehicle, they'd ask where I would like to put it to get the best [results] or be able to use it in the best way. Yes, and also other questions related to my experience.

Or as SL.4.CH put it: 'They can be . . . questions about anything, really. I mean "can you help me calculate x here" or – yes, it could be anything really'.

Another type of problem solving was to try to match one's own knowledge with firm challenges via what we consider a more advanced form of informal discussion, in which the industrial PhD students are actively seeking relevant outlets for their knowledge and research results. Five informants reported engaging in such knowledge matching, usually when opportunities to contribute to ongoing firm activities presented themselves during other activities. Usually this happened when the students realized that they possessed knowledge that could benefit firm activities, as S.3.CH described:

> I saw that they were using methods I didn't think would work, and they had problems getting things to work. I realized we could do it another way and talked to them about it. So we tried my suggestion, and I wrote the code and ran a small test and saw that it worked.

Another example was described by S.6.CH: 'The supervisors at the company were trying to enhance the performance, and I was taking a [relevant] course and I directly saw that some of my knowledge could perhaps be applied, so that's happening right now'.

When developing tools and methods, this is an important outcome, useful for advancing engineering research and development. Clearly, one desired outcome of their research projects is that the industrial PhD students should learn new tools and methods that could potentially be used later in their firms when developing new products and processes. As S.5.CH pointed out, 'Most likely I'll be learning new tools and methods in the university this half year, and potentially I can see that there are applications where they could be used'. Another contribution is by solving an old problem in a new way, as described by S.3.CH: 'You can contribute by, that is, you can suggest new ways of doing the same thing . . . or solving the same problem with new solutions'.

Enriching the technological vision and base at their firms is a longer-term impact that the industrial PhD students perceive that they can have. Several students reported wanting to be involved in developing a particular technical vision that their firm set out to achieve. The informants said that they could help fulfil a piece or part of those particular visions. For example, informant S.3.CH stated:

> I see that if there is a vision of doing something, you need to break it down into smaller things, and I can contribute to one of those things. You know what needs to be done but not how it should be done, and I see I can contribute to solving that.

Similarly, while the research conducted by industrial PhD students might not result in specific products or processes, the informants described their contribution in terms of developing a technology base serving as the foundation for many different products in the future. Informant S.6.CH described it as an ongoing contribution:

> I will be part of the long-term technological road map, so what I've been working on is a block within that future map. So basically the experts have been discussing how they can establish their architecture, and then there are these blocks, and each block has to be filled in, and I think I can contribute to one of the blocks or to multiple blocks.

The informants also noted the uncertainty inherent in research, stressing that their research could end up in new products or processes, as L.4.CH put it: 'I can't promise anything, it's a bit unclear . . . it's research and that's a bit like gambling – you never know what works beforehand. You've just got to have hope'.

Another aspect was being able to play a different role within the firm, by representing a more global view and by being future leaders. Several informants stated that one of the most important contributions they brought to their firms was a broader outlook, in terms of both the academic and global perspectives. As an illustration, S.5.CH noted that, 'Bringing the academic perspective and the global perspective into industry are two main contributions I see for the research at the firm. Because otherwise we do our research in a closed circle, we don't engage with external parties'. Therefore,

> You can have really critical discussion of what's the best way to do things, and that has led to interesting conversations for us, to just not be defensive but to be open and to accept criticism when it's due. So I think that's a positive thing . . . using the academy as a medium to enable this kind of discussion.

Moreover, informant S.5.CH perceived clear expectations on the part of the firm: 'They expect you to be a PhD student because they want future research leaders in the fields that they identified'.

Finally, the industrial PhD students reported many ways in which they contributed insight into external organizations and networks. Through these students' projects, firms get insights into external players. Based on the informants' experiences, three such external organizations can be identified: academia, other industries, and competitors. In terms of academia, it is easier to know what is going on at the universities if you can get insider information. The firms monitor this, and as L.4.CH expressed it, '[The firm] wants to know what's going on at the University. Who is close to graduation and which of them might be good to hire'. It is especially important to be up to date on the universities in some cases: 'The real pioneering is happening in certain labs, for instance, in [a certain foreign university] . . . they have been working on that topic for, like, 20 years, and then of course it would help to share those experiences'. Getting insight into other industries and how they are solving similar problems can also be very helpful. In S.5.CH's case, such input comes through the University, which has a long tradition of collaborating with many different industries. As an industrial PhD student, it is also possible to get access to market competitors. This was the situation of S.7.CH: '[Co-finance Foundation A] organizes trips. I went to the USA on one of those two weeks ago and had the opportunity to visit competitors of my company'.

Networking is thus a broad category of activities, often related to technological development, whereby the industrial PhD students affect their firms more indirectly. Both universities and firms want the industrial PhD students to take part in networking activities. Extended networks can be useful in technological development and future recruitment, as S.7.S stated:

> You find valuable contacts, both for yourself and the company. You might find someone working on a problem we need to solve at the company, then you can start to think about whether you should hire that person, read their research, or see if you can develop it on your own.

In terms of establishing contacts in the collaborating university and firm, the informants described different scenarios. In some cases, it was more common for firm employees to request contact details for people within the University rather than the reverse. However, when people at the University asked for contact details, they were usually for someone in a parallel group or other activity at the University. In other cases, it seemed that even University employees were reaching out to the firms. Another form of networking activity was found when the University organized courses for firm employees. S.5.CH cited an example of this: 'I would say that [the University] is well integrated with industry . . . because they hold these courses for industry people, so that represents another channel for networking'. Sometimes the co-financing organization also enabled networking, as in the case, described previously in this chapter, of Co-finance Foundation A and S.7.CH: It was through Co-finance Foundation A that the informant had the opportunity to travel to the USA and meet competitors of Firm A.

In summary, we have organized our in-depth exploration of the activities and perceptions of industrial PhD students into three broad categories, each further divided into many sub-categories and illustrations. The first category is directly working on products and processes, the second is discussing science and technology inside and outside the firm, and the third is problem solving, articulating visions, and networking at the firm.

5. ANALYSIS OF INDUSTRIAL PHD STUDENTS AND THEIR IMPACT ON FIRM INNOVATION

This section reports the analysis of our own results, in contrast to the existing literature and in relation to our empirical findings.

Regarding the first research question about providing a definition of industrial PhD students, in the theoretical section we proposed conceptualizing industrial PhD students as individuals who embody a specific type of academic engagement with industry. Given the notion of knowledge networks, we propose that industrial PhD students are at the university–firm interface, and that they may stimulate the absorptive capacity of the firm, helping it develop new technologies. Our empirical study went on to identify various specific attributes and issues to be considered, both theoretically and empirically. Using the three defined levels of academic engagement with industry, we find that the following empirical attributes are vital for understanding the empirical phenomenon.

At the institutional and organizational level of academic engagement for these industrial PhD students:

- There are differences between academic and industrial PhD students, although both receive the same degrees.
- Industrial PhD students are more common in certain fields, such as engineering.
- The collaboration for PhD studies lasts at least four years.
- The collaboration is usually formal, and involves senior supervisors at both the university and the firm.

At the individual level of academic engagement for these industrial PhD students:

- Each industrial PhD student is employed at a firm, which has implications for labour market contracts, etc.
- Different industries are represented, generally large multinationals or their joint ventures.
- The most common financing arrangement is that the firm's support is co-financed with another external organization (not the university).
- The contract states that academic work takes 90–100 per cent of the student's time.
- The contract states that firm work takes 0–10 per cent of the student's time.
- Having previous work experience and competences reportedly benefits students' involvement in their firms.

We found some categories that are consistent, such as the definition and financing. In terms of how to define collaborative research, empirically, for this study, we suggest that the common factors are: engineering studies at one university; collaboration lasting a minimum of four years; an individual employment contract at a firm; co-financing with a research council or foundation; and a 90–100 per cent focus on academic work, though students spend much of their academic work time (e.g., research project) seeking ways to benefit their firm, especially in terms of technological development. Moreover, we also found many areas in which the industrial PhD students differ, especially regarding previous experience and competences. Although the industrial PhD students may act as boundary spanners (Allen 1977), there is diversity in how different sets of individuals can play that role, as well as diversity inside the firms that is likely to shape the university–student relationship. We propose that such students should be called 'industrial PhD students', to emphasize the similarities and differences with other PhD students.

Regarding the second research question, concerning the activities of industrial PhD students and how they are perceived to affect firm innovation, we also explored this through our qualitative research. Starting with an existing conceptual framework that distinguishes direct and indirect routes of exerting impact on firms (McKelvey and Ljungberg 2016), we enriched the framework to make it relevant to our narrower focus on industrial PhD students. In terms of the empirical material, we concentrated on understanding the activities of industrial PhD students, identifying the following main categories, and how they perceived they contributed to firm innovation (Table 7.5).

Table 7.5   Linking main categories to the activities of industrial PhD students

Identified broad category	Activities of industrial PhD students
Working directly on products and processes	Product development
	Working on research and product development, which deliver results on different time scales
	Filing patents
Discussing science and technology inside and outside the firm	Technical meetings at firm
	Presentations at firm
	Written reports to firm
	Firm-level coordination of industrial PhD students
	Seminars and conferences
	Papers and publications
Problem solving, articulating visions, and networking at the firm	Informal problem solving
	Matching own knowledge with firm challenges
	Developing tools and methods
	Contributing to technological vision and base
	Role of representing a more global view and being future leaders
	Networking with external organizations

Let us relate our empirical findings to the conceptual framework, specifically considering the direct and indirect routes by which collaborative research influences firm innovation.

When analysing these activities, we do not find any that we consider would correspond to the direct route to influencing innovation, as mentioned in McKelvey and Ljungberg (2016). Neither do we find statements about their role in identifying business opportunities (Broström 2010; Gustavsson et al. 2016), nor about participation in process development. The way our informants reported their activities and perceptions in relation to directly influencing innovation is somewhat contradictory. Some informants clearly stated that they did not take part in product development within their firms, whereas others stated that it would be fairly easy to go from research to practical implementation. This may have to do with the institutional level related to the type of discipline and knowledge.

Our view is that, through their activities, these industrial PhD students contributed to tangible and direct innovation outcomes in three ways: (1) *They assisted in problem solving* at their firms when they identified opportunities to do so. Some informants revealed that they could sometimes identify situations in which their knowledge could be matched with firm challenges. There are clearly situations in which industrial PhD students can step in and help firm employees with specific technological problems. Even though these students do not work directly on product development as such, they can occasionally identify opportunities to assist in problem solving (Bishop et al. 2011), particularly relating to technology. (2) *They could file patents.* Patent filings are rare events, primarily undertaken by individuals already working at firms as engineers. (3) *They could take part in firm-specific work activities.* Two informants were explicitly assigned firm work (10 per cent) in their study contracts. It is also clear that some of the other informants participated in firm-specific activities as well, and that such work is usually somewhat related to their research projects. The industrial PhD students from firms not formally stipulating time for firm work thus also participated in firm-specific work activities to some extent. We believe that these three activities should be included among direct innovation outcomes due to their tangible character, especially as they are stipulated in some of the informants' contracts.

Regarding the indirect route to influencing innovation, we found that the industrial PhD students contributed in a wide variety of ways, with some overlap with the direct problem solving identified above. We discuss these in terms of (1) knowledge transfer and learning, (2) networking, and (3) signalling effects.

Regarding knowledge transfer and learning, our empirical findings are that these industrial PhD students interacted with their firms in several ways. For example, activities such as supervision at the firm, meetings, presentations, report filing, academic writing, seminars and conferences all represent formal modes of interaction. However, it was not only through formal interaction that the industrial PhD students contributed to knowledge transfer and learning; this also happened through informal interactions, such as conversations and discussions with firm employees as well as occasionally assisting in problem solving.

The industrial PhD students' natural connection to their universities facilitates access to scientific knowledge (Thune 2009; Gustavsson et al. 2016) for firms. This is confirmed by the present empirical evidence, which shows that firms want to learn what is going on in academia. It is also clear in the empirical findings that industrial PhD students develop technological competences (Thune and Børing 2014; Gustavsson et al. 2016) and can serve as 'windows' on new technologies (Perkmann and Walsh 2008). For example, the informants described helping their firms develop visions and technological roadmaps as well as learning new tools and methods that could be applied in their firms. In some cases, the latest development within specific fields happens at universities. Firms access this pioneering knowledge by having close connections with the academic sector, for example, via industrial PhD students. In terms of developing internal R&D activities (Gustavsson et al. 2016), the empirical findings indicate that industrial PhD students make two main contributions, by bringing an academic perspective as well as a global perspective to firms. These perspectives enable firms to open their internal research to external influence, instead of keeping it confined within a closed circle. For example, the academic perspective enables critical discussions of the best way forward without overemphasizing commercial aspects. Bringing in the global perspective facilitates learning about how firms in other industries and sectors address similar problems. Moreover, in theory, firms experience human capital management benefits in terms of recruiting and training employees (Bishop et al. 2011) when collaborating with universities (Broström 2010). These two outcomes can also be identified in the present empirical data. For example, Firm D clearly expected informant S.5.CH to become a future research leader in the firm. In terms of recruitment, several informants agreed that it was an important outcome of the research collaboration.

Regarding networking and network development, our empirical data indicate that these together constitute an important aspect of industrial PhD students' activities. Firms are thought to benefit from their students' studies in terms of network development. For example, the firms could access people in the University by asking their industrial PhD students for contact details or suggestions about whom to contact in academia. Another way of strengthening the connection to academia was to attend courses that the University organized for industry. Finally, the co-financing organizations could foster opportunities for network development. Although the empirical material does not contain specific examples of new or strengthened contacts with other firms, there are some indications that this was happening. For example, S.7.CH's trip to the USA enabled visits to competitors of Firm A, which could be categorized as new firm contacts although they might not be very collaborative. Also, the courses the University offered to industry actors entailed opportunities to network with other firms. Even though there are no explicit examples of new and strengthened contacts with other firms, the empirical findings seem aligned with theory regarding network development.

Concerning signalling effects, our empirical findings do not suggest that the research and PhD studies of the individual students had much impact on third parties. The only clear statement we found in the empirical material was connected to papers and publication. S.5.CH referred to prestige: 'I think they look at it as a prestige thing, if something is published by the section, because it brings more value to the company as well as the research area, so they favour publication'. Increased prestige and reputation can be considered to accrue from scientific publications.

In summary, we conclude that these industrial PhD students bolstered their firms' knowledge transfer and learning through giving access to scientific knowledge, developing technical competencies, promoting internal R&D activities, and influencing human capital management. In terms of network development, they contributed by opening doors to new networks and by strengthening the relationship with universities and other firms. Lastly, industrial PhD students also affected their firms via signalling effects; more precisely, through the prestige accrued by publishing scientific studies.

6.   FUTURE RESEARCH AND LIMITATIONS

This qualitative research has explored the activities of industrial PhD students and how they are perceived to affect firm innovation. This chapter relates to the larger question of how academic engagement with industry through collaborative research can influence firm innovation. We have specifically defined these industrial PhD students, both theoretically and empirically. Moreover, our empirical results suggest that industrial PhD students are more involved in developing firm capabilities for innovation than directly involved in developing product innovations or patents.

Future research could usefully address some of these questions through a qualitative study of the intermediary impacts of organizational and individual factors. In the present qualitative research, we identified certain areas of coherence as well as considerable diversity. This suggests that a range of factors such as sub-areas of engineering, firm characteristics, gender, and industry characteristics may matter, because such factors have been found to influence innovation in general. Therefore, these factors could be studied qualitatively through a large-scale survey, and fields other than engineering, such as the medical health, and natural sciences, could be quantitatively investigated.

Second, future research could consider industrial PhD students as intermediaries between firms and universities, thereby also taking account of the perceptions and actions of firms and universities. This would enable us to obtain a more holistic view of the phenomenon and gain more insight into the dynamics between industry and universities. Future qualitative research on this topic should include relevant informants from universities and firms and should situate the results more explicitly in relation to the conceptual framework used here. Longitudinal studies of this phenomenon would help clarify when and how indirect innovation outcomes lead to product innovations, which is of interest to firms, public policy, and society as a whole.

A third interesting area for future research would be to move beyond the perspective of the industrial PhD student as such, as was the present focus. By this, we mean that future qualitative and quantitative research should consider the industrial PhD student as just one part of a much larger set of activities between firms and universities, which together constitute academic engagement. One such activity would be firms' coordination of all industrial PhD students, and how that affects their research. As firm employees, industrial PhD students undergo advanced engineering education at universities, and we have proposed that they act as boundary spanners by creating, developing and absorbing new technology. However, we propose that their ability to act in this way may differ depending on their firms' absorptive capacity (Cohen and Levinthal 1990), due to various organizational- and individual-level factors.

Finally, we acknowledge that this research has limitations. We have chosen an explorative qualitative research design to examine a phenomenon subject to limited previous research. It was therefore necessary to begin by formulating theoretical and empirical definitions, and by identifying and categorizing activities. We recognize these limits, and therefore have not attempted to generalize from the results due to the narrow case selection and limited number of interviews. Moreover, the current study focused on how the activities and perceptions of the industrial PhD students could be interpreted in terms of the direct and indirect routes for influencing firm innovation. This explorative study is therefore limited in how much we can claim about firm innovation as such.

ACKNOWLEDGEMENTS

Funding for this project was provided by: (1) a donation to the Professorship in Industrial Management and Economics at the University of Gothenburg, held by M. McKelvey and financed by Carl Bennet AB, SKF, and Volvo Group; and (2) the research programme 'The Long-Term Provision of Knowledge', financed jointly by the Bank of Sweden Tercentenary Foundation, Formas, Forte, and the Swedish Research Council. Specifically, we acknowledge support from the Bank of Sweden Tercentenary Foundation (Riksbankensjubileumsfond) for the project 'How Engineering Science Can Impact Industry in a Global World', with project leader M. McKelvey.

We would like to acknowledge comments and suggestions from Daniel Ljungberg and Astrid Heidemann Lassen, assistant supervisors of Karin Berg as well as colleagues at the Institute of Innovation and Entrepreneurship, Department of Economy and Society, University of Gothenburg, Sweden. We would also like to thank participants in the DRUID PhD Academy Conference 2018 and the 21st Uddevalla Symposium 2018 for sharing valuable and insightful comments with us.

REFERENCES

Ahuja, G. (2000a). Collaboration networks, structural holes, and innovation: A longitudinal study. *Administrative Science Quarterly.* **45**(3), 425–55.

Ahuja, G. (2000b). The duality of collaboration: inducements and opportunities in the formation of interfirm linkages. *Strategic Management Journal.* **21**(3), 317–43.

Allen, T. (1977). *Managing Flow of Technology*, Cambridge, MA: The MIT Press.

Ambos, T.C., Makela, K., Birkinshaw, J. and D'Este, P. (2008). When does university research get commercialized? Creating ambidexterity in research institutions. *Journal of Management Studies.* **45**(8), 1424–47.

Ankrah, S. and Al-Tabbaa, O. (2015). Universities–industry collaboration: A systematic review. *Scandinavian Journal of Management.* **31**(3), 387–408.

Bishop, K., D'Este, P. and Neely, A. (2011). Gaining from interactions with universities: Multiple methods for nurturing absorptive capacity. *Research Policy.* **40**(1), 30–40.

Borrell-Damian, L., Brown, T., Dearing, A., Font, J., Hagen, S., Metcalfe, J. and Smith, J. (2010). Collaborative doctoral education: University–industry partnerships for enhancing knowledge exchange. *Higher Education Policy.* **23**(4), 493–514.

Bozeman, B., Rimes, H. and Youtie, J. (2015). The evolving state-of-the-art in technology transfer research: Revisiting the contingent effectiveness model. *Research Policy.* **44**(1), 34–49.

Broekel, T. and Boschma, R. (2012). Knowledge networks in the Dutch aviation industry: The proximity paradox. *Journal of Economic Geography.* **12**(2), 409–33.

Broström, A. (2010). Firms' rationales for interaction with research universities and the principles for public co-funding. *The Journal of Technology Transfer.* **37**(3), 313–29.

Campbell, T.S. and Kracaw, W.A. (2012). Information production, market signalling, and the theory of financial intermediation. *The Journal of Finance.* **35**(4), 863–82.

Chemmanur, T.J. (2012). The pricing of initial public offerings: A dynamic model with information production. *The Journal of Finance.* **48**(1), 285–304.

Chemmanur, T.J. and Fulghieri, P. (2012). Investment bank reputation, information production, and financial intermediation. *The Journal of Finance.* **49**(1), 57–79.

Chesbrough, H. (2003). The logic of open innovation: Managing intellectual property. *California Management Review.* **45**(3), 33–58.

Cohen, W.M. and Levinthal, D.A. (1990). Absorptive capacity: A new perspective on learning and innovation. *Administrative Science Quarterly.* **35**(1), 128–52.

Cruz-Castro, L. and Sanz-Menéndez, L. (2005). The employment of PhDs in firms: Trajectories, mobility and innovation. *Research Evaluation.* **14**(1), 57–69.

D'Este, P. and Patel, P. (2007). University–industry linkages in the UK: What are the factors underlying the variety of interactions with industry? *Research Policy.* **36**(9), 1295–313.

Eisenhardt, K.M. (1989). Building theories from case study research. *The Academy of Management Review.* **14**(4), 532–50.

Etzkowitz, H. (2004). The evolution of the entrepreneurial university. *International Journal of Technology and Globalisation.* **1**(1), 64–77.

Etzkowitz, H. (2013). Anatomy of the entrepreneurial university. *Social Science Information.* **52**(3), 486–511.

Freeman, C. (1974). *The Economics of Industrial Innovation*, Harmondsworth: Penguin Books.

Garcia-Quevedo, J., Mas-Verdú, F. and Polo-Otero, J. (2011). Which firms want PhDs? An analysis of the determinants of the demand. *Higher Education.* **63**(5), 607–20.

Gibbons, M., Limoges, C., Nowotny, H., Schwartzman, S., Scott, P. and Trow, M. (1994). *The New Production of Knowledge: The Dynamic Science and Research in Contemporary Societies*, London: SAGE Publications.

Granstrand, O. (1998). Towards a theory of the technology-based firm. *Research Policy.* **27**(5), 465–89.

Gustavsson, L., Nuur, C. and Söderlind, J. (2016). An impact analysis of regional industry–university interactions. *Industry and Higher Education.* **30**(1), 41–51.

Higgins, M.J., Stephan, P.E. and Thursby, J.G. (2011). Conveying quality and value in emerging industries: Star scientists and the role of signals in biotechnology. *Research Policy.* **40**(4), 605–17.

Lam, A. (2007). Knowledge networks and careers: Academic scientists in industry –university links. *Journal of Management Studies.* **44**(6), 993–1016.

Laredo, P. (2007). Revisiting the third mission of universities: Toward a renewed categorization of university activities? *Higher Education Policy.* **20**(4), 441–56.

Leland, H.E. and Pyle, D.H. (1977). Informational asymmetries, financial structure, and financial intermediation. *The Journal of Finance.* **32**(2), 371–87.

Mansfield, E. (1995). Academic research underlying industrial innovations: Sources, characteristics, and financing. *The Review of Economics and Statistics.* **77**(1), 55–65.

McKelvey, M. and Holmén, M. (eds) (2009). *Learning to Compete in European Universities*, Cheltenham, UK and Northampton, MA, USA: Edward Elgar Publishing.

McKelvey, M. and Ljungberg, D. (2016). How public policy can stimulate the capabilities of firms to innovate in a traditional industry through academic engagement: The case of the Swedish food industry. *R&D Management.* **47**(4), 534–44.

Nerkar, A. and Paruchuri, S. (2005). Evolution of R&D capabilities: The role of knowledge networks within a firm. *Management Science.* **51**(5), 771–85.

Nicholson, S., Danzon, P.M. and McCullough, J. (2005). Biotech–pharmaceutical alliances as a signal of asset and firm quality. *The Journal of Business.* **78**(4), 1433–64.

Perkmann, M. and Walsh, K. (2008). Engaging the scholar: Three types of academic consulting and their impact on universities and industry. *Research Policy.* **37**(10), 1884–91.

Perkmann, M., Tartari, V., McKelvey, M., Autio, E., Broström, A., D'Este, P., Fini, R. et al. (2013). Academic engagement and commercialisation: A review of the literature on university–industry relations. *Research Policy.* **42**(2), 423–42.

Ponomariov, B.L. (2007). Effects of university characteristics on scientists' interactions with the private sector: An exploratory assessment. *The Journal of Technology Transfer.* **33**(5), 485–503.

Ponomariov, B.L. and Craig Boardman, P. (2007). The effect of informal industry contacts on the time university scientists allocate to collaborative research with industry. *The Journal of Technology Transfer.* **33**(3), 301–13.

Roach, M. and Sauermann, H. (2010). A taste for science? PhD scientists' academic orientation and self-selection into research careers in industry. *Research Policy.* **39**(3), 422–34.

Rosli, A. and Rossi, F. (2016). Third-mission policy goals and incentives from performance-based funding: Are they aligned? *Research Evaluation.* **25**(4), 427–41.

Salter, A.J. and Martin, B.R. (2001). The economic benefits of publicly funded basic research: A critical review. *Research Policy.* **30**(3), 509–32.

Statistics Sweden (2017). Universitet och högskolor. Doktorander och examina på forskarnivå 2016. Third-cycle students and third-cycle qualifications 2016. UF 21 SM 1701.

Thune, T. (2009). Doctoral students on the university–industry interface: A review of the literature. *Higher Education.* **58**(5), 637–51.

Thune, T. and Børing, P. (2014). Industry PhD schemes: Developing innovation competencies in firms? *Journal of the Knowledge Economy.* **6**(2), 385–401.

Tushman, M. (1977). Special boundary roles in the innovation process. *Administrative Science Quarterly.* **22**(4), 587–605.

Wang, C., Rodan, S., Fruin, M. and Xu, X. (2014). Knowledge networks, collaboration networks, and exploratory innovation. *Academy of Management Journal.* **57**(2), 484–514.

Yin, R. (2014). *Case Study Research: Design and Methods.* London: SAGE Publications.

8. Globalizing startups: business development organizations in the Bay Area

David Bartlett and Tomasz Mroczkowski

INTRODUCTION

In spring 2018, Startup Genome published a comprehensive report on the rise of global startup companies (Gauthier et al., 2018). Drawing on surveys of 10 000 startups worldwide, the report examines the repercussions of current shifts in global technology. The original products of the Information Technology revolution of the 1990s–2000s (e.g., digital media, gaming) have reached maturity. The highest growth rates of startup-related activities (new company formation, early stage financing, exit events) now appear in new and emerging technologies: artificial intelligence, data analytics, blockchain, advanced manufacturing, robotics. This "Third Wave" of technological change is disrupting the business models of industry incumbents and hastening the ascent of a new generation of startup companies seeking rapid integration into global markets.

This chapter focuses on a critical component of the global startup phenomenon: the growing visibility of *business development organizations* in the globalization of startup companies. Drawing on field research in the San Francisco Bay Area (widely regarded as the world's leading innovation ecosystem), we examine the role of four types of startup organization: Business Incubators, Business Accelerators, International Bridge Organizations, and Corporate Innovation Centers.

Scholarly research indicates that these organizations have proven largely ineffectual in hastening the globalization of startup firms. Only a small number of elite business accelerators have empirically demonstrated records of successful launches of global startups. This result underscores the importance of revamping the business development capacity of accelerators, incubators, and related organizations whose portfolios comprise startup companies with high global potential.

To that end, our empirical investigation identifies ways of refining and strengthening the global startup capabilities of the four organizational types noted above. Through our comparative analysis, we propose a model of startup globalization to enable high potential new ventures to capitalize on the growth opportunities arising from disruptions of the economic and technological environment. In this way, the chapter makes an original contribution to the extant literature on global startups.

The chapter is organized as follows. We begin with a review of recent scholarly research on global startups, noting the gap in that literature regarding business development organizations. We then survey the four organizational forms of startup globalization under consideration. We continue with an assessment of the expansion of global startups in the San Francisco Bay Area. We describe our research design, which features field interviews at a select group of startup organizations in the Bay Area. We then summarize the preliminary results of our field research, profiling representative entities in each of the organizational categories. We conclude with a comparative analysis of the effectiveness of these models of startup globalization and a summary of directions of future research on global startups.

RESEARCH ON GLOBAL STARTUPS

We situate our investigation at the intersection of two spheres of scholarly research on global startups.

Global Entrepreneurship

The first research sphere comprises theoretical papers and empirical studies of the rise of global entrepreneurship in the 21st century. This research includes works on the strategic drivers of entrepreneurial internationalization (Autio, 2017; Kollmann and Christofor, 2014; Mainela et al., 2014; Petrova, 2013; Prashantham et al., 2018; Stayton and Mangematin, 2016; Symeonidou et al., 2017); the liabilities of newness and outsidership facing global entrepreneurial firms (Fiedler et al., 2017; Fernández-Olmos and Ramírez-Alesón, 2017); the performance of internationalizing new ventures (Fernhaber, 2013; Turcan and Juho, 2014); the role of innovation in early internationalizing companies (Lamotte and Colovic, 2013; Hagen et al., 2014; Protogerou et al., 2017); the governance structures of global startups (Li et al., 2015; Zahra, 2014); and the internal capabilities and cognitive attributes of early globalizing firms (Kyvik et al., 2013; Saemundsson and Candi, 2017).

Other works in the global entrepreneurship domain address the internationalization processes of business startups (Casillas and Acedo, 2013;

Chandra et al., 2012; Etemad, 2016; 2017; 2018; Pehrsson et al., 2015; Reuber et al., 2017; Santangelo and Meyer, 2017) and the experiences of global startups in emerging markets (Dai et al., 2018; Klonowski, 2016; Smallbone et al., 2013). The global entrepreneurship literature also provides a rich body of empirical and theoretical work on the "born global" phenomenon (e.g., Cavusgil and Knight, 2016; Coviello, 2015; Norbäck and Persson, 2014; Romanello and Chiarvesio, 2017; Taylor and Jack, 2013; Trudgen and Freeman, 2014; Zander et al., 2015).

Global Accelerators and Incubators

The second domain of research on global startups explores the role of accelerators and incubators in speeding the internationalization of high-potential young companies. Charry et al. (2014) provide a survey of empirical and theoretical work on this subject, which includes studies of technology business incubators (Mian et al., 2016); the selection criteria and exit policies of business incubators (Bruneel et al., 2012); the service offerings and value propositions of incubators (Fernández et al., 2015; Köhler and Baumann, 2015); the role of networking and peer relationships in incubators (Ebbers, 2013; Redondo-Carretero and Camareno-Izquierdo, 2017); the determinants of the efficacy of accelerators/incubators (Harper-Anderson and Lewis, 2018); the business outcomes of incubators (Patton, 2013; Stokan et al., 2015; Wise and Valliere, 2014), and the growing visibility of corporate accelerators (Mahmoud-Jouini et al., 2018).

Other scholars focus on the role of accelerators/incubators in developed market economies, including multi-country studies of business development organizations in Europe (Aerts et al., 2017; Pauwels et al., 2016) and single country studies in Australia/Israel (Rubin et al., 2015), Denmark (Bøllingtoft, 2012), Italy (Lukeš et al., 2019), Spain (Albort-Morant and Oghazi, 2016), Sweden (Barrehag et al., 2012), Switzerland (DaSilva and Gurtner, 2017), and the United Kingdom (Dushnitsky, 2018).

Another group of scholars examine the operations of accelerators and incubators in emerging markets. Building on the pioneering work of Khanna and Palepu (2010) on the "institutional void" of emerging markets, Dutt et al. (2016) describe emerging market business incubators as "open system intermediaries" that boost local entrepreneurs via market infrastructure development and business capabilities development. Other scholars provide single-country studies of the role of accelerators/incubators in filling gaps in local institutional capacity: Egypt (Mrkajic, 2017), Kosovo (Mulolli et al., 2017), Nigeria (Iyortsuun, 2017), Poland (Pietrasienski, 2013), Russia (Rogova, 2014).

The scholarly research summarized above yields the following conclusions about global startups:

1. Shifts in the economic and technological landscape are intensifying pressure on entrepreneurial firms for rapid internationalization. For startup companies situated in globally competitive industries, the Uppsala model of gradual, incremental internationalization that guided previous generations of entrepreneurs is no longer feasible (Forsgren, 2016; Hagen and Zucchella, 2014; Hennart, 2014; Patel and Naldi, 2018; Vahlne and Johanson, 2017).
2. Globally oriented startups in high-technology industries are particularly well positioned for fast internationalization. Operationally lean and strategically agile startups can quickly adopt new and emerging digital technologies (artificial intelligence, data analytics, blockchain, Internet of Things, robotics), launching differentiated products and services in niche global markets that may be too small to be interesting to large industry incumbents. Such firms are also poised to develop innovative business models to guide their penetration of complex, rapidly growing international technology sectors (Onetti et al., 2012).
3. Accelerators/incubators offer a range of services that promise to speed the globalization of high-potential startup companies: administrative/financial/legal support, mentoring by experienced entrepreneurs, networking with venture capitalists and strategic investors, and so on. But empirical research on the actual business outcomes of these organizations shows weak results. Hallen et al. (2014) find that only the top global accelerators (e.g., Y Combinators, TechStars) produce statistically significant effects on the acceleration paths of portfolio companies. The relative success of these elite accelerators reflects their rigorous selection processes (3 percent admission rate) that filter out all but the highest quality startups. Completion of the intensive programs of those accelerators certifies graduates for follow-up venture capital funding and jump starts their globalization campaigns (Smith and Hannigan, 2015; Yin and Luo, 2017). However, empirical studies of other accelerators (500 Startups, AngelPad, Dreamit, Excelerate, Launchbox Digital, Seedcamp, et al.) indicate limited or no demonstrable effects on the business development of portfolio companies compared to non-portfolio peers. Van Weele et al. (2017) report similarly disappointing results of business incubators, where startups often fail to exploit the organizational assets of their host organizations.
4. The above-cited works do not fully account for recent trends in business development organizations, whose global footprint has expanded well beyond pioneers like Y Combinator and whose current service offerings

indicate refinements of the traditional accelerator/incubator model. The extant literature also lacks comparative analyses of other organization forms (international bridges, corporate innovation centers) that play an important role in the globalization of startup companies.

Our chapter fills this gap in the global startup literature by examining the current operations of business development organizations in the San Francisco Bay Area, one of the world's leading hosts of entrepreneurial firms pursuing rapid globalization.

TYPOLOGY OF BUSINESS DEVELOPMENT ORGANIZATIONS

We develop a framework that permits a comparative analysis of four types of business development organization.

Business Incubators

Business Incubators are a well-recognized and widely established organizational form that provides the following services to startups:

Incubation of startup companies

- Supporting entrepreneurial ventures from inception to commercialization;
- Launching new enterprises.

Economic infrastructure

- Co-location of businesses in a single physical space to lower overhead costs;
- Shared office space to realize economies of scale.

Networking

- Internal: Cross-fertilization between incubatees;
- External: Links with prospective investors, customers, and partners.

Support services

- Legal, administrative, and technical support;
- Accounting and marketing services.

Enterprise development

- Coaching, mentoring, and business advisory support;
- Knowledge sharing.

Business Accelerators

While "incubators" and "accelerators" are commonly viewed as syn-onymous terms, recent scholarly research treats *Business Accelerators* as a distinctive organizational form committed to the development of early stage companies that have graduated from the incubation phase.

Barrehag (2012), Cohen (2013), and Pauwels et al. (2016) specify the particular attributes of accelerators that distinguish such organizations from business incubators.

Business model
Whereas incubators are typically structured as non-profit entities that do not take equity positions in incubatees, accelerators are usually for-profit organizations that provide selected companies with upfront investment (starting with seed capital in exchange for equity positions; proceeding to early stage venture funding for portfolio companies with demonstrated commercial potential).

Selection
While business incubators apply forgiving or no selection criteria, accelera-tors undertake rigorous competitions to select the most promising applicants. In contrast to incubators' concentration on individual entrepreneurs, accel-erators use cyclical application procedures to assemble cohorts of growth-oriented early stage companies with common features and aspirations.

Composition
Incubators engage pre-revenue startups with promising business ideas that hopefully progress to commercialization. By contrast, accelerators engage early stage companies that have reached commercial status but require external assistance to realize their growth objectives.

Services
Accelerators and incubators provide a number of common services to par-ticipating companies: knowledge sharing, mentoring, training, network-ing, and so on. However, the business development services of accelerators are more intense, focused, and programmatic to hasten the realization of the growth potential of selected companies.

Duration

While business incubators retain incubatees for 1–5 years, accelerators offer brief fixed terms of 3–6 months that end with "demo days" when graduating companies deliver pitches to investor audiences. The short, finite duration of accelerators concentrates the attention of portfolio companies and forces them to make quick decisions on market positioning. This approach lowers the risk of co-dependency on the accelerator, speeds time to market, and enables founders of failed entrepreneurial ventures to pivot to other, higher-value opportunities.

Business accelerators first appeared in 2005 with the launch of Silicon Valley-based Y Combinator and Boulder-based TechStars (Hathaway, 2016a; 2016b). By 2017, some 200 accelerators were operating worldwide, supporting over 7000 early stage companies. To date, accelerators have provided $43 billion of funding and managed company exits worth $8.6 billion (SeedDB, https://www.seed-db.com/accelerators).

International Bridge Organizations

In recent years, another organizational form has emerged to support born global startups and other entrepreneurial companies seeking rapid penetration of world markets. *International Bridge Organizations* promote transnational partnerships (government institutions, NGOs, universities, research institutions, private sector agents) to spur the global expansion of locally based companies and to speed local market entry by foreign-based companies (Pietrasienski and Bitka, 2015).

In contrast to business incubators (whose geographic domain is often limited to the home economy), international bridge organizations are explicitly designed to hasten the globalization of high-potential startup companies. And unlike business accelerators, bridge organizations typically do not take equity positions in their portfolio companies.

International bridge organizations perform the following functions:

- Coordinating governmental support of bilateral commercial/ technological ventures, including relations with ministerial, diplomatic agencies, and economic development agencies;
- Forging technology partnerships between business organizations and academic institutions in the host and home countries;
- Providing business development services (advertising, branding, marketing, etc.), mentoring/advisory services, and legal/administrative/ logistical support to young foreign-based companies preparing to enter the local market;
- Delivering intermediary and matchmaking services to expand

foreign companies' access to local customers, investors, and strategic partners;

- Facilitating the transfer of market knowledge, business intelligence, and operational best practices between globally oriented enterprises in the host and home countries;
- Showcasing the local city/region as a destination for foreign-based small and medium-sized enterprises, multinational corporations, and born global startups.

Corporate Innovation Centers

Corporate Innovation Centers represent the fourth type of business development organization addressed in this chapter. Unlike incubators, accelerators, and international bridges (which are independent organizations), corporate innovation centers are managed and funded by leading multinational corporations. And in contrast to corporate R&D centers (which are internally staffed by full-time company employees), corporate innovation centers focus on the development of external companies holding promising technologies of potential commercial value to the parent MNC. Through such "innovation outposts", multinationals seek to transcend the internal barriers to innovation (bureaucratic, cultural, organizational) that often beset large, mature companies.

Corporate innovation centers grew out of the "open innovation" movement first documented by Henry Chesbrough (2005) and elaborated in subsequent scholarly research (Chesbrough et al., 2014; Gobble, 2016; Wright, 2016; Chesbrough, 2017; Brunswicker and Chesbrough, 2018) and case studies (Lakhani et al., 2015; Edmondson and Harvey, 2016).

Broadly understood, open innovation is a "distributed innovation process" through which established companies transcend organizational boundaries by engaging external providers of innovative technologies and business processes. Open innovation takes two basic forms: (1) *inside-out open innovation* whereby the incumbent engages external partners to commercialize idle patents and other unused internal assets; and (2) *outside-in open innovation* whereby the company leverages specialized assets of outside entities that are not available internally.

Through these channels, mature companies fill capabilities gaps, monetize underutilized intellectual property (IP), and tap the entrepreneurial energy and innovative drive of nimbler startups on the outside. Leading multinational corporations use the open innovation model to forge partnerships with agile, fast moving startups to spur innovation amid exponential shifts in the technological landscape.

GLOBAL STARTUPS IN THE SAN FRANCISCO BAY AREA

As the world's leading innovation hub, the San Francisco Bay Area is a magnet for foreign technology startups seeking rapid penetration into global markets.

World-class innovation ecosystems are concentrated in a small number of "superstar" cities that exhibit dense institutional networks of multinational corporations, technology developers, entrepreneurs, investors, and research universities. Using a benchmarking framework employing five metrics (performance, funding, market research, talent, startup experience) Startup Genome ranks the San Francisco Bay Area *first* among global ecosystems. Joining the Bay Area in the first tier of ecosystems are New York, London, Beijing, Boston and Tel Aviv. Major technology/innovation hubs have also appeared in Shanghai, Berlin, Stockholm, Singapore, Bangalore, Sydney, Vancouver, Amsterdam and other cities (Gauthier et al., 2019).

The San Francisco Bay Area's comparative advantages as a global ecosystem took decades to build and remain prohibitively difficult to emulate. The region hosts nearly 18000 startup companies, supported by the world's foremost venture capital industry (Accel Partners, Kleiner Perkins Caufield, etc.) and leading research universities (Stanford and UC Berkeley). The Bay Area serves as the global headquarters of leading US multinational technology companies (Apple, Cisco, eBay, Google, Hewlett-Packard, Intel, Oracle, etc.) and the North American headquarters of multiple foreign-based multinationals.

Illustrating the region's outsized role in launching global startups, the Bay Area captures nearly 30 percent of global investments in early stage companies, generates nearly one-third of the value of company exits globally, and hosts a quarter of the world's "unicorn" (startups valued at more than $1 billion). The Bay Area also hosts the world's highest share of companies founded by immigrants (46 percent), demonstrating the region's attractiveness to foreign-born entrepreneurs (Gauthier et al., 2017).

RESEARCH DESIGN

Our investigation focuses on the Bay Area operations of the organizational types described above: Business Incubators, Business Accelerators, International Bridge Organizations and Corporate Innovation Centers. The study also addresses the expanding role of hybrid accelerators/incubators.

Our research draws on two sources: (1) databases on global entrepreneurship including Crunchbase (https://www.crunchbase.com/), SeedDB (https://www.seed-db.com/accelerators), and Techcrunch (https://techcrunch.com); and (2) interviews of senior managers of a select group of incubators/accelerators/bridge organizations/corporate innovation centers in the San Francisco Bay Area, conducted in spring 2018.

In selecting subjects for the field interviews, we limited our target list to business development organizations with (1) ongoing operations in the Bay Area and (2) a demonstrated commitment to global entrepreneurship. For inclusion on the target list, locally based organizations must be systematically engaged in the recruitment of foreign-based startups, holding portfolios with significant shares of foreign companies. Foreign-based organizations must have a physical presence in the Bay Area, with resources dedicated to supporting the US market entry of startup companies headquartered in the home country.

This screening exercise yielded *58 target organizations* in the Bay Area, whose geographic origin is indicated in Figure 8.1.

The profiles of our target organizations are indicated in Table 8.1 (US-based), Table 8.2 (European-based) and Table 8.3 (Asian-based).

PRELIMINARY FINDINGS

Our interviews with these organizations focused on the following issues:

- Criteria for the recruiting and selection of startups;
- Activities of participating companies during their Bay Area stays;
- Mechanisms of knowledge transmission and technology transfer;
- Processes and procedures to support startup firms;
- Funding vehicles for startups and early stage companies;
- Business outcomes of graduating companies.

The following is a summary of the findings of our initial round of organizational interviews in the San Francisco Bay Area.

Business Incubators

Located in San Francisco's Mission District, Impact Hub (https://sanfrancisco.impacthub.net/) is a for-profit, fee-based incubator whose membership comprises a variety of local and foreign companies. Impact Hub is a registered B Corporation, an internationally recognized certificate for companies committed to social, economic, and environmental goals ("*business*

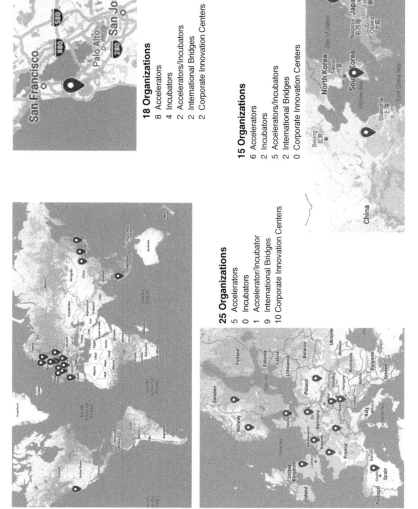

18 Organizations

- 8 Accelerators
- 4 Incubators
- 2 Accelerators/Incubators
- 2 International Bridges
- 2 Corporate Innovation Centers

15 Organizations

- 6 Accelerators
- 2 Incubators
- 5 Accelerators/Incubators
- 2 International Bridges
- 0 Corporate Innovation Centers

25 Organizations

- 5 Accelerators
- 0 Incubators
- 1 Accelerator/Incubator
- 9 International Bridges
- 10 Corporate Innovation Centers

Figure 8.1   Global accelerators in the San Francisco Bay Area: geographic distribution

Table 8.1   Global accelerators in the San Francisco Bay Area:
            organizational profiles: United States

Organization	Headquarters	Organizational Type	Foreign Operations	Company Portfolio
500 Startups	San Francisco, CA	Accelerator	Global	Digital technology, healthcare, fintech, education
Boost VC	San Mateo, CA	Accelerator	Global	Virtual reality, blockchain
BRIIA	San Ramon, CA	Accelerator	Global	Digital technology
Envestnet/ Yodlee	Redwood City, CA	Incubator	India, Australia, UK	Fintech
Founders Space	San Francisco, CA	Accelerator + Incubator	China, Austria, Taiwan, South Korea, South Africa	Digital technology, healthcare, automotive, fintech, agtech
Google Launchpad	Mountain View, CA	Corporate Innovation Center	Global	Software development, cloud computing
GSV Labs	Redwood City, CA	Accelerator	Global	Education, entertainment, big data
Impact Hub	San Francisco	Incubator	Global	Digital technology, financial services, consumer products
Indie Bio	San Francisco, CA	Accelerator	Global	Biotechnology
Mind the Bridge	San Francisco, CA	International Bridge	Italy, Spain, UK	Social media, sports & entertainment
Plug and Play	Sunnyvale, CA	Accelerator	Global	IoT, fintech, healthcare, materials, energy, real estate
Rocket Space	San Francisco, CA	Accelerator	Global	Agtech, mobility, supply chain
Runway	San Francisco, CA	Incubator	Global	Higher education
Singularity University	Moffett Field, CA	Corporate Innovation Center	Global	Artificial intelligence, robotics, digital medicine
Tarmac SF	San Francisco, CA	Incubator	Global	Biomedical technology, cloud computing, gaming
The Refiners	San Francisco, CA	Accelerator + Incubator	Global	Digital technology, social media, cloud computing, healthcare

Table 8.1   (continued)

Organization	Headquarters	Organizational Type	Foreign Operations	Company Portfolio
US Market Access Center	Menlo Park, CA	International Bridge	Global	Digital technology, media, financial services, healthcare, automotive
Y Combinator	San Francisco, CA	Accelerator	Global	Digital technology, healthcare, augmented reality, materials, fintech, food tech

as a force for good"). With this designation, Impact Hub attracts startups dedicated to sustainability, social enterprise, and community development. In addition to shared office space at the San Francisco office, incubatees enjoy access to Impact Hub branches in New York and Washington as well as foreign affiliates in Johannesburg, Madrid, Singapore, and other locales. As a membership-based organization, Impact Hub does not take equity positions in incubatees. However, it does facilitate introductions to prospective Bay Area investors.

KIC Silicon Valley (https://www.kicsv.org/) is the US outpost of Korea Innovation Center, a global incubator network dedicated to supporting South Korean-based small and medium enterprises (SMEs) in "4IR" (Fourth Industrial Revolution) technologies: artificial intelligence, data analytics, cloud computing, cyber security, financial technology, Internet of Things (IoT), augmented/virtual reality. KIC Silicon Valley annually hosts 10–20 South Korean SMEs for a three-phase program. The first phase ("Technology Revolution Together") focuses on collaboration between KIC incubatees and global corporations. The second phase ("Soaring") addresses corporate structure, technology commercialization, and market validation. The third phase ("Beyond Soaring") provides customized executive mentoring and go-to-market support for globally minded South Korean SMEs, some of which obtain venture capital funding and strategic investments.

Founded in 2005, Digital Garage (http://www.garage.co.jp/en/) is a Tokyo-based publicly listed investment company that manages a global digital technology portfolio. Digital Garage is organized into four business units: Incubation Technology, Financial Technology, Marketing Technology, and Long-Term Incubation. The Incubation Technology segment includes Digital Garage US, which operates an incubator ("DG717")

*Table 8.2   Global accelerators in the San Francisco Bay Area:
organizational profiles: Europe*

Organization	Headquarters	Organizational Type	Foreign Operations	Company Portfolio
Open Austria	Vienna, Austria	Accelerator	US	Digital technology
EIT Digital	Brussels, Belgium	International Bridge	Global	Digital technology
Enrich	Brussels, Belgium	International Bridge	Brazil, China, US	Digital technology
Innovation Center Denmark	Copenhagen, Denmark	International Bridge	US	Artificial intelligence
AXA Innovation Lab	Paris, France	Corporate Innovation Center	US, China	Financial services
French Tech Hub	Paris, France	Accelerator	US	Digital technology, healthcare
L'Atelier BNP Paribas	Paris, France	Corporate Innovation Center	US, China	Digital technology, fintech
Orange Silicon Valley	Paris, France	Corporate Innovation Center	US	Digital technology, fintech
Parisoma	Paris, France	Accelerator + Incubator	US	Digital technology, social media
Schneider Electric Innovation Center	Rueil Malmaison, France	Corporate Innovation Center	US	Electronics, industrial automation
Winnovation	Paris, France	Corporate Innovation Center	US	Telecommunications, media
Axel Springer Digital Ventures	Berlin, Germany	Corporate Innovation Center	US	Digital technology, fintech
German Accelerator Tech	Berlin, Germany	Accelerator	US	Digital technology, healthcare
Siemens Next47	Munich, Germany	Corporate Innovation Center	Sweden, France, UK, China, US	Digital technology, IoT, robotics, energy, healthcare
SAP Innovation Center	Walldorf, Germany	Corporate Innovation Center	Singapore, India, China, Australia, US	Cloud computing, blockchain
Innovation Norway	Oslo, Norway	International Bridge	Global	Digital technologies. clean tech

Table 8.2 (continued)

Organization	Headquarters	Organizational Type	Foreign Operations	Company Portfolio
Polska Silicon Valley Acceleration Center	Warsaw, Poland	International Bridge	US	Digital technologies, social media
US-Poland Innovation Hub	Katowice, Poland	International Bridge	US	Digital technologies, healthcare
ABC Accelerator	Ljubljana, Slovenia	Accelerator	Germany, US	Digital technology, healthcare
Spain Tech Center	Madrid, Spain	International Bridge	US	E-commerce, mobility, healthcare
Ericsson Garage	Stockholm, Sweden	Corporate Innovation Center	Europe, US	Digital technology
Nordic Innovation House	Stockholm, Sweden	International Bridge	Nordic states, US	Healthcare, sports tech
Nestlé Silicon Valley Innovation Outpost	Vevey, Switzerland	Corporate Innovation Center	US	Food tech
Swissnex	Bern, Switzerland	International Bridge	Brazil, China, India, US	Energy, intelligent machines
Startupbootcamp	London, UK	Accelerator	Global	Digital health, food tech, IoT

in downtown San Francisco. The San Francisco incubator hosts 25 companies, which pay fees for access to shared office space, technical support, and business development events. Along with locally based startups, incubatees include early stage Japanese companies seeking to enter the US market. To support its incubation programs, DG 717 has cultivated ties with the Bay Area subsidiaries of Japanese multinationals. Some of the San Francisco incubatees go on to receive growth capital from the Digital Incubation, the parent company's digital investment fund that comprises 130 companies from Japan, US, and the rest of the world.

Business Accelerators

Our field research included interviews at four globally active accelerators in the San Francisco Bay Area.

Table 8.3   Global accelerators in the San Francisco Bay Area:
             organizational profiles: Asia

Organization	Headquarters	Organizational Type	Foreign Operations	Company Portfolio
H Camp	TI Park Silicon Valley	Accelerator	Global	Digital technology, IoT, fintech, video
HanHai investment	Beijing, China	Accelerator + Incubator	US	Artificial intelligence, IoT, robotics, healthcare, big date
Hax Accelerator	Shenzhen, China	Accelerator	US	ICT hardware
Innospring	Shanghai, China	Accelerator + Incubator	US	ICT, healthcare, real estate
Hysta	Shanghai, China	International Bridge	US	Digital technology
KIC Silicon Valley	Seoul, South Korea	Accelerator	US	Artificial intelligence, fintech, big data
Digital Garage	Tokyo, Japan	Incubator	US	Digital technology, social media
Shanghai Valley	Shanghai, China	Accelerator	US	Digital technology
Shanghai Yangpu US Innovation Center	Shanghai, China	International Bridge	US	Digital technology
Shenzhen Valley Ventures	Shenzhen, China	Accelerator + Incubator	US	ICT hardware, engineering services
Sinovation Ventures	Beijing, China	Accelerator	US	IoT, robotics, software, education technology
Small World Group	Singapore	Accelerator + Incubator	US	Photonics, materials
TechCode Accelerator	Beijing, China	Accelerator + Incubator	US	Artificial intelligence, robotics, transportation
TI Park Silicon Valley	Beijing, China	Incubator	US	ICT
TI Park Silicon Valley	Beijing, China	Accelerator	US	Digital technology

HAX Accelerator (https://hax.co/) is funded by SOSV, a $300 million global asset management company. In contrast to other digital technology accelerators whose portfolios include software developers, HAX deals exclusively with hardware manufacturers: consumer products, health and fitness devices, industrial equipment, enterprise sensing and connectivity solutions. The accelerator process at HAX comprises two stages: (1) product development and prototyping in Shenzhen, in anticipation of eventual commercial-scale manufacturing in China; and (2) formulation of a go-to-market strategy at HAX's San Francisco office, including training in sales, marketing and distribution in collaboration with StartX, the startup accelerator of Stanford University. HAX provides participating companies with $250 000 seed funding in exchange for 10 percent equity. Forty percent of HAX companies come from North America, 20 percent from Europe, and 40 percent from the rest of the world (Asia, Latin America, Middle East).

Also funded by SOSV, Indie Bio (https://indiebio.co/) specializes in the global acceleration of biotechnology startups. Indie Bio selects pre-clinical biotech firms from the US and abroad for 4-month programs at its San Francisco office, which houses a "wet lab" for development of advanced therapeutics, genomics, synthetic biology, and food technology. Indie Bio provides selectees with $250 000 seed funding for 8 percent equity.

Open Austria (http://www.open-austria.com/) is the private sector complement to Advantage Austria, the country's official trade promotion agency. Collaborating with local venture capitalists and entrepreneurs, Open Austria selects 10–15 Austrian companies for quarterly residencies in San Francisco. Open Austria focuses on the global scaling of early stage companies that are approaching commercialization.

Headquartered in Singapore with an office in San Francisco, Small World Group (http://smallworldgroup.com/) focuses on three industries commonly neglected by startup investors: advanced materials, clean technology, and optics. Small World Group provides selected startups with seed funding ranging from $50 000 to $500 000. The organization has close ties with the venture capital community in Silicon Valley that facilitates the migration of high-potential startups from seed to Series A/B funding. Demonstrating its preference for startups targeting niche markets, Small World Group managed the successful exit of Rapsodo, a Singaporean developer of a specialized spin measuring system for baseball pitchers, now adopted by all major league baseball teams in the US.

Accelerators/Incubators

By virtue of its engagement with seed-stage and post-seed companies, The Refiners (http://www.therefiners.co/) qualifies as a hybrid accelerator/ incubator. The Refiners is the only Bay Area organization in our interview set that is 100 percent dedicated to foreign companies. Illustrating the business ethos of Silicon Valley, this San Francisco-based company displays a more aggressive business strategy than other organizations in our field research, prioritizing the development of foreign startups with "unicorn" valuation potential.

The Refiners taps a global network to recruit high-potential startups to come to San Francisco for an intensive program comprising three phases. The first phase focuses on acclimatizing foreign-based startups to the distinctive business culture of the San Francisco Bay Area. For European-based startups (which represent the majority of The Refiners' company portfolio), this cultural training is intended to break the incubatees from the conservative, risk-averse milieu of their home countries. The second phase of the program concentrates on business networking, featuring one-on-one meetings between incubatees and seasoned local entrepreneurs. The third phase is dedicated to fund-raising, including investor "fire side chats" and concluding with a "Pitch Night" during which incubatees deliver presentations to Silicon Valley investors.

In contrast to the fee-based incubators profiled above, The Refiners takes a direct financial interest in its portfolio companies, providing selected companies with $100 000 seed funding in exchange for 5 percent equity. The Refiners retains the option of raising its equity position in companies that proceed to early stage funding, strategic acquisitions, and initial public offerings. Of the 45 companies that have graduated from the seed program since the launch of The Refiners, half have obtained Series A/B funding.

Similar to other accelerators/incubators in the Bay Area, The Refiners emphasizes development of startups engaged in advanced digital technologies: AI, IoT, blockchain, AR/VR. However, the organization's portfolio covers a wide of industries, including apparel, cosmetics, music, education, hospitality, and shipping. The one industry The Refiners deliberately excludes from its portfolio is biotechnology, for which company principals lack requisite experience and technical expertise.

International Bridge Organizations

As indicated in Table 8.2, International Bridge Organizations have become a favored mode of entry for European companies in the San Francisco Bay Area. Both developed European countries (Belgium, Norway, Spain, Sweden, Switzerland) and emerging markets in Central and Eastern Europe (e.g., Poland) have established bridge organizations in the Bay Area to speed the globalization of startups (Bartlett and Mroczkowski, 2019).

EIT Digital (https://www.eitdigital.eu/) is part of the European Institute of Innovation and Technology, formed by the European Commission to spur the development of a pan-European digital economy. EIT Digital operates innovation hubs in nine European locales (Berlin, Budapest, Eindhoven, Helsinki, London, Madrid, Paris, Stockholm, Trento) and one hub in the United States (San Francisco). Through these transnational hubs, EIT promotes the scaling of digital startups whose commercial potential would otherwise be limited to their domestic markets. Launched in 2017, EIT's San Francisco office has hosted 15 European startups seeking to enter the Bay Area as a gateway to the US and global markets. EIT San Francisco also supports locally based US industrial companies aiming to expand in the European Union.

As a non-EU country, Norway relies on national governmental initiatives to spur the globalization of locally based startups. One such program is Innovation Norway (https://www.innovasjonnorge.no/en/start-page/), which operates in a wide range of countries in Europe, Asia and the Americas. Innovation Norway shares a facility with the other Nordic countries in the Nordic Innovation House in Palo Alto. In collaboration with the Norwegian Consulate Office in San Francisco, Innovation Norway provides business development services to Norwegian startups in healthcare, financial technology, and other industries.

Corporate Innovation Centers

Along with international bridges, Corporate Innovation Centers are now the preferred entry for European companies in the Bay Area. A number of leading European multinationals have established innovation outposts in the region, including companies headquartered in France (Orange, Schneider Electric, Orange), Germany (SAP, Siemens), and Switzerland (Nestlé).

Our field interviews featured a visit to Ericsson Garage (https://www.ericsson.com/en/tech-innovation/ericsson-garage), the corporate innovation center of the Stockholm-based networking/telecommunications company. Ericsson faces powerful global competitors, notably Alcatel-Lucent (France), Cisco (US), Nokia (Finland), and Samsung (South Korea) as well as China-based Huawei and ZTE. Amid mounting industry consolidation, Ericsson has undertaken a number of strategic acquisitions, including Marconi, Nortel and Redback Networks. The company meanwhile divested its share of Sony Ericsson, signaling Ericsson's exit from handset manufacturing to focus on its core mobile infrastructure unit. In that segment, Ericsson holds a 27 percent global market share, just behind industry leader Huawei.

Ericsson's growth trajectory in coming years hinges on (1) its capacity to speed development of emerging digital technologies, particularly 5G broadband, Big Data, and the Internet of Things; and (2) the company's ability to leverage its installed mobile infrastructure network for commercial applications of advanced digital technologies across a diverse range of industries.

As a large, mature global business, Ericsson is vulnerable to organizational inertia amid disruptions in the landscape of information and communications technology. In this milieu, Ericsson launched Ericsson Garage to spur entrepreneurship, innovation, and creativity outside the procedural and bureaucratic strictures of the company's internal R&D division.

Ericsson Garage is an open innovation platform organized around the company's "5Is": Initiate, Investigate, Incubate, Ignite, Integrate. Managed by a small team at Ericsson's global headquarters in Stockholm, Ericsson Garage engages four stakeholder groups (customers, employees, academia and external startups). The organization has spearheaded applications of digital technology in healthcare, public transportation, personalized wearables, mining, retail, energy, and manufacturing.

Ericsson's startup program offers six-month residencies to early stage companies in 13 "garages" in Europe, Asia and North America, including an office in Silicon Valley. Ericsson Garage recruits startups possessing innovative technologies, strong founding teams, and global market potential. Incubatees receive customized coaching, business development support, and use of Ericsson's infrastructure and testbed facilities. The portfolio companies of Ericsson Garage include Airmee (transportation), Build-R (construction), Evertracker (logistics), GreenWake Technologies (wireless power), Plantagon (vertical farming), SarvAI (machine learning), and Sensefarm (precision agriculture).

Ericsson Garage undertakes licensing agreements and equity investments in selected startups whose technology solutions align with the parent company's immediate strategic priorities. In most instances, graduating companies exit the garage with no direct relations with Ericsson. In these cases, Ericsson's benefit from the engagement is not financial but technological: that is, validation of disruptive technologies at early stages of development that present potential long-term competitive advantages and/or competitive threats to Ericsson.

Ericsson Garage Silicon Valley partners with Skydeck, a startup accelerator/incubator managed by the Haas School of Business and Department of Engineering at the University of California Berkeley. Through this partnership, Ericsson Garage companies receive a $100 000 investment from the Berkeley Skydeck Fund, undergo instruction in the Berkeley Acceleration Method, and gain access to the university's extensive corporate network in the Bay Area.

MODELS OF STARTUP GLOBALIZATION

The findings reported in this chapter are based on a limited number of mini case studies that provide guidance for future research on the globalization of startup companies. Our preliminary research in the San Francisco Bay Area illuminates the effectiveness of alternative models of startup globalization amid rapid changes in the economic and technological landscape.

Drawing on our initial round of field interviews, Table 8.4 summarizes the attributes of the five organizational types addressed in this chapter. Drawing on qualitative evidence from our research, this table rates the relative effectiveness (coded as low–medium–high) of these business development organizations along key components of startup development (mentoring, networking, funding, technology acquisition, exit opportunities, etc.).

Incubators are useful vehicles for pre-commercial startups that seek exposure to global ecosystems like the San Francisco Bay Area. But as

Table 8.4   Effectiveness of global accelerators: Comparison of models

	Incubators	Accelerators	Accelerators/ Incubators	International Bridge Organizations	Corporate Innovation Centers
Administrative Support	• •	• • •	• • •	• •	• • •
Local Networking	• •	• • •	• • •	• •	• •
Global Connectivity	• •	• • •	• • •	• •	• • •
Funding	•	• •	• • •	•	• •
Mentoring	• •	• • •	• • •	• •	• •
Technology Development	•	• •	• •	• •	• • •
Knowledge Acquisition	• •	• • •	• • •	• •	• • •
Cultural Alignment	• •	• • •	• • •	• •	• •
Business Development	• •	• • •	• • •	• •	• • •
Exit Opportunities	•	• •	• • •	•	• •

METRICS   Low •   Medium • •   High • • •

fee-based organizations that do not take equity positions, incubators do not have a financial stake in the eventual business outcomes of incubatees. The arm's-length relationship between incubators and incubatees and the short duration of residencies limit their impact on startup companies with global aspirations.

Our research indicates that *Accelerators* are more effective globalization mechanisms for high-potential startup companies than Incubators. This finding reflects: (1) the competitive process of admission to accelerators, which permits the selection of startups with demonstrated global commercial potential; (2) the structured and focused design of accelerator programs, which strengthens the business development capacity of startups; and (3) the host organization's provision of seed funding to selected firms, which creates a vested interest in the success of portfolio companies and prepares them to pursue Series A/B funding.

The hybrid *Accelerator/Incubator* model blends the attributes of the two forms while providing the foundation for a deeper and more enduring relationship between the host organization and participating companies. As seen in our case study of The Refiners, the hybrid model allows for the host's participation in both seed-stage and post-seed funding, positioning high-potential startups for successful exits via initial public offerings (IPOs) and strategic acquisitions.

International Bridge Organizations are distinguished from the other organizational types by their engagement of both private and public sector actors in transnational business development programs. The expansion of European bridge organizations in the San Francisco Bay Area underscores the challenges of entrepreneurship and innovation in Europe, where startups confront economic, financial and cultural impediments to global scaling. Immersion in bridge organizations in the Bay Area hastens the business development and deepens the global connections of European startups. But the international bridge model is less effective than Accelerators and Accelerators/Incubators at generating private sector investment in European startups, whose seed funding typically emanates from governmental and supranational agencies in Europe. To improve their effectiveness, European bridge organizations should better prepare companies for presentations to Silicon Valley private investors with demanding return on investments (ROI) expectations.

Corporate Innovation Centers play a distinctive role in the Bay Area ecosystem. They share a number of the attributes of Accelerators and Accelerators/Incubators: strong administrative and technical support; opportunities for local networking; extensive global connectivity; and effective business development services. By virtue of their ties with multinational parent companies, Corporate Innovation Centers exhibit knowledge acquisition and technology development capabilities that match or exceed those of Accelerators and Accelerator/Incubators. They clearly surpass Incubators and International Bridge Organizations in the metrics of funding and exit opportunities. The foremost challenge facing Corporate Innovation Centers is preserving their autonomy and entrepreneurial drive amid competing priorities of the parent's internal R & D divisions.

Our research reveals interesting connections between the type and geographic origin of business development organizations. The startup accelerator model is best established among US-based organizations, underscoring the central role of American pioneers of that organizational form (e.g., Y Combinator, Plug & Play, 500 Startups) that have built global startup portfolios from their Bay Area headquarters. Corporation Innovation Centers and International Bridge Organizations figure prominently among European-based organizations, compensating for the relative weakness of accelerators and incubators where American and Asian entities have achieved greater traction. Asia displays a mixture of organizational types, with the hybrid Accelerator/Incubator serving as the favored business development model of Chinese-based entities such as HanHai Investment, Innospring and TechCode.

Synthesizing these findings, Figure 8.2 conceptualizes a hypothetical model of startup globalization. Incubators are an appropriate vehicle

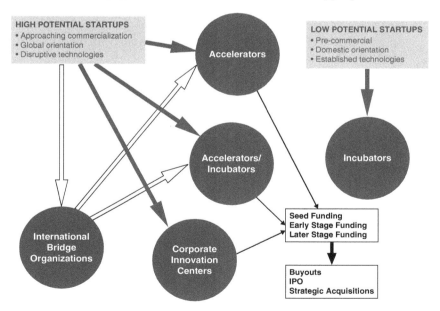

Figure 8.2   A conceptual model of startup globalization

for pre-commercial startups with a domestic market orientation and established technologies. High potential startups possessing strong global mindsets and disruptive technologies enjoy several paths to globalization. Accelerators and Accelerators/Incubators offer business development services that can prepare highly capable startups for funded exits and early globalization. Corporate Innovation Centers provide global connections and technological assets to hasten the global expansion of startups, albeit with some risk of loss of autonomy operating within large parent companies. International Bridge Organizations present an alternative path for promising startups that are beyond the incubation stage but not yet ready for admission to accelerators or corporate innovation center, providing business development support to guide their eventual transition to the latter organizations.

FUTURE RESEARCH

The initial findings reported in this chapter point to the following topics of future research on global startups and business development organizations.

Role of Business Development Organizations in Startup Globalization

- Analyses of the structure and operations of alternative types of global business development organizations in North America, Europe, and other regions;
- Tracking of the funding and exits of startup companies, sorted by organizational type and lead investors;
- Evaluation of the business outcomes of graduating startups, based on financial performance metrics and case studies of target companies.

Comparative Analyses of Global Startups and Business Development Organizations

- Regional comparisons (e.g., efficacy of Silicon Valley accelerators vs. European-based organizations);
- Industry comparisons (e.g., impact of business accelerators on startups in digital technology vs. manufacturing);
- Economic development comparisons (e.g., globalization paths of startup companies in developed vs. emerging markets).

Elaboration and Refinement Models of Startup Globalization

- Analyses of the business effects of sequencing in startup globalization (e.g., international bridge–accelerator–funding–exit);
- Investigations of the mechanisms of knowledge acquisition, technology development, and other components of startup globalization;
- Field studies of the processes of startup globalization, drawing on interviews and site visits at business development organizations and portfolio companies.

REFERENCES

Aerts, K., Matthyssens, P. and Vandenbempt, K. (2017). Critical role and screening practices of European business incubators. Unpublished manuscript.

Albort-Morant, G. and Oghazi, P. (2016). How useful are incubators for new entrepreneurs? *Journal of Business Research.* **69**, pp. 2125–9.

Autio, E. (2017). Strategic entrepreneurial internationalization: a normative framework. *Strategic Entrepreneurship Journal.* **11**, pp. 211–27.

Barrehag, L., Fornell, A., Larsson, G., Mårdström, V., Westergård, V. and Wrackefeldt, S. (2012). Accelerating success: a study of seed accelerators and their defining characteristics. Thesis in Industrial Engineering and Management, Department of Technology Management, Chalmers University of Technology, Gothenburg, Sweden.

Bartlett, D. and Mroczkowski, T. (2019). Emerging market startups engage Silicon Valley: cases from Central and Eastern Europe. *Journal of Small Business Strategy.* **29**(1), pp. 48–63.

Bøllingtoft, A. (2012). The bottom-up business incubator: leverage to networking and cooperation practices in a self-generated, entrepreneurial-enabled environment. *Technovation.* **32**, pp. 304–15.

Bruneel, J., Ratinho, T., Clarysse, B. and Groen, A.J. (2012). The evolution of business incubators: comparing demand and supply of business incubation services across different incubator generations. *Technovation.* **32**, pp. 110–21.

Brunswicker, S. and Chesbrough, H. (2018). The adoption of open innovation in large firms. *Research-Technology Management.* **61**(1), pp. 35–45.

Casillas, J. and Acedo, F. (2013). Speed in the internationalization process of the firm. *International Journal of Management Review.* **16**, pp. 105–29.

Cavusgil, S. and Knight, G. (2016). The born global firm: an entrepreneurial and capabilities perspective on early and rapid internationalization. *Journal of International Business Studies.* **46**, pp. 3–16.

Chandra, Y., Styles, C. and Wilkinson, I. (2012). An opportunity-based view of rapid internationalization. *Journal of International Marketing.* **20**(1), pp. 74–102.

Charry, G., Arias Perez, J.E. and Lozada Barahona, N.E. (2014). Business incubator research: a review and future directions. *Pensamiento & Gestión.* No. 37, pp. 41–65.

Chesbrough, H. (2005). *Open innovation: the new imperative for creating and profiting from innovation.* Cambridge, MA: Harvard Business Review Press.

Chesbrough, H. (2017). The future of open innovation. *Research-Technology Management.* **60**(1), pp. 29–35.

Chesbrough, H., Sohyeong, K. and Agogino, A. (2014). Chez panisse: building an open innovation ecosystem. *California Management Review.* **56**(4), pp. 144–71.

Cohen, S. (2013). What do accelerators do? Insights from incubators and angels. *Innovations.* **8**(3/4), pp. 19–25.

Coviello, N. (2015). Re-thinking research on born globals. *Journal of International Business Studies.* **46**, pp. 17–26.

Dai, Y., Goodale, J.C., Byun, G. and Ding, F. (2018). Strategic flexibility in new high-technology ventures. *Journal of Management Studies.* **55**(2), pp. 265–94.

DaSilva, C. and Gurtner, P. (2017). Accelerators: an assessment of accelerator models. *Academy of Management Proceedings.* **2017**(1), p. 1.

Dushnitsky, G. (2018). Variance decomposing of accelerator and cohort effects among London startups. *Academy of Management Annual Meeting Proceedings.* **2018**(1), pp. 747–52.

Dutt, N., Hawn, O., Vidal, E., Chatterji, A., McGahan, A. and Mitchell, W. (2016). How open system intermediaries address institutional failures: the case of business incubators in emerging market countries. *Academy of Management Journal.* **59**(3), pp. 818–40.

Ebbers, J. (2013). Networking behavior and contracting relationships among entrepreneurs in business incubators. *Entrepreneurship: Theory & Practice.* February, pp. 1–23.

Edmondson, A. and Harvey, J. (2016). Open innovation at Fujitsu. Harvard Business School, Case # 9-616-034, January.

Etemad, H. (2016). The promise of granularity theory in simplifying challenges of entrepreneurial internationalization. *Journal of International Entrepreneurship.* **14**, pp. 473–82.

Etemad, H. (2017). Towards an emerging evolutionary life-cycle theory of internationalized entrepreneurial firms: from born global to borderless firms. *Journal of International Entrepreneurship.* **15**, pp. 111–20.

Etemad, H. (2018). Growth and learning mechanisms in the evolving multilayered and multidimensional view of international entrepreneurship. *Journal of International Entrepreneurship.* **16**, pp. 1–11.

Fernández, M., Blanco Jiménez, F.J. and Cuadrado Roura, J.R. (2015). Business incubation: innovative services in an entrepreneurship ecosystem. *The Service Industries Journal.* **35**(14), pp. 783–800.

Fernández-Olmos, M. and Ramírez-Alesón, M. (2017). How internal and external factors influence the dynamics of SME technology collaboration networks over time. *Technovation.* **64–5**, pp. 16–27.

Fernhaber, S. (2013). Untangling the relationship between new venture internationalization and performance. *Journal of International Entrepreneurship.* **11**, pp. 220–42.

Fiedler, A., Fath, B. and Whittaker, D. (2017). Overcoming the liability of outsidership in institutional voids: trust, emerging goals, and learning about opportunities. *International Small Business Journal.* **35**(3), pp. 262–84.

Forsgren, M. (2016). A note on the revisited Uppsala internationalization process model – implications of business networks and entrepreneurship. *Journal of International Business Studies.* **47**, pp. 1135–44.

Gauthier, J.F. et al. (2017). Global startup ecosystem report 2017. Startup Genome, Global Entrepreneurship Network.

Gauthier, J.F. et al. (2018). Global startup ecosystem report 2018: succeeding in the new era of technology. Startup Genome, Global Entrepreneurship Network.

Gauthier, J.F. et al. (2019). Global startup ecosystem report 2019: with new life sciences ecosystem ranking. Startup Genome, Global Entrepreneurship Network.

Gobble, M. (2016). Defining open innovation. *Research-Technology Management.* **59**(5), pp. 63–7.

Hagen, B. and Zucchella, A. (2014). Born global or born to run? The long-term growth of born global firms. *Management International Review.* **54**, pp. 497–525.

Hagen, B., Denicolai, S. and Zucchella, A. (2014). International entrepreneurship at the crossroads between innovation and internationalization. *Journal of International Entrepreneurship.* **12**, pp. 111–14.

Hallen, B., Bingham, C.B. and Cohen, S. (2014). Do accelerators accelerate? A study of venture accelerators as a path to success. *Academy of Management Annual Meeting Proceedings.* **2014**(1), pp. 747–52.

Harper-Anderson, E. and Lewis, D. (2018). What makes business incubators work? Measuring the influence of incubator quality and regional capacity on incubator outcomes. *Economic Development Quarterly.* **32**(1), pp. 60–77.

Hathaway, I. (2016a). Accelerating growth: startup accelerator programs in the United States. Brookings Institution, February.

Hathaway, I. (2016b). What startup accelerators really do. *Harvard Business Review.* March, pp. 2–7.

Hennart, J. (2014). The accidental internationalists: a theory of born globals. *Entrepreneurship Theory and Practice.* January, pp. 117–35.

Iyortsuun, A. (2017). An empirical analysis of the effect of business incubation process on firm performance in Nigeria. *Journal of Small Business & Entrepreneurship.* **29**(6), pp. 433–59.

Khanna, T. and Palepu, K. (2010). *Winning in emerging markets: road map for strategy and execution.* Cambridge, MA: Harvard Business Review Press.

Klonowski, D. (2016). Venture capital and entrepreneurial growth by acquisitions: a case from emerging markets. *Journal of Private Equity.* Summer, pp. 21–9.

Köhler, R. and Baumann, O. (2015). Organizing a venture factory: company builder incubators and the case of Rocket Internet. Unpublished manuscript.

Kollmann, T. and Christofor, J. (2014). International entrepreneurship in the network economy: internationalization propensity and the role of entrepreneurial orientation. *Journal of International Entrepreneurship.* **12**, pp. 43–66.

Kyvik, O., Saris, W., Bonet, E. and Felício, J. (2013). The internationalization of small firms: the relationship between the global mindset and firms' internationalization behavior. *Journal of International Entrepreneurship.* **11**, pp. 172–95.

Lakhani, K., Hutter, K., Healy Pokrywa and Fuller, J. (2015). Open innovation at Siemens. Harvard Business School, Case # 9-613-100, March.

Lamotte, O. and Colovic, A. (2013). Innovation and internationalization of young entrepreneurial firms. *Management International.* September, pp. 87–103.

Li, L., Qian, G. and Qian, Z. (2015). Should small, young technology-based firms internalize transactions in their internationalization? *Entrepreneurship Theory and Practice.* July, pp. 839–62.

Lukeš, M., Longo, M. and Zouhar, J. (2019). Do business incubators really enhance entrepreneurial growth? Evidence from a large sample of innovative Italian startups. *Technovation.* **82**, pp. 25–34.

Mahmoud-Jouini, S., Duvert, C. and Esquirol, M. (2018). Key factors in building a corporate accelerator capability. *Research-Technology Management.* **61**(4), pp. 26–33.

Mainela, T., Puhakka, V. and Servais, P. (2014). The concept of international opportunity in international entrepreneurship: a review and a research agenda. *International Journal of Management Reviews.* **16**(1), pp. 105–29.

Mian, S., Lamine, W. and Fayolle, A. (2016). Technology business incubation: an overview of the state of knowledge. *Technovation.* **50–51**, pp. 1–12.

Mrkajic, B. (2017). Business incubation models and institutional void environments. *Technovation.* **68**, pp. 44–55.

Mulolli, E., Islami, X. and Skenderi, N. (2017). Business incubators as a factor for the development of SMEs in Kosovo. *International Journal of Management, Accounting and Economics.* **4**(6), pp. 659–66.

Norbäck, P. and Persson, L. (2014). Born to be global and the globalisation process. *The World Economy.* May, pp. 672–89.

Onetti, A., Zucchella, A., Jones, M.V. and McDougall-Covin, P.P. (2012). Internationalization, innovation and entrepreneurship: business models for new technology-based firms. *Journal of Management & Governance.* **16**(3), pp. 337–68.

Patel, P. and Naldi, G. (2018). Geographic diversification and the survival of bornglobals. *Journal of Management.* **44**(5), pp. 2008–36.

Patton, D. (2013). Realising potential: the impact of business incubation on the absorptive capacity of new technology-based firms. *International Small Business Journal.* **32**(8), pp. 897–917.

Pauwels, C., Clarysse, B., Wright, M. and Van Hove, J. (2016). Understanding a new generation incubator model: the accelerator. *Technovation.* **50–51**, pp. 13–24.

Pehrsson, T., Ghannad, N., Pehrsson, A., Abt, T., Chen, S., Erath, F. and Hammarstig, T. (2015). Dynamic capabilities and performance in foreign markets: developments within international new ventures. *Journal of International Entrepreneurship.* **13**, pp. 28–48.

Petrova, K. (2013). The effects of globalization on entrepreneurship. *International Advances in Economic Research.* **19**, pp. 205–206.

Pietrasienski, P. (2013). Silicon Valley Acceleration Center – a case study of the first Polish governmental "bridge". Warsaw: Warsaw School of Economics, August.

Pietrasienski, P. and Bitka, K. (2015). European bridge organizations in Silicon Valley: organizational structures, activity profiles, best practices. Trade and Investment Section of the Polish Embassy, Washington, DC, February.

Prashantham, S., Eranova, M. and Couper, C. (2018). Globalization, entrepreneurship and paradox thinking. *Asia Pacific Journal of Management.* **35**, pp. 1–9.

Protogerou, A., Caloghirou, Y. and Vonortas, N. (2017). Determinants of young firms' innovative performance: empirical evidence from Europe. *Research Policy.* **46**(7), pp. 1312–26.

Redondo-Carretero, M. and Camarero-Izquierdo, C. (2017). Relationships between entrepreneurs in business incubators: an exploratory case study. *Journal of Business-to-Business Marketing.* **24**(1), pp. 57–74.

Reuber, A., Dimitratos, P. and Kuivalanen, O. (2017). Beyond categorization: new directions for theory development about entrepreneurial internationalization. *Journal of International Business Studies.* **48**(4), pp. 411–22.

Rogova, E. (2014). The effectiveness of business incubators as the element of the universities' spin-off strategy in Russia. *International Journal of Technology Management & Sustainable Development.* **13**(3), pp. 265–81.

Romanello, R. and Chiarvesio, M. (2017). Turning point: when born globals enter post-entry stage. *Journal of International Entrepreneurship.* **15**, pp. 176–206.

Rubin, T., Aas, T. and Stead, A. (2015). Knowledge flow in technological business incubators: evidence from Australia and Israel. *Technovation.* **41–2**, pp. 11–24.

Saemundsson, R. and Candi, M. (2017). Absorptive capacity and the identification of opportunities in new technology-based firms. *Technovation.* **64–5**, pp. 43–9.

Santangelo, G. and Meyer, K. (2017). Internationalization as an evolutionary process. *Journal of International Business Studies.* **48**, pp. 1114–30.

Smallbone, D., Welter, F. and Ateljevic, J. (2013). Entrepreneurship in emerging market economies: contemporary issues and perspectives. *International Small Business Journal.* **32**(2), pp. 113–16.

Smith, S. and Hannigan, T. (2015). Swinging for the fences: how do top accelerators impact the trajectories of new ventures? Paper presented at the Druid Society Conference, 15–17 June.

Stayton, J. and Mangematin, V. (2016). Startup time, innovation and organizational emergence: a study of USA-based international technology ventures. *Journal of International Entrepreneurship.* **14**(3), pp. 373–409.

Stokan, E., Thompson, L. and Mahu, R. (2015). Testing the differential effect of business incubators on firm growth. *Research and Practice.* **29**(4), pp. 317–27.

Symeonidou, N., Bruneel, J. and Autio, E. (2017). Commercialization strategy and internationalization outcomes in technology-based new ventures. *Journal of Business Venturing.* **32**(3), pp. 302–17.

Taylor, M. and Jack, R. (2013). Understanding the pace, scale and pattern of firm internationalization: an extension of the "born global" concept. *International Small Business Journal.* **31**(6), pp. 701–21.

Trudgen, R. and Freeman, S. (2014). Measuring the performance of born-global firms throughout their development process: the roles of initial market selection and internationalisation speed. *Management International Review.* **54**, pp. 551–79.

Turcan, R. and Juho, A. (2014). What happens to international new ventures beyond startup: an exploratory study. *Journal of International Entrepreneurship.* **12**, pp. 129–45.

Vahlne, J. and Johanson, J. (2017). From internationalization to evolution: the Uppsala model at 40 years. *International Small Business Journal.* **48**, pp. 1087–102.

Van Weele, M., Van Rijnsoever, F.J. and Nauta, F. (2017). You can't always get what you want: how entrepreneur's perceived resource needs affect the incubator's assertiveness. *Technovation.* **59**, pp. 18–33.

Wise, S. and Valliere, D. (2014). The impact of management experience on the performance of start-ups within accelerators. *The Journal of Private Equity.* Winter, pp. 9–19.

Wright, R. (2016). The magical side of open innovation. *Research-Technology Management.* **59**(5), pp. 57–8.

Yin, B. and Luo, J. (2017). Why do accelerators select startups? Shifting decision criteria across stages. Unpublished manuscript.

Zahra, S. (2014). Public and corporate governance and young global entrepreneurial firms. *Corporate Governance: An International Review.* **22**(2), pp. 77–83.

Zander, I., McDougall-Covin, P. and Rose, E. (2015). Born globals and international business: evolution of a field of research. *Journal of International Business Studies.* **46**(1), pp. 27–35.

9. As an element of the regional innovation cluster, the citizen/non-profit sector fulfills the "seedbed function" of the new industry

Masashi Imase

1. INTRODUCTION

Regionally, it is not only commercial companies but also the citizen/non-profit sector that create innovation and new business. In regions that have deep-seated problems, innovation and new business become easy to create. When serious problems occur frequently in the region, businesses and initiatives by the citizen/non-profit sector may be actively developed to solve such problems.

These are projects and activities that neither commercial companies nor government have engaged in before. The citizen/non-profit sector creates innovation in response to the latent potential of a dysfunctional market, conducts its business activities as "social experiments", and develops new business models. For example, the citizen/non-profit sector created information technology (IT) businesses (internet-related business), nursing care services, welfare/nursing care businesses, environmental businesses, education support businesses and so on before commercial enterprises did.

In this chapter, using one case study, the author reports on the circumstances surrounding the creation of IT business. When the Great Hanshin-Awaji Earthquake happened in January 1995, there were almost no companies using the internet in Japan. In Kobe and Osaka, the citizen/non-profit sector pioneered the use of the internet to support the earthquake victims in the period from January to March 1995. In Kobe, Osaka and even in the whole of Japan, this was groundbreaking, and commercial companies began to introduce the internet as a consequence of that initiative.

Based on these specific case studies, the author discusses that the citizen/non-profit sector fulfills a "seedbed function" of regional new industry and

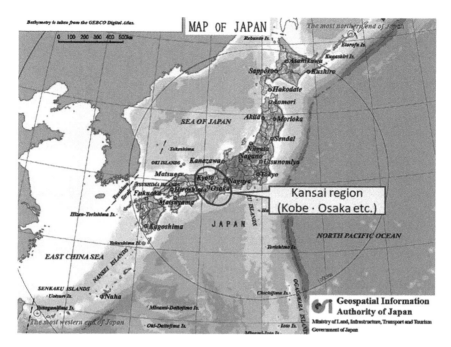

Source: Geospatial Information Authority of Japan (Ministry of Land, Infrastructure, Transport and Tourism (Government of Japan)). Map of Japan. Accessed 12 September 2017 at: http://www.gsi.go.jp/common/000102099.pdf.

Figure 9.1 Kansai region

it also plays an important function as an element of "regional innovation clusters".

2. THE CREATION OF NEW INDUSTRIES THROUGH THE "BUSINESSIZATION" OF THE CITIZEN/NON-PROFIT SECTOR

2.1 The Seriousness of Regional Problems and "Businessization" of the Citizen/Non-profit Sectors

In Japan, since the 1980s, potential demand for services such as welfare, nursing care, child rearing support, environmental conservation, and informationization support became manifest as a social problem in its regions. Despite this, there was little effort to supply these industries in order to satisfy demand. This was because market mechanisms have been hard to actualize, and so there have been few companies that have attempted to commercialize these industries. Further, despite being "non-profit" and "public", administrative agencies have created little policy because this has been considered a low priority and difficult to implement.

Under such circumstances, since the second half of the 1980s, the social and economic environment in the regions has undergone various changes, and citizen/non-profit sector initiatives have been activated. In an effort to solve social problems in regions, the citizen/non-profit sector has been working increasingly to supply such "unsatisfied demand".

The citizen/non-profit sector can also function as an "economic entity" as well as functioning as a "public interest entity". The citizen/ non-profit sector, which includes private, non-profit organizations and volunteer groups, is of great benefit to the public in addition to being non-profit, and is also in a position to test new ground using an experimental approach. The citizen/non-profit sector is divided into two major types of initiative in the process of activity development. One type of initiative, known as a "citizen public benefit organization", is structured around grassroots action or volunteerism. Another type of initiative is an organization that develops like a business as the organization and activities expand. This is an organization that "businessizes" non-profit and volunteer activities.

In the mid-1990s, the author gave the term "community business" to businesses where "businessization" has progressed in those community contribution activities that are carried out by the citizen/non-profit sector. The author defined this as follows. In the regions, local residents and business owners themselves provide social services, manufacture and sell products, with great public benefit and non-profitability. By doing so, it is a regional problem-solving business that revitalizes local communities.

2.2 Citizen/Non-profit Sector Targeted by the Government's "Economic and Industrial Policy"

In 1998, the "Specific Non-profit Activity Promotion Law" was enacted. The law enabled citizens' public interest groups to adopt a legal personality. In 2001, the Ministry of Economy, Trade and Industry established the "NPO Committee" of the Industrial Structure Council. In 2002, the author formulated an interim report titled "Toward the Realization of the New Public Interest" in "NPO Committee". As a result, the citizen/non-profit sector was positioned as a national economic and industrial policy, and was to be considered not only as a public interest entity but also as an economic entity. The citizen/non-profit sector has become an important driver of community business. Various support policies were developed by the government and local governments.

2.3 Creation of New Industries by the Citizen/Non-profit Sector

Regionally, the citizen/non-profit sector has been conducting civic public interest activities that solve social problems and revitalize the community in various ways. These civil public interest activities will be businessized as "community businesses". Sections of the citizen/non-profit sector that supplied goods and services corresponding to "unsatisfied demand" began to appear. Thereafter, general corporations also began to engage in such new business, imitating the business models of the citizen/non-profit sector. As they spread, they grew as new industries and began to form new markets.

The following businesses are case examples of new industries created by this citizen/non-profit sector:

- IT business (internet-related business) that supports the introduction of personal computers and the internet;
- Long-term care services for the elderly and disabled;
- Welfare and nursing-related businesses such as wheelchair and nursing care services;
- Environmental businesses promoting renewable energy such as solar and wind power generation;
- Educational support businesses that tackle truancy.

As one example in this chapter, we will report on the results of the survey and analysis on the cases in the Kansai region where the citizen/non-profit sector created IT businesses (internet-related business) and thus facilitated the opportunity to create a new industry.

At the time of the Great Hanshin-Awaji Earthquake, support activities by information volunteers using the internet were actively conducted from January to March 1995. As a result, the usefulness of the internet became widely known. This became an opportunity to promote the usefulness and potential of adopting the internet for commercial enterprises.

3. CASE STUDY: THE CITIZEN/NON-PROFIT SECTOR CREATING AN IT BUSINESS (INTERNET-RELATED BUSINESS) (JANUARY–MARCH 1995)

On 17 January 1995, the Great Hanshin-Awaji Earthquake occurred in the Kansai region, primarily in Kobe, Osaka and Awaji (see Figure 9.1).

It claimed many victims, resulting in significant changes to the social and industrial structure of Japan, as well as the values of its people. Earthquake relief efforts promoted social recognition of volunteers and citizen/non-profit sectors and triggered the development of those organizations and activities. One of them was the creation of "information volunteers" who utilized information technology (IT) such as the internet and contributed to the strengthening of activities of citizen/non-profit sectors through the use of this technology.

The citizen/non-profit sectors used IT to support the disaster victims, and contributed to the informationization by the private non-profit organizations (NPOs/NGOs). These were initiatives that neither commercial companies nor the government had previously utilized, becoming social experiments and leading to the creation of a new business model. In addition, the project to support the informationization by the citizen/non-profit sector triggered an increase in the number of general corporations that imitated this business model, resulting in the creation of new industries and markets.

3.1   Hanshin-Awaji Earthquake and "First Year of the Volunteer"

The "citizen/non-profit sector", comprising many volunteers, citizen public benefit organizations, and private non-profit organizations (NPOs/NGOs) all supported people in the affected regions who were in a state of disarray. The year of the Great Hanshin-Awaji Earthquake, 1995, became known as the "first year of the volunteer" in Japan.

As a result of the earthquake, many people were affected, precious lives were lost, and everything, including houses, office buildings and roads, was destroyed (see Figure 9.2). Utilities including electricity, water, gas

Source: Photo by Masashi Imase.

Figure 9.2   The great Hanshin-Awaji earthquake

and telephones were either disabled or interrupted for a long time. Also, many administrative agencies were affected and their operational capacity paralyzed. Local municipalities who were responsible for supporting the affected citizens were also unable to fulfill their functions adequately.

3.2   The Birth of "Information Volunteers" to Support the Earthquake Disaster Using Information Communication Means

In the Great Hanshin-Awaji Earthquake, all kinds of lifelines were cut off, but the blocking, depletion and biasing of "information" became a particularly large problem. At that time, telephone and fax, newspapers, television, CATV and radio, which were daily means of communication and information sources, could not fully respond to the needs of people in the disaster affected area. Under such circumstances, small community comic magazines, amateur radio, and word of mouth supplemented the flow and access of information. In addition, in those days the internet was almost unknown and hardly used in Japan. But personal computer communication by computer buffs played a major role.

NTT's telephone lines to the affected regions such as Kobe and Osaka were difficult to connect due to congestion caused by call restriction measures. However, information communication via the internet, even in regions where it was difficult to connect telephone lines, had unique capabilities that enabled connection by changing the access points. Utilizing these characteristics, communication was no longer impeded by congestion, meaning that the disaster region was connected to each of the other regions and to the world. Those who volunteered by utilizing information communication systems such as the internet and personal computer communication came to call themselves "information volunteers" from this time onwards.

3.3   Unused Internet in Companies and Administrative Organs

In Japan, as of January 1995 when the Great Hanshin-Awaji Earthquake struck, the use of personal computers as communication devices, the use of electronic networks, and the introduction of so-called IT (information technology) lagged behind compared with other countries such as the United States. The use of electronic networks was extremely limited, and was only found in information exchange between research institutes, or in companies in a few special industries or in the hobby world. There were almost no commercial companies or administrative agencies using them.

"Personal computer communication" was fairly popular, but the internet had not penetrated society at all. Internet servers could only be found in organizations such as Osaka University, Tsukuba University and Keio University. There were only a few provider companies engaged in internet-related services. Only a few people, such as university researchers, were internet users. Personal computer users were known as "otaku", or "weird people", and in many cases were seen in a negative light by the general population.

Since internet email software was not sold in Japan, it was acquired overseas. There was no Japanese version of the software, so foreign language software was used. The common use of the term "IT" or "information technology" was only adopted years later.

3.4   Activity of Information Volunteers Utilizing Electronic Networks

3.4.1   Development and practice of new applications of the electronic network

As a result, through their support of the victims of the Hanshin-Awaji Earthquake, individuals or people in the citizen/non-profit sector who utilized personal computer technology and electronic networks became known as "information volunteers". Information support initiatives by information volunteers were a completely new form of activity, which companies and administrative agencies had never engaged in before. The information volunteer activities were driven by volunteers who worked for universities such as Osaka University and Keio University, or major companies such as NEC and Panasonic.

Information volunteers visited shelters one by one on bicycles or motorcycles, surveyed the scene, and consulted with those affected. They assessed what was needed in the afflicted regions, examined how the people were suffering, and asked for support and cooperation by sending this data via the internet. Those who couldn't go to the disaster affected region effectively sorted the information into sectors, districts and so on, and shared it on the electronic network.

In addition, information volunteers were able to search effectively for important data from the abundant information accumulated on the electronic network in response to requests from people in the afflicted region. This data was then printed and handed to those who were in need. In addition, they coordinated support supplies based on requests for support information.

An electronic bulletin board (Net News) on the electronic network and earthquake information news groups (featuring different bulletin boards for each topic type) were created as a matter of urgency. A vast range of information flowed on the electronic bulletin board. For example, the following information was shared: information on shops that were open, bathing locations, hospitals that offered treatment, transportation time-tables, detailed changes to information on college entrance examinations, information released by administrative agencies, information on sup-porter supplies, support information by volunteer organizations, support information by companies, shelter information, lists of deceased persons, voice messages confirming the safety/whereabouts of people in the disaster affected region, detailed information on the disaster situation, support information on animals and pets, recruitment and reports of volunteers, donation information, amateur radio information, information for people with disabilities, information in English.

3.4.2   Internet information that brought support from the world

Immediately after the earthquake, there were various kinds of offers of support from overseas. One of the factors that brought about such support was information shared on the internet by information volunteers regard-ing the disaster affected region. People from all over the world learned about the situation in afflicted areas such as Kobe, Osaka and Awaji via the internet – faster and more realistically than through television and newspapers. Information volunteers photographed the situation in the affected region with digital cameras, and from the morning of the day after the earthquake occurred, video information was sent via the internet to global networks.

3.5   "Information Volunteer Organizations" that Worked According to their Characteristics

3.5.1   "Information volunteer organizations" with various characteristics

Immediately after the disaster, around the same time, some information volunteer groups were created and started the activity. In the process of these activities, role sharing advanced according to the specialization and characteristics of each organization. The following were the main organizations.

3.5.1.1   World NGO Network (WNN)   WNN mainly utilized the internet as a communication tool and carried out the following support activities: mediation of information between what the victim needed and what the supporter was able to provide. Construction and operation of the website of a private non-profit organization (NPO) that was carrying out sup-port activities in the disaster affected region. Visiting such organizations and educating people on how to use the internet and personal computer communication.

*3.5.1.2   Shiminkatsudou Information Center – Civic action clearinghouse –
(SIC)*   SIC is an organization that evolved from WNN about six months
after the earthquake (August 1995). SIC expanded to private non-profit
organizations (NPOs) in addition to earthquake support organizations as
targets of its support activities. As an "intermediate support organization"
specializing in communications support to NPOs, SIC principally carried
out the following activities: supporting information technology acquisition
for NPOs in various fields; mutual cooperation of each NPO and support
of information networking.[1]

3.5.1.3   Information Volunteer Group (Information VG)   Information
VG mainly conducted the following activities in the early days after
the earthquake: in personal computer communication (Nifty Serve),
dissemination of information for "lifeline" support of victims; printing of earthquake support information from the electronic network;
distribution of printed support information to affected regions; investigation of actual conditions and needs of affected people in evacuation
centers.

3.5.1.4   Inter Volunteer Network (IVN)   IVN is a network of information volunteer organizations consisting mainly of users of Nifty Serve
and mainly conducting the following activities: support for collaboration
between evacuation centers, government agencies and external organizations; collection and dissemination of useful information mainly for the
victims of evacuation centers.

3.5.1.5   Volunteer Assist Group (VAG)   VAG mainly utilized personal
computer communication and shared the following three support activities with each regional collaborator: "collect" information related to
living support in disaster affected regions; "aggregate and organize" that
large amount of information; "digitize" that information and "present
(dispatch)" it on the electronic network.

3.5.1.6   Inter V Net   Inter V Net conducted the following activity mainly
as a potential support activity from Tokyo, away from the disaster affected
region: building infrastructure as a common information exchange location between the internet and various personal computer communications.
This mechanism allows for any information input from any electronic
network to be referred to by any other electronic network. It facilitated the
"collection, arrangement, and transmission" of information and promoted
its effective use.

3.5.2 Collaboration among various "information volunteer organizations"

While these "information volunteer organizations" promoted their support activities, they were able to share roles among these groups. In order to advance networking between shelters, administrative agencies and external agencies, IVN and VAG connected by personal computer communication, which was an easy way to connect. WNN connected using the internet to advance the networking of the victims evacuated from their homes and the private non-profit organizations (NPOs/NGOs) with external organizations.

Inter V Net provided a mechanism for connecting to the internet (WNN is part of its users) and personal computer communication (IVN and VAG are part of its users). VAG and WNN supported the training of human resources of different users. VAG provided support to train operators of personal computer communications mainly in evacuation centers. WNN conducted activities to teach internet technologies to staff from NPOs/NGOs.

3.6 Social Experiment Project of NPO Creating IT Business (Internet-related Business): The Birth of an NPO that Carries out the Project of "Informationization Support"

Among such information volunteer organizations, the author looked at the activities of "World NGO Network (WNN)" and "Shiminkatsudou Information Center – Civic action clearinghouse – (SIC)" as a more detailed case study. These organizations conducted support activities utilizing the internet, and also conducted activities and projects to support the informationization of private non-profit organizations (NPOs/NGOs).

3.6.1 Promotion of volunteer activities by internet engineers

Immediately after the earthquake in late January 1995, some information volunteers recruited internet engineers as information volunteers. They urged Osaka YMCA and Osaka University's large computer center to cooperate. Osaka YMCA had been conducting earthquake disaster support activities by recruiting many volunteers. At that time, Osaka University's large computer center had cutting-edge internet technology.

Nearly a hundred people, including university researchers and employees of major electric manufacturers, gathered as information volunteers in response to the call. At that time, internet engineers were still rare in Japan. Then in February 1995 the "World NGO Network (WNN)" was formed. The author was the secretary general of WNN. In addition, about six months after the earthquake (August 1995), the "Shiminkatsudou Information Center – Civic action clearinghouse – (SIC)" was established as an organization developed from WNN (2018).

At that time, users of electronic networks and personal computer technicians were called "geeks", a pejorative term, by members of the public. None of the private non-profit organizations (NPOs) and volunteers used electronic networks. The author wanted to connect the world of these technicians with the world of volunteers. Technological knowledge possessed by "geek" technicians who were considered to have fewer contact points with society became useful for society directly through volunteer activities. Furthermore, depending on the results, there was also the possibility that new businesses and industries could be created. The author wanted to share such ideas and turn them into reality.

3.6.2 Information volunteer activities for earthquake assistance utilizing the internet

Information volunteers posted queries on the internet based on information contained within reports of the victims' support activities by NPOs (including unresolved needs and desired information etc.) and received responses (resolution information). They organized the information posted on the electronic network bulletin board (Net News), and searched and sent the information requested by the earthquake victims among themselves.

Information volunteers made their own homepage on the internet and posted electronic maps. On these electronic maps, they posted the following useful information for people in the disaster affected regions based on item/region: information on bus stops, hospitals offering treatment, public health centers, evacuation centers, relief centers and so on in the afflicted regions. Sumitomo Electric Systems Co. Ltd cooperated in utilizing these electronic maps. Some of the earthquake disaster volunteers from overseas printed electronic maps which included information on the disaster affected regions, and used them when they visited these areas.

3.6.3 "Informationization support" project by NPO

WNN and SIC conducted a project of "digital information support" for NPOs/NGOs so that private non-profit organizations (NPOs/NGOs) could perform activities efficiently. They strengthened the information communication function using the internet, and promoted the information network between NPOs/NGOs. WNN also conducted the "digital information" project of three NPOs/NGOs that provided support activities in the disaster affected region.

For example, an information volunteer using internet technology visited various NPOs'/NGOs' project locations and offices and taught NPO/NGO staff how to use personal computers and internet technology. Technical guidance was conducted so that NPO/NGO staff could use the internet by themselves, such as emailing and website creation.

3.6.4   "Informationization support" project of NPO providing earthquake support

For example, the following activities were carried out as support for digital information services to private non-profit organizations (NPOs) conducting earthquake disaster support.

3.6.4.1   Visiting technical guidance and preparation of Japanese operation manual   Information volunteers visited NPOs' project locations and offices and instructed NPO staff about how to use internet technology. To make it easy for anyone to master the internet, they independently created Japanese operation manuals, personal computers and email software. At that time (February 1995), there were no Japanese versions of software, only English versions. Also, there was almost no commercially available software.

3.6.4.2   Utilization of the internet video conference system   The information volunteers carried out support activities using the simple and inexpensive video conference system "CU – SeeMe" which ran through the internet and a personal computer. "CU – SeeMe" was used in conjunction with a simple video camera "QuickCam" (cost: US$100). Osaka YMCA conducted a homestay program in New Zealand to provide care services for children far from the disaster affected region. Information volunteers accompanied them and assisted the children and their Japanese parents to talk with each other remotely.

3.6.4.3   Development of a volunteer automatic acceptance system by email   Information volunteers developed a volunteer automatic acceptance system (software) by email. Since the reception of volunteers did not proceed smoothly immediately after the disaster, NPOs that were providing disaster relief support requested this.

3.6.4.4   Knowledge   and   know-how   learning   from   American FEMA   Information volunteers thought that development of emergency response information systems and wide region networks were necessary to deal with future disasters. Through the internet they received knowledge and know-how cultivated through the US FEMA's (Federal Emergency Management Agency) experiences when dealing with the Los Angeles earthquake.

In the United States, the San Francisco earthquake occurred in 1906. Similar to the Great Hanshin-Awaji Earthquake, there were major disasters in urban areas. After that, major disasters such as earthquakes and hurricanes occurred one after another. Therefore, FEMA was established in 1979 as a government agency to deal with major disasters. In the Los Angeles earthquake of 1994, FEMA contributed to the support activities of the victims. FEMA is a model for disaster relief for countries around the world.

3.6.4.5 Recommendation of "Public Access Point Concept" Information volunteers wanted to create regional electronic networks as social capital in various regions. They created research named "Public Access Point Concept" and made recommendations. They wanted to create an environment where citizens could easily use the internet by using personal computers located in familiar places such as stations and public facilities.

3.7 Collaboration with NPOs/NGOs for Companies to Enter New Businesses

There were many difficult problems with new activities and projects utilizing the internet, such as earthquake support activities and NPOs'/NGOs' informationization projects. However, due to positive social conditions for community contribution activities after the earthquake, many of the difficulties could be overcome. Cooperation (free of charge) from many companies promoted activities and projects.

Cooperation from companies interested in developing new businesses using the internet also promoted activities and projects. Looking for mutual benefits with NPOs/NGOs that created new businesses, companies and other organizations conducted collaborative businesses. The following are examples of cooperation of companies and other organizations in the "Informationization support" project of WNN and SIC.

3.7.1 Support for introducing ISDN from NTT
NTT and WNN collaborated in a joint research project. At that time, NTT was just beginning to roll out ISDN services. NTT had internal rules which meant they could not donate to volunteer groups.

3.7.2 Donation of dozens of personal computers from Apple Computer Co. Ltd
A personal computer was offered to NPOs that were the focus of the "informationization support" project.

3.7.3 Providing dozens of email accounts and website servers from NEC Corporation (NEC)
In cooperative work with NEC ("meshnet" business provider), for example, the following promises were exchanged: supporting NPO/NGO creates

homepage of activity information and continuously updates it. Frequent use of mail. Printing the mail addresses containing the word "meshnet" on an NPO/NGO's business cards etc. For NEC, this was a social contribution activity, a trial experiment and a PR activity before their full entry into the new business of the internet.

3.7.4   Providing servers and classrooms from Osaka University's large computer center

As a part of Osaka University's social contribution activities, this became an advanced case of a collaborative project between community and university.

In addition, SIC was able to obtain cooperation from many companies and other organizations, and was able to pioneer the NPOs'/NGOs' "informationization support" project. These various projects have become pioneering models of collaborative work between private non-profit organizations (NPOs/NGOs) and commercial companies. Through collaboration with NPOs/NGOs, companies carried out regional contribution activities for earthquake support. Companies were also able to develop new products and services in their profitable business (main business) through community contribution activities.

3.8   Creation of an IT Business (Internet-related Business) by Citizen/ Non-profit Sectors

3.8.1   Utility of the internet revealed by NPO activities

As a result of the citizen/non-profit sector using the internet in their support activities at the time of the Great Hanshin-Awaji Earthquake, the usefulness of the internet can be summed up as follows:

- Even small pieces of information not featured by the mass media can be edited from the user's standpoint, transmitted in real time, with a large amount of information able to be conveyed as is. (Example: Detailed change information on university entrance examinations etc.)
- Individuals can easily transmit their information to many people.
- When contacting a disaster affected region, information such as a message is transmitted to the other party via the nearest access point.
- Anyone can exchange information with a wide range of people.
- Anyone can save and communicate regional information such as transportation timetables, hospitals offering treatment, bathing locations, etc.

- Anyone can search for such information when necessary and can update it easily.
- Even people who are far away from the disaster affected region, or those who cannot go to the afflicted regions for work, can do support activities to compile and disseminate information as background support.

Until that time, the networks between organizations had often been limited to those between leaders or between certain members. However, it became clear that by utilizing email and the internet, it was easy for any member of the organization to communicate flexibly with members of other organizations and to construct a network equally.

Collaboration and cooperation among organizations cannot be established without "common benefits and objectives" for each organization. Even in earthquake disaster support activities, this became an issue. However, it became clear that the establishment of mutual benefit among organizations would be facilitated by the fact that anyone could easily share information using the internet.

3.8.2 "Businessization" of the internet created by NPO activities

In this way, at the time of the Great Hanshin-Awaji Earthquake in January 1995, the internet, which was not used at all in Japan, was used for the earthquake support activities by the citizen/non-profit sector. As a result, the method of utilizing the internet and its usefulness became clear, and the internet spread rapidly afterwards.

It has been demonstrated that the internet can function as a "means of communication" in emergency situations, a "means for sending and receiving information" and as a new activity tool for private non-profit organizations (NPOs/NGOs). The possibility to dramatically increase NPOs'/NGOs' activity and abilities through "informationization" has been shown. It has also been shown that human networks that are spontaneously created on the internet function organically. Regarding the internet, the citizen/non-profit sector demonstrated this possibility and direction afterwards.

In the industrial world, hardly any companies had introduced the internet at that time in Japan. Nobody knew about the application and utilization of internet technology and functions for business. It was under such circumstances that the internet was utilized for support activities by citizen/non-profit sectors in the Great Hanshin-Awaji Earthquake. By doing so, it became empirically evident for the first time, including: "which technology and function can be used", "which application can be used", "how to use it", and "how useful it is", and so on.

3.8.3 Citizen/non-profit sector that fulfilled the "seedbed function" of IT business (internet-related business)

Indeed, the activities of the citizen/non-profit sectors for earthquake disaster support and information conversion support became a social experiment. That created the foundation for a new IT business (internet-related business) that supported the introduction of personal computers and the internet. That fulfilled the "seedbed function" that created the IT industry and the new market. If the citizen/non-profit sector had not had an active part in the Great Hanshin-Awaji Earthquake, the spread of the internet in Japan would have been delayed for many years.

3.9 Development of IT Business (Internet-related Business) as a New Industry (after Late 1995)

3.9.1 Internet use expanded further with Windows 95 release

After that, the release of Microsoft's Windows 95 also brought about a synergistic effect, and the use of the internet spread rapidly to commercial enterprises and government. At the Asia-Pacific Economic Cooperation (APEC) Osaka Conference held in November 1995, the experiences, technologies, know-how, human networks, etc. of the citizen/non-profit sector accumulated through activities of earthquake disaster and information conversion support were utilized in the management of the meeting.

3.9.2 Creation of IT-related companies in the Kansai region

Due to IT-related activities in the citizen/non-profit sector (NPO, information volunteer), phenomena were seen to accumulate at an early stage in the Kansai region such as in Osaka and Kobe. For example, the following happened: the accumulation of multimedia-related companies in the Tanimachi district of Osaka was evident at an early stage. The Digital Hollywood Osaka School was opened in 1996. IT-related human resource development and corporate foundations became active after the late 1990s.

3.9.3 Information volunteer activities in the Great East Japan Earthquake utilizing the experience of the Great Hanshin-Awaji Earthquake

The Great East Japan Earthquake occurred in 2011, 16 years after the Great Hanshin-Awaji Earthquake. In the Tohoku region such as the Fukushima prefecture, Miyagi prefecture and Iwate prefecture, there was a large earthquake and a large tsunami, resulting in many casualties. At this time, the internet was fully developed and was used on a daily basis in all social and economic activities. With support activities for the Great East Japan Earthquake, know-how based on the experience of information volunteer activities in the Great Hanshin-Awaji Earthquake was utilized.

The citizen/non-profit sector used the internet effectively to carry out support activities in collaboration with the government and commercial companies.

4. CITIZEN/NON-PROFIT SECTOR AS REGIONAL INNOVATION CLUSTER

4.1 Regional Innovation and New Industry Creation

Regionally, various management resources and regional resources are necessary to create innovation, new business and new industries. With demand becoming obvious in the region, companies supply products and services, and new businesses are created. However, even if there is a potential demand, companies will not supply products and services unless a relationship between demand and supply is established.

Even if there are management resources and regional resources, companies cannot develop new businesses unless market mechanisms work. In other words, with regions, as innovation is created, potential demand is found, it becomes obvious, and the market mechanism works by establishing a balance between supply and demand. In addition, companies have management and regional resources, utilize them, supply products and services, and create new businesses.

Global innovation is triggered by regional innovation. The needs of products and services that people demand in the region will become the needs of products and services that people around the world want. Global business and global markets are born first from local businesses and regional markets. Products and services are created to meet the needs of people in some regions or to solve social and economic problems somewhere in the region. In some cases, they spread all over the world.

4.2 "Input Resources" of Regional Innovation Clusters and the Process of Creation of New Industries: Citizen/Non-Profit Sector Fulfilling the "Seedbed Function" of New Industry

Based on examples such as IT business (internet-related business), what kind of regional resources are being introduced into the region by regional innovation clusters? The author has clarified the input resources and outlined the process by which new business and industry are created. The role that the citizen/non-profit sector contributes has also been summarized.

4.2.1 Revealing social and economic problems in the region: factors of regional innovation creation

There are various social or economic problems in the region. Regional innovation is sought to solve regional problems, and it is created by the needs of residents, consumers and businesses who are members of the region.

4.2.2 Citizen/non-profit sector activities to solve regional problems: revealing latent demand

The citizen/non-profit sector is the one that finds the potential demand, reveals it, and makes the market mechanism work. Citizen/non-profit sectors are private non-profit organizations (NPO/NGO), volunteer organizations and so on who develop businesses and activities to solve regional problems. They have high public benefit/non-profitability, are pioneering and carry out social experimental activities.

4.2.3 Innovation by social experimental activities of the citizen/non-profit sector

The citizen/non-profit sector functions as an "economic entity" as well as a "public interest entity". Citizen/non-profit sectors create innovation and develop businesses and activities in regions which have a demand for services but where the market mechanism does not work. The citizen/non-profit sector pioneers the development of business, conducts social experiments, and harnesses the advantages of non-profit characteristics and volunteer power.

4.2.4 Progress of "businessization" of citizen/non-profit sectors and creation of market mechanisms

As its business and activities expand, the organization also expands, and "businessization" progresses. Potential demand due to the market mechanism not working is revealed, and supply to it will expand (see Figure 9.3).

4.2.5 Collaboration between companies and citizen/non-profit sectors

Citizen/non-profit sectors conduct various pioneering activities and projects to solve regional problems. On the other hand, companies will cooperate as part of social contribution activities and social responsibility. In addition, there are cases where such a business can also benefit the company's commercial business (main business). In such a case, the company develops a social experimental business in collaboration with the citizen/non-profit sector.

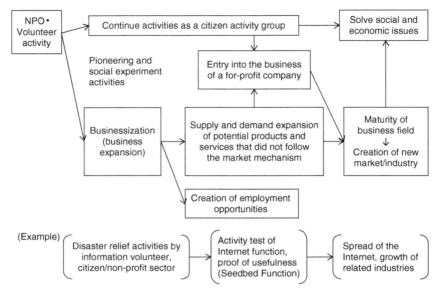

Source: Masashi Imase (author), June 2000.

Figure 9.3 *"Seedbed function" of new industry creation by citizen/non-profit sector*

4.2.6 Administrative agencies' support for social experimental projects by citizen/non-profit sector

Administrative bodies develop various support policies for social experimental projects aimed at solving regional problems by the citizen/non-profit sector. For example, consider the following support policy:

- Provision of subsidies from administrative agencies to private non-profit organizations (NPOs/NGOs) and others;
- Outsourcing of administrative services to NPOs/NGOs;
- Development of collaborative projects between NPOs and administrative agencies.

4.2.7 Companies entering new businesses and creating new industries

Through such processes, companies will enter the business field. By increasing the number of companies engaged in the business, new industries and new markets will be created.

5.   CONCLUSION

In this way, the citizen/non-profit sector functions as an "economic entity" as well as a "public benefit agent", and has created new business in the region. Social experimental projects by citizen/non-profit sectors are initially very small and operate as individual projects. However, they have the power to create new business models in the region. They have the ability to create new industries and markets by accumulating and collaborating with many in the region.

In other words, due to the activation of citizen/non-profit sector activities and "businessization", the supply–demand relationship of potential products and services is identified and expands. In addition, in the products and services fields where market mechanisms did not work well before, an environment is created where companies can easily enter. And as companies start to do business one after another, such new products and service fields will mature. Through such processes, new markets and industries are created.

In this way, the citizen/non-profit sector has a very high pioneering ability and is more challenging and pioneering as an entrepreneur than a startup company (venture company). In the region, the citizen/non-profit sector fulfills the "seedbed function" of a new industry.

NOTE

1.   It should be noted that WNN and SIC are the organizations the author has been involved with.

REFERENCES

Geospatial Information Authority of Japan (Ministry of Land, Infrastructure, Transport and Tourism (Government of Japan)). *Map of Japan.* Accessed 12 September 2017 at: http://www.gsi.go.jp/common/000102099.pdf.

Imase, M. (1995). Information volunteer activity utilizing electronic network – Internet and personal computer communication. Japan: Regional Development Center, "Regional Development".

Imase, M. (2011). *New state / public in the regional sovereignty era – NPO to open up hope and autonomy / cooperative reform.* Japan: Gakei Publishing Company.

Imase, M., Takahashi, M. & Takayanagi, D. (2002). Quantifying the economic benefits of the non-profit organization in Japan – setting the non-profit performance to the I-O table. *DP RIETI Discussion Paper Series 02-J-010*, Tokyo: The Research Institute of Economy, Trade and Industry.

METI-KANSAI (2001). *Survey research report for the construction of 'autonomous circulation type regional economic system'* in the Kinki region. Osaka: Kansai Bureau, Ministry of Economy, Trade and Industry (METI-KANSAI).

METI-KANSAI (2002). *Interim summary towards the realization of 'new public interest'*. Osaka: Industrial Structure Council NPO Subcommittee, Ministry of Economy, Trade and Industry (METI-KANSAI).

Osaka Economic Promotion Liaison Committee (1997). *Research on promotion measures of the next generation type growth industry in Osaka – Multimedia Contents related industries*. Osaka: Osaka Economic Promotion Liaison Committee.

Osaka Economic Promotion Liaison Committee (1997). *Research on promotion measures of the next generation type growth industry in Osaka – Social service related industry*. Osaka: Osaka Economic Promotion Liaison Committee.

RIETI (2002). *Survey research report on NPO as a new economic entity*. Tokyo: The Research Institute of Economy, Trade and Industry (RIETI).

Shiminkatsudou Information Center (2018). Civic action clearinghouse website. Accessed 20 September 2018 at: http://sicnpo.jp.

10. The factors in the establishment of the Shizuoka sake brewing cluster: regional human resources enabling open innovation

Nobuyuki Kishida

1. INTRODUCTION

Innovation affects the rise and fall of regional industries so much. Hence, when we think about such a regional scientific issue like the establishment or transformation of regional industrial clusters, it is necessary to argue what clusters supply to their own innovations. This study takes the Shizuoka sake producing region as a case and discusses the contributions of regional inputs toward regional industry cluster innovation.

Regional science is one of Gibbons et al.'s (1994) Mode 2 sciences which intends to create knowledge that will contribute to solve real contemporary regional problems by means of consolidating multidisciplinary academic theories. So, we must be careful not only about the properness of the theories from various disciplines, but also the adequateness of the way to consolidate them. Especially in social sciences, there are several classic standards that were created from or verified by the facts and cases that were gathered during the Second Industrial Revolution or earlier. Industrial cluster theory, which this chapter relies upon, may be one of those examples. Although the essence of a theory will remain true, the drastic changes in the knowledge bases and the social infrastructures since the last century may affect the characters of classic theories. Because of this, when applying such theories for regional scientific considerations, those contemporary limits of application or applicability should be examined beforehand, so as to fit other latest academic knowledge.

Based on the industrial cluster theory of Marshall (1923) and Porter (1990), this chapter initially expected the regional inputs in question would be found among the clustering prerequisite conditions listed by those two standard studies. After analyzing the case intensively, these conditions are to be examined one by one as to how important they were on the context of the case. It is notable that this study is neutral from the impacts of the internet, because it is a 1980s' case.

Yoshikawa (2001) summarizes Marshall's and Porter's discussions on the factors behind the clustering of a particular industry in a particular region, indicating that the region will have the following six factors suited to the industry:

1. labor, human resources;
2. investment factor conditions excluding labor and human resources;
3. development of related and supporting industries;
4. spread of technology and knowledge particular to the industry;
5. presence of customers (state of demand);
6. competition between companies within the same industry.

In the Japanese sake brewing industry, in addition to the two major production regions of Nada and Fushimi, the industry also features regional sake clusters that have established their positions in the market through high-quality sake that stands apart from the products of major producers. This study discusses the conditions that led to the establishment of the newer sake industry cluster in Shizuoka, which emerged around the end of the Showa era (1926–1989) among the traditional brewing regions such as Niigata, Hiroshima, Miyagi and Hokuriku. The methods for brewing sake are said to have been established in the Muromachi period (14th to 16th centuries) by Buddhist monks in the Kinai area (around modern-day Kyoto/Osaka), and there are records of quality sake being brewed in Shizuoka as early as the mid-16th century. It is only since the mid-1980s, however, that Shizuoka has come to be recognized as one of Japan's regional quality sake brewing clusters. Numerous other regions have aimed for market participation in a fashion similar to Shizuoka's industry, but most of the success has been had by the leading brewers rather than by the regions themselves. Thus, Shizuoka presents a notable case: though small-scale, it has gained recognition as a region.

The Japanese government began providing directives on sake brewing and improved quality management with a view to securing tax income starting in the Meiji period (late 19th century). As a result, many regions, including Shizuoka, came to possess the six factors listed above. Based on these six industrial cluster factors, this study discusses several related particularities in the formation of the Shizuoka regional sake cluster, as well as verifying the modern meaning of the six factors.

2. A BRIEF HISTORY OF THE SAKE PRODUCTION INDUSTRY

Sake (*nihonshu* or *seishu* in Japanese) is a traditional Japanese alcoholic beverage made from rice. Its origin may be traced back as far as the time when rice farming was introduced to the Japanese archipelago. The basic techniques for sake brewing were complete in the Muromachi period (14th to 16th centuries). In medieval times, sake from Nara received the highest praise. By the Edo period (17th to 19th centuries), the broad framework of Japan's sake culture had crystallized. The development of the shipping industry and the vast consumer demand in Edo, which is called Tokyo now and was one of the world's largest-scale cities at the time, encouraged the growth of the Ikeda and Itami brewing regions near Oosaka, cultivating what was still Japan's largest sake brewing cluster region: Nada. Fushimi, in Kyoto, is a brewing cluster dating back to the Heian period (8th to 12th centuries), but it was behind Nada in terms of logistics and fell into decline during the warfare at the end of the Edo period. From the start of the Meiji period, Japan's sake brewers were placed under the control of the Ministry of Finance in order to obtain tax revenue. In 1904, the Brewing Testing Institute (now the National Research Institute of Brewing; NRIB for short) was set up as a national research institution. The Institute's engineers visited sake production sites and achieved much significant success in process innovation, such as in techniques for preventing quality changes (mash spoilage) during production and deterioration (bacterial contamination) during maturation, as well as establishing techniques for mass production (e.g., rapid *soku-jō* brewing method). Meanwhile, progress in improving brewing methods was being made in regional and private circles, and, following successful research into soft water preparation techniques in the mid-Meiji period, areas such as Hiroshima and Kyoto's Fushimi came to be recognized as national centers of quality brewing to rival Nada. Governments and citizens worked together to almost double national sake production, from 515 160 kl in 1877 to a prewar peak of 996 300 kl in 1925.

Following World War II, Japan's sake brewing industry restarted amidst warfare and famine, achieving growth in step with the recovery of the Japanese economy. By 1963, sake production volumes, which had been as low as 121 000 kl in 1948, had mostly caught up with their 1925 levels. At this time, to respond to the strong demand, priority was given to securing volume, and markets were dominated by sake made through the mass production process implemented by the Brewing Testing Institute during the war based on the "synthetic sake" (*gōseishu*) techniques. Then, in 1973, the highest annual figures in history were recorded for both production volumes, at 1 421 000 kl, and taxable shipping volumes, at 1 766 000 kl. Meanwhile, the population diversified its consumption habits due to rapid economic growth. After 1973, however, sake production volumes began to enter a gradual decline.

The number of sake breweries, indicated by the number of sites licensed for sake brewing, has also been in constant decline from its level of around 4000 sites in the late 1950s. In 1973, when production volumes peaked, there were 3303 sites. Looking at base company figures, Japan's sake brewers numbered 2356 in 1988 and 1709 in 2012. Over 99 percent of these are small to medium-sized firms ("smaller brewers" hereafter).

After World War II, smaller brewers were for a long time protected by regional production volume limits. These limits were relaxed around 1975, and smaller brewers were thus exposed to price competition from large-scale production goods. Compared with the time of peak sake production volumes in 1973, the number of sites licensed to brew sake has been more than halved. Most of the smaller brewers are engaged in developing new, high-quality sake products that are distinctive. The companies have transitioned from being production subcontractors to developing their own products.

3.   OVERVIEW OF THE SAKE BREWING PROCESS

According to Japan's Liquor Tax Act, sake (*seishu*) is defined as a fermented product made from the base ingredients of rice, koji and water, or from the base ingredients of rice, koji, water, and other goods designated by government ordinance.

Below is a summary of the elements of the traditional sake brewing process:

1.   rice milling process;
2.   making steamed rice;
3.   making koji from steamed rice;
4.   making seed mash from koji, steamed rice and water;
5.   sake main mash (fermentation) process;
6.   pressing process;
7.   filtration process;
8.   pasteurization process;
9.   maturation process.

One cycle of the whole process, excluding the maturation period, takes around 50 days.

Multiple tanks will often be prepared at the same time in parallel, but there will often be minute differences in the sake produced even between tanks, which should have been prepared under the same conditions. Blending will thus be undertaken with the aim of securing the quality of the product for shipment.

In recent years, large-scale brewing manufacturers have aimed to mass-produce sake at low cost by using liquefaction methods, whereby enzymes are added to white rice, which is then heated to induce glycation, instead of using the traditional fermentation processes described above. In this method, the seed mash process is combined with the sake main mash process within the tank.

4. TOJI GROUPS AND SAKE BREWING CLUSTERS

A sake brewing company's human resources can be broadly divided into managers, technicians and laborers. Progress was made early on in separating capital from management in the sake brewing industry. In the Meiji and Taisho years, following the government calls for greater industry development policy, many breweries were founded based on the capital of rich families and merchants. We refer to these owner-managers as Kuramoto brewers. The technical aspects of brewing that made this possible were supported by groups of seasonal laborers called Kurabito, led by brewing technicians called Toji (*tōji*). This study refers to these groups as "Toji groups".

Traditionally, sake brewing would occur from around October through to the following March each year, and teams of sake-producing laborers led by Toji would lodge at the brewery during this period. This is because conditions such as the temperature of around 1.5°C, the new rice available from early autumn, and the availability of seasonal laborers during the agricultural slack season were considered suitable for sake brewing.

Since the cold environment in winter was well-suited for controlling microbes in traditional brewing processes, farmers who had finished rice production could be seen working in sake brewing in the winter throughout Japan. Toji groups would work in rice farming in their hometowns from spring until autumn, and from late autumn until early spring, they would stay in breweries in remote regions and work in sake production. In their hometowns, Toji would often be heads of family houses and influential figures in the community; as well as being brewing technicians who would guide the entire sake-brewing process, they would also be supervisors of work teams formed by Kurabito (aspiring Toji from the same region). While Kuramoto brewers would sometimes recruit locally for peripheral duties such as transportation and business operations, all vital brewing processes would be undertaken by Toji as a rule. The Kurabito would return to their hometowns from spring to autumn and vie with each other to share their experiences from various regions; they would compete with other Toji groups and improve their brewing techniques.

Some larger brewers have introduced modern equipment and are able to brew sake throughout the year, but it is common for smaller brewers producing high-quality sake to undertake this sort of seasonal sake production even now. However, Toji groups of agriculture-based seasonal laborers are having difficulty finding next-generation successors, and increasing numbers of brewers are training up full-time Tojis.

The feudal system was dismantled and labor made a free matter in the Meiji period, and many Toji groups were set up, primarily in regions with harsh winters, such as Iwate (Nanbu), Niigata (Echigo), Yamagata (Sannai), Ishikawa (Noto), and San'in (e.g. Tamba, Tajima, Iwami). Toji groups were also created in comparatively warm regions, such as Hiroshima and Okayama, where traditional sake brewing skills had accumulated as a profitable source of cash income during the winter. The basin of the Ōigawa River in central Shizuoka was also home to the Shida Toji group.

The Shida Toji's most prosperous period was from the Taisho years to the early Showa era, when members numbered over 800, but it is thought to have entered into decline early on after the war. When sake brewed with Shizuoka yeast began in the early 1980s, by then Shida Tojis were employed only at brewers within the prefecture seasonally, and dispatches to remote regions had almost completely stopped. While the Shida Toji group has disappeared in terms of its seasonal laborers now, its traditional techniques and trade name have been inherited by Takashi Aoshima, a Toji, and the managing director of the Aoshima Shuzō brewery (the Kikuyoi sake brewer).

Traditional sake production by Kurabito teams involves physical labor starting early every morning from around November until the end of March the following year. While farmers who faced difficulties in cultivating crops during the winter in areas prone to snow were able to get comparatively good work in the milder regions to which they may have been dispatched, in Shizuoka, a warmer region, it was also possible to cultivate fruit and vegetables alongside the spring wheat, a secondary crop, and since industrialization had also begun early along the Tokaido strip, there was also the option of seasonal factory work. Moreover, the common opinion of the Shida Toji was not always better than that of other groups. Since there are records of some Shida Toji having been called from a Japanese American brewery to Hawaii before the war, their capabilities in brewing in warm regions are seen as having been somewhat advanced.

But traditional warm-region brewing techniques placed priority on safe brewing, for instance in preventing spoilage, and the quality of taste and bouquet produced could not match that of the cold-weather production sake boasted by Toji groups from colder regions. It had led to less favorable opinions from the domestic market. In technical terms, cold-weather brewing as typified in Nada uses a production technique called the kimoto method, whereby the main mash, prepared over three stages, is kept at a low temperature for a comparatively long period. Meanwhile, the mizumoto method, a traditional brewing technique effective even in warmer regions for example, may also easily create a seed mash starter, but since it makes more lactic acid, the sake becomes more acidic.

The combination of these effects meant that Shida Toji had already started to be taken on as full-time and seasonal company employees of local brewers during the period when Shizuoka yeast sake was being established. Now that the Toji system has declined, full-time Tojis are not uncommon at regional breweries, but company employees with Toji experience and expertise had begun taking root at breweries within Shizuoka prefecture during Japan's era of rapid economic growth. This can be considered a particular feature of labor and human resources from the time when Shizuoka yeast sake was being established.

5. THE SYSTEM OF SPECIFIC-DESIGNATION SAKE AND THE NATIONAL NEW SAKE AWARDS

Sake is classified according to stipulations in the Sake Brewing Quality Labeling Standards (announced in November 1989 by Japan's National Tax Administration Agency, NTA). Among these classifications, specific-designation (*tokutei-meishō*) sake is the high-quality category of importance to regional sake clusters. The classifications first divide sake into ordinary (*futsū*) sake and specific-designation (*tokutei-meishō*) sake, and specific-designation sake is then broadly divided into three subcategories: *ginjo*, *junmai* and *honjōzō*. Labels such as *ginjo* and *junmai* were in use before the specific-designation sake system was introduced, but, when the system was enacted, standards of objective criteria were made statutory (see Table 10.1).

The key for successful regional brewing clusters is the production of specific-designation sake that stands out and is of better quality than the products of major brewers in Nada and Fushimi, and competition has focused on sake belonging to the *ginjo* category, seen as being of the highest quality sake during 20th century in general. This competition took place at sake contests. These events presented ideal marketing opportunities

Table 10.1   Requirement standards for specific designations

Type	Specific designation	Ingredients[1,2,3]	Degree of polishing[4]	Other requirements[5]
Ginjo: premium	Junmai Daiginjo	Rice, Koji	50% or less	Gijo-zukuri method, characteristic flavor and high clarity
	Junmai Ginjo	Rice, Koji	60% or less	
	Daiginjo (honjōzō)	Rice, Koji, Jozo- alcohol	50% or less	
	Ginjo (honjōzō)	Rice, Koji, Jozo- alcohol	60% or less	
Junmai: pure rice	Tokubetsu Junmai	Rice, Koji	60% or less, or specially processed	Good flavor and best clarity
	Junmai	Rice, Koji	none	Good flavor and high clarity
Honjōzō: Authentically brewed	Tokubetsu Honjōzō	Rice, Koji, Jozo- alcohol	60% or less, or specially processed	Good flavor and best clarity
	Honjōzō	Rice, Koji, Jozo- alcohol	70% or less	Good flavor and high clarity

Notes:
1. Water is omitted from the ingredients lists.
2. All types must be more than 15% Koji relative to the rice by weight.
3. There should be no more than 10% jozo-alcohol relative to the rice by weight. The jozo-alcohol, which is a vodka-like clear distilled ethanol fermented from sugar cane or etc., is used to adjust the flavor of non-*junmai* sakes.
4. The degree is the weight ratio between the brown rice and the polished rice.
5. There is no clear definition of the *ginjo*-zukuri method. However, it usually means the process of using the rice polished to a low degree and fermenting at a low temperature to create the characteristic fragrance.

Source: National Research Institute of Brewing (2013), *Glossary of Terms on Sake Bottle Labels ver.3*, NRIB.

for smaller regional breweries to contend fairly with Nada and Fushimi's national brand sake in quality and to raise their public profile. Here, Tojis from each brewery poured their hearts and souls into their *ginjo* sake and submitted it for exhibition. Among many contests, the National New Sake Awards (NNSA) has kept its authoritative position as the only national public sake contest. It was first held in 1911 at the old Ministry of Finance Brewing Testing Institute, which was now reorganized as the NRIB. The NNSA is held annually in May, and the judging examines sake produced in that given year. In an average year, there will be around 800 to 1000 submissions from brewing companies. The number of gold awards has increased since 1989; now, just under 30 percent of all submissions a year obtain a gold award. For a recent example, nearly 30 percent, a total of 232 sakes, won a gold award out of the 850 submissions in the NNSA 2017. In contrast, only about 15 percent, about 100 sakes, were given a gold award out of 600–800 submissions during the 1980s. There was less chance of winning a gold award at the time. Despite this, at the NNSA 1985, 21 companies submitted the Shizuoka yeast *ginjo* sake discussed in this chapter; they performed notably well, even nationally, with 10 of these submissions receiving gold awards and seven others winning prizes.

A gold award from the most authoritative contest in the sake world not only grants breweries a favorable reputation but also serves as a certification of excellence for smaller breweries. This has led to the gradual expansion of the market for Shizuoka sake around the Tokyo metropolitan region.

6. THE STRATEGY OF KAWAMURA, AN ENGINEER AT THE SHIZUOKA PREFECTURAL INDUSTRIAL TESTING CENTER

Nishimura (2003) indicates that from the Meiji period (late 19th century) until before the war, "universities in Japan at the time, and in particular Tokyo Imperial University, were devices for adopting western civilization" and at the same time "functioned as a switchboard for distributing it to citizens, to regional areas, and to lesser schools." He claims that advanced technology from the West "would first be adopted by the public sector, namely through public universities, specialist colleges, national testing and research institutes, and then be transferred to the private sector, for instance to companies." This study looks at the Shizuoka Prefectural Industrial Testing Center (the "Prefectural Testing Center" hereafter; it is now the Shizuoka Prefectural Industrial Technology Center), which was founded in 1906 and thus created during Japan's period of "advanced cooperation between industry and academia", as indicated by Nishimura. Even if they no longer function as a "switchboard" for advanced technology from the West, public regional testing centers remain close and important collaborators with Japan's smaller businesses.

Denbei Kawamura (1943–2016) obtained an Agricultural Chemistry degree from the Faculty of Agriculture at Shizuoka University in 1965, and then entered the Shizuoka Prefectural Industrial Testing Center. He learnt the core techniques of microorganism cultivation at the university, but it was through his work after having joined the Center that he gained the technical knowledge required for sake brewing. At the time, Toshiro Amano, a Shida Toji from Shidaizumi Brewery, was employed as a temporary worker at the brewing division of the Prefectural Testing Center in Shizuoka City. Before long, Kawamura distinguished himself as a brewing engineer; in the late 1970s, he planned to develop high-quality *ginjo* sake using new sake yeast in order to promote sake production within the prefecture, and he intended to show the prefecture's strengths by acquiring an unprecedented number of gold awards, reaching double-digits, at the NNSA.

The target qualities for Shizuoka yeast sake were a high sake meter value (SMV; nihonshu-do) and low acidity. The aim was to produce "sake which is clean, rounded, refreshing and pleasant to drink." These are the qualities that were settled upon in pursuit of good sake as a result of the accumulation of tasting experience and furthered interaction between breweries, Tojis and researchers from the National Brewing Testing Institute after members of the brewing division of the Prefectural Testing Center invited an ex-sake inspector at the Nagoya Tax Bureau to begin the guidance service on brewing in 1955, a decade before Kawamura joined. At the time, there was increasing criticism of the sweeter, mass-produced sake made through the synthetic sake techniques that spread after the war and the quality of sake shifted toward drier styles. Meanwhile, Aji-*ginjo*-style sake emerged, which is both better in bouquet and taste, and won awards at the NNSAs. Thus, Shizuoka's configuration of sake qualities also stood out from the NNSA trends at the time.

Yeast choice and koji creation are important for producing unique sake qualities. Kawamura negotiated with the Shizuoka Brewers' Association and organized a yeast project as a joint research endeavor with the Prefectural Testing Center to search for new yeast by collecting the best main mash from the prefecture's breweries. As a result, around 1980, the Shizuoka yeast HD-1 was found from the main mash at Doi Brewery. The Shizuoka yeast has been cultivated and kept at the Prefectural Testing Center, and is distributed amongst the Association's members only.

There are limits on how far the sake's qualities can be made to stand out through differences in sake yeast when the yeast used is *kyokai-kobo*,[1] which is obtainable by any brewer. By the same logic, if a brewer is able to obtain and use yeast superior to *kyokai-kobo*, the product can be expected to differ fundamentally in quality. Shizuoka yeast is distributed as a prefectural association project to association members only; the yeast is used as a key resource in distinguishing sake made within the prefecture from the products of other regions.

7. THE DISCOVERY AND DEVELOPMENT OF THE SHIZUOKA YEASTS

Nowadays, most major brewers have an in-house central research base for research and development (R&D), as in other food and chemical industries, and some have produced research results of a high standard, even in academic terms. Meanwhile, for smaller brewers, research and development has historically been conducted through affiliation with public technical testing centers. Broadly speaking, the National Brewing Testing Institute under the NTA (now NRIB) has come to handle basic scientific research, public technical guidance organizations in each area (the NTA's regional inspection offices; prefectural technology testing centers), and handle applied research, and individual smaller breweries handle new product development. Separate bodies preside over each stage of the linear R&D model. Close links are built between each stage through guidance visits, technical consultations, education and training, interactions between personnel, and so forth; a wealth of cooperative research and joint development also occurs. This system has produced great results in process innovation, such as in improved preservation properties and defect prevention as described before. Meanwhile, sake yeast development plays an important role in product innovation. Two types of microorganisms are used in sake brewing: koji mold, which turn the starch in the base rice into sugar, and yeast bacteria, which ferment the sugar and create ethanol. The latter was discovered at the end of the 19th century, when artificial selection and improvement began. Sake yeast not only causes fermentation but also creates fragrance substances, esters, and several types of organic acids and amino acids, which greatly influence the palate. A large part of the flavor of sake, particularly its bouquet, is determined by the characteristics of the sake yeast used. Aspiring brewers from public and private circles had begun striving to find and develop new types of sake yeast that would create better tastes and bouquets since the late Meiji period. Under the brewing licensing system, these were generally collected and catalogued by the Brewing Society of Japan, an organization under the National Brewing Testing Institute, and then sold to brewers across Japan as *kyokai-kobo* yeast.

Since HD-1 is the property of the Shizuoka Brewers Association, its genetic analysis results are kept as trade secrets and not publicly available. Thus, the discussion on its source origins below does not extend beyond the author's estimations.

It is certain that HD-1 is a new strain of sake yeast separated from Doi Brewery's K9 *ginjo* mash, with high fragrance properties. Since all the traditional *ginjo* sake yeasts were the house sake yeast of some renowned regional breweries, HD-1 may be either Doi Brewery's house sake yeast or a wild yeast that happened to enter into the mix by chance.

HD-1 yeast is said to be less robust during fermentation than standard *kyokai-kobo* yeasts. Although its use requires a high degree of skill in the production of koji by the Toji, HD-1 sake that is adequately produced has a low acidity (between 1.0 and 1.2) and a retronasal bouquet that is abundant with bananas. The main components of its bouquet are some varieties of *kyokai-kobo* (sake yeast strain) like K9 and others that are reminiscent of the native *ginjo* yeast. The fragrance characteristics of HD-1 arise from the ratios of the ester components, which are aromatic compounds, and because there is a preponderance of isoamyl acetate over ethyl caproate ester, it is classified as an isoamyl acetate-predominant variety. The fact that it is clearly different from ethyl caproate ester-predominant varieties allows its significance to be confirmed through the use of statistical analysis comparing it to the Alps yeast,[2] which is a typical caproate ester-predominant variety of sake yeast. Caproate ester-predominant varieties are noted for their luxurious green apple-like top notes which differ considerably from the more sensual bouquet of isoamyl acetate-predominant varieties. K9, like K14, is classified as an isoamyl acetate-predominant variety. Judging from the fact that HD-1 is also an isoamyl acetate-predominant variety, it is likely that HD-1 is closely related to K9. Continuing this line of reasoning, it is likely that it is a strain that is a cross-breed of Doi Brewery's house sake yeast or a wild yeast and K9. It is also likely that it is a natural variant of one of these yeasts.

Although there is only a slight chance that it is a natural variant of K9, this cannot be ruled out. This is because of the fact that it is possible to create a hybridized diploid-predominant strain from a parent strain that is highly productive and has a good balance of aromatic components. Hybridizing dominant strains selected from monoploid strains separated from the same types of parent strains has been reported by studies of K7.[3] *Kyokai-kobo* yeasts include a range of pure diploids that were cultivated by the Brewing Society of Japan. Therefore, it is highly unlikely that these hybridized strains found their way into *kyokai-kobo* ampules. If this was the case, it would mean that some K9 remained somewhere in Doi Brewery, where sake made with K9 was brewed, spores were then created, which led to the appearance of monoploid yeast strains that cross-bred. These elite yeast strains with dominant characteristics would have had to cross-breed with each other by chance to create a "super K9" strain. This then would have somehow become mixed into the sake main mash prior to being used in the brewing of sake. According to an anonymous person connected to a brewery in Shizuoka Prefecture, during the "golden age" of Shizuoka yeast, a brewer in Shizuoka Prefecture secretly brought the HD-1 strain to an old friend at one of the major breweries in Nada. According to the rumor, a detailed examination of the strain was conducted there and showed that it was indistinguishable from K9. If true, this would support the idea that a "super K9" exists. However, at the time this was supposed to have occurred it was not yet possible to conduct testing at the genome level to match different strains, and therefore if it did occur according to the rumor, it is likely that the results were obtained through the use of more conventional testing methods such as gene electrophoresis or saccharide resourcability tests. Strictly speaking, these methods would not always have been able to distinguish between sake yeasts that include a large number of closely related strains.

In addition, Shokichi Hase (1932–2009), who brewed the sake main mash in which Kawamura discovered HD-1 at Doi Brewery, was a Toji in Noto (Ishikawa Prefecture). One can assume that its discovery was related in some way to *ginjo* yeasts used in the Hokuriku region of Japan. The Liquor Inspection Office of the Kanazawa Regional Taxation Bureau, which had jurisdiction over the three prefectures within the Hokuriku region, began research into *ginjo* yeasts early in the Showa era (1926– 1989). They are known to have discovered multiple unique high-grade yeast strains, as they were very active in the selection and preservation of these strains. They were also said to provide quality-related guidance to the brewers under their jurisdiction by giving their special *ginjo* yeasts. One of these high-grade yeast strains has been adopted as the *kyokai-kobo* K14. Therefore, one can speculate that it would have been either Hase Toji or one of the Kurabitos following him from Noto that somehow secretly passed on the Kanazawa high-grade yeast. Thereby, it is possible that HD-1 is a hybrid strain that is a cross-breed between one of the Kanazawa high-grade yeasts and K9 or the Doi house sake yeast.

Sake brewing using HD-1, which is not very active during fermentation, requires a high degree of skill in the making of koji. Kawamura utilized the incremental process innovation approach in order to identify and standardize the optimum conditions for a koji-making process that would facilitate the stable brewing of HD-1 sake. At the same time, he improved the breeding method for this strain so as to work toward improving its fermentation characteristics while maintaining the unique characteristics of sake brewed using HD-1 yeast. He cross-bred HD-1 with other sake yeasts that were more active during fermentation. He then selected a method that allowed him to cultivate a cross-bred yeast that maintained both the sake characteristics associated with HD-1 and the active fermentation of one of the parent strains. One of the strains that were crossed with HD-1 was the yeast known as NO-2. NO-2 is a natural variant of the non-foaming variety of K10, which Kawamura discovered during the process of cultivating and separating K10 at the Prefectural Testing Center. The non-foaming strain of K10 was placed on the market by the Brewing Society of Japan in 1984 under the name of K1001. However, Kawamura had already put NO-2 into practical use prior to the launch of K1001. The genetic differences between NO-2 and K1001 are still unknown. The creation and test brewing of new yeast that was a cross-breed between HD-1 and NO-2 were carried out and the yeast known as New-5 was completed around 1984, and its use began in sake brewing in 1985 after its distribution and adoption by sake breweries in the prefecture. That year the total number of breweries using Shizuoka yeast that adopted the use of HD-1 and New-5 reached double-digits. Specifically, they numbered 21 breweries, or almost 40 percent of the breweries in the prefecture.

Comparisons of the sensory features of New-5 sake and HD-1 sake indicated that, although HD-1 sake had a comparatively low acidity, the acidity of New-5 sake was even lower. Examination of their bouquet qualities indicated that HD-1 sake had a prominent bouquet and that New-5 sake was lighter and more fragrant. These differences, along with the increased activity during fermentation, were the result of cross-breeding of the characteristics of the K10 parent strain of NO-2 with the HD-1 yeast.

The major advantage of New-5 is that it can be easily brewed by any brewery using the standard koji-making techniques. The fact that the use of HD-1 required the Toji to be highly skilled in koji-making techniques was an obstacle that prevented the widespread use of HD-1. As of 1985, however, breweries that were able to use HD-1 and those that were previously unable to use HD-1 began using New-5, which led to its rapid diffusion.

8.   ESTABLISHMENT OF THE SHIZUOKA *GINJO* PROCESS

During the first half of the 1980s, early in the development process of HD-1, Kawamura introduced the new strain to cooperative breweries he had become closely associated with. He wanted to learn the techniques used by the Tojis at the breweries. Around 1985, from early in the morning he began traveling by car to four or five breweries a day. At this small number of cooperative breweries, the Tojis used their skills to work out ways to create a number of prototype HD-1 sake varieties. One of these was a sake with an extremely high sake meter value of +12 that was created by chance at the Iso-Jiman Brewery. Although they believed this sake would not sell very well, it was highly praised by sake vendors in Tokyo. As a result, they began shipping it to Tokyo. This is how Shizuoka sake came to be associated with its three characteristics: high bouquet, low acidity, and high SMV, which suggests the drier taste.

Shizuoka yeast was originally intended for use in the brewing of low-acidity sake. There is data from brewing laboratories that supports the fact that the selection of the yeast and a moderate amount of stirring of the fungal threads during the making of koji are required to make *ginjo* sake with low acidity. However, Kawamura believed that:

> for the most part, science is only concerned with the types of yeast, the temperatures, and the amounts of water. So, in a sense, it is quite simplistic. However, at breweries where sake is actually made, it is important to have a level of technical skill that allows one to control sake brewing so that it remains at the optimum level in accordance with a variety of initial conditions and subsequent environmental changes that occur. This ability cannot be understood simply as a "technique". The world of sake brewing is one in which technical skills are subordinate to individual know-how.

Thus, he believed he should learn the brewing methods used in as many breweries as possible. "There are hints even in the unconscious actions taken by Kurabitos early in the morning" said Kawamura.

> Through these, I learn about the difference between good and bad sake main mash, and how to handle the canvas squeezing bags. Many of these things are which the Toji and Kurabitos would be unable to explain to me if I simply asked them. I learned particularly a lot about the brewing of *ginjo* sake because the Toji is involved in the entire process. (Kishida, 2005)

Kawamura frequently visited the sake brewing facilities of the cooperative breweries. Koji making is an "analog" technique, and as such it is slightly different at each brewery. Thus, Kawamura spent the early part of his studies observing how koji was made at a number of cooperative breweries. During the winter sake brewing season, Kawamura spent nearly every day running back and forth from one brewery to the next. His typical schedule was as follows: he would start around 5 o'clock in the morning when the gate of the Masuichi Brewery, located near the Prefectural Testing Center, was opened to allow the Kurabitos who commuted to come in. Kawamura would enter the brewery and observe the koji making. Then he would go to the Prefectural Testing Center around 8:30 in the morning when operations there would start. On some days, the only brewery he would visit would be Kanzawagawa Brewery in the town of Yui, in which one of the outstanding Shizuoka yeast users, Jun'etsu Yamakage Toji, was brewing. When he traveled to the eastern part of the prefecture, he might go to Eikun Brewery, also located in the town of Yui, and Sanwa Brewery in Shimizu. When traveling to the west, he might visit

Shidaizumi Brewery in Fujieda, Iso-Jiman Brewery in Yaizu, and then continue on to Omura-ya Brewery in Shimada around 5 o'clock in the afternoon. Shizuoka Prefecture stretches east to west, and therefore there is a distance of approximately 180 kilometers from Miyazaki Brewery in the extreme west to Bandai Brewery in the east. However, all the breweries that Kawamura visited were all within a 30 kilometer radius of the Prefectural Testing Center. They were all located within a sake brewing industry cluster in the center of the prefecture; this allowed for frequent face-to-face communications during the most active stage of the effort to optimize techniques suitable for Shizuoka yeast. This method of providing guidance in brewing through close cooperation with actual brewing facilities continued through the late 1980s.

Sake breweries in temperate Shizuoka provide a good working environment for Toji groups from the regions where winters are harsh. To this day, skilled Tojis come to Shizuoka from Nanbu, Noto, Echigo, Hiroshima and other areas. Kawamura acted as the central figure who collected the knowledge and the data these Tojis gained through their process of trial-and-error. Then he consolidated them to create the optimum brewing process of the ideal Shizuoka *ginjo* sake. Kawamura's academic paper on *ginjo* sake brewing that was published in the *Journal of the Brewing Society of Japan* in 1988 was considered a valuable treasure at that time and was referred to by no-Shizuoka brewers who were planning to enter the *ginjo* sake market as the "Kawamura Manual".

The small number of cooperative sake breweries that introduced the use of HD-1 early on did well at the NNSA. However, in order to achieve Kawamura's dream of gold awards totaling double-digits being won in a single year by Shizuoka breweries, more breweries would have to introduce the use of Shizuoka yeast. Nevertheless, attempts to develop a better product that exploited the advantages of the HD-1 yeast and that would be accepted by the market continued. Around the second half of the 1970s, there was a peak in the popularity of *ginjo* sake produced in Ishikawa Prefecture. This factor led Kawamura, who had begun to focus on high-grade sake as a commercial base, to shift his focus to *ginjo* yeasts. Thus, from the beginning he viewed Shizuoka yeast sake from the perspective of the NNSA and the perspective of the market in Tokyo.

Kawamura introduced Shizuoka sake in such a way that it could be sold on the market as sake varieties that had a quality that was comparable to sake varieties that were recognized in the NNSA. Thus, the products almost never disappointed customers who tried them. Quite a few sake breweries in other prefectures entered the NNSA with a supernatant liquid that is the first that naturally trickles out of the unpressed sake main mash and that had just been bottled. After gathering this "top layer" sake, it was manually pressed and then mechanically pressed with automated machinery. However, the more a sake is pressed, the more its quality suffers. As a result, it is easy to identify differences in quality with sake varieties that have been machine pressed.

In addition, retailers began to appear who enthusiastically followed the development of Shizuoka sake and sold it actively. Their efforts cannot be overlooked. For example, starting around 1980, the Yamazaki Liquor Store in Shizuoka City each year stocked its shelves and actively sold the top five winners at the NNSA; this means it was one of the earliest stores in the nation to do so. Around this same time it became common practice for liquor stores in Shizuoka Prefecture to store *ginjo* sake at a low temperature (7°C). Although efforts were made to create a distribution system that was suited to high-quality *ginjo* sake, it was limited to only a few liquor stores.

The dream of Shizuoka *ginjo* sake varieties capturing gold medals numbering in double-digits at the NNSA, which Kawamura set as a goal designed to improve the reputation of Shizuoka sake, was finally realized at the Brewing Year[4] 1985 NNSA, which was held in the spring of 1986. Twenty-one breweries located in Shizuoka Prefecture entered *ginjo* sake varieties made with Shizuoka yeast in the awards that year. They won 10 Gold Medals and seven lower level prizes. Although there were previous cases of other prefectures winning a higher number of prizes, the fact that breweries from Shizuoka Prefecture won prizes numbering in double-digits was such a remarkable achievement that they had thought it could not be done.

The prefectures that were awarded prizes numbering double-digits in a single year during the seven-year period at the end of the Showa era (three years before and after BY1985) were only Shizuoka (1 time), Hyogo (4 times), and Hiroshima (6 times). When looking at data limited to the number of prizes awarded by prefectures, the number that achieved double-digit totals in the Showa era and the Heisei era were markedly different. This is because the number of gold awards given by the NNSA that were over 100 items each year over long periods of time began to increase significantly in 1989. As a result, the winners started to garner anywhere from 200 to 300 items, which more than doubled the previously seen scores. The award rate, which indicates the award-winning products as a percentage of the total number of products that were entered into the contest, was 19 percent in 1979 and 16 percent in 1988, but rose to 38 percent in 1993. In BY1985, 119 products out of a total of 836 entries won awards, which meant that the award rate was a mere 14.2 percent. In 1985, Shizuoka *ginjo* sake varieties were clear stand-outs.

9.   EXAMINATION USING THE FRAME OF INDUSTRIAL CLUSTERS

Below, we examine cases in Shizuoka Prefecture using the above-mentioned six factors related to industrial clusters.

1.   The separation of capital investors and management from the workers and staff members in the sake brewing industry began during the Meiji era, as many of the capital investors who founded breweries were wealthy land owners or wealthy merchants who were known as Kuramoto. Brewing technologies were maintained by Tojis and a group of Kurabitos who were employed seasonally. Since the cold environment during winter was optimal for controlling the microorganisms used in the traditional brewing processes, it was common in Japan for farmers who had finished harvesting their rice to go and work at sake breweries during the winter. Tojis would return to their home in spring in order to do farm work, and then from late autumn to early spring they would be hired as live-in employees by a Kuramoto and work brewing sake. Tojis are the skillful, experienced Kurabitos who directed the entire process of sake brewing, and at the same time they are also "supervisors" of work teams of Kurabitos that used to be composed of men in the Tojis' hometown who wanted to learn the trade. The Tojis and Kurabitos who live in their hometowns from spring to autumn exchange their brewing experiences in various regions so as to improve their brewing skills to compete with other Toji groups. Many Toji groups were formed mainly in regions with harsh winters in the Meiji era. However, during times when there was great demand for Tojis from breweries, several Toji groups were formed in relatively warm regions of Japan. Thus, Shida Tojis were in the warmer Shizuoka. The peak of Shida Tojis' activity is said to be in the early Showa era, but by the 1970s, when development of Shizuoka yeast began, Shida Tojis were employed by nearby Kuramotos in Shizuoka on a seasonal basis and thus the practice of going outside the prefecture in search of work had all but ceased. This was because there were many job opportunities during the winter in Shizuoka, where the weather was mild and industrialization had continued to progress. Although they are thought to have been recognized for their skill in brewing sake in warm climates because Shida Tojis were invited to a Japanese American sake brewery in Hawaii prior to World War II, the flavor quality produced using traditional warm-climate brewing techniques that place a great deal of importance on safe brewing by, for example, preventing spoilage, did not match the high-quality

flavor of sake produced using cold production techniques, and the sake varieties they produced were not well regarded. Thus, soon after the post-World War II economic growth had started, the Shida Tojis began to be absorbed into local Shizuoka Kuramoto breweries as full-time employees. This meant that employees with the experience and know-how of Tojis started to become commonplace at Shizuoka breweries around the time of Japan's high economic growth following World War II. These are the specific Shizuoka characteristics that are related to labor and workers, although full-time Tojis are no longer unusual all over Japan today.

2. Another factor other than labor and workers is the sake brewing yeast known as Shizuoka yeast. This yeast was separated from a premium sake main mash in Shizuoka and cultivated by Kawamura at the Prefectural Industrial Testing Center as part of a subcontracted research project run by the Shizuoka Brewers Association. Thus, the investments and judgments of the Association that subcontracted this project can also be considered input factors. Shizuoka yeast is a premium sake yeast whose use is limited to sake brewers located in Shizuoka Prefecture, and therefore it is the brand equity of the Shizuoka *ginjo* sake. Although there are a number of estimations regarding its actual genetic origins, this is a trade secret of the Association officially.

3. The development of related industries and supporting industries, such as the Brewers Association and the Industrial Testing Center, have no distinguishing factors when compared to developments in other regions.

4. The transfer of the technologies and knowledge that are unique to this industry can be attributed to the hard work and discipline of Tojis in a wide range of differing traditions that were transferred to Kawamura of the Shizuoka Prefectural Industrial Testing Center. In the early 1980s, Kawamura promoted the use of "volunteer breweries" in the development of the *ginjo* sake that utilized Shizuoka yeast. With its mild climate, Shizuoka was a good place for Tojis in colder regions to come to earn money, and this led to a long tradition of the highly skilled Tojis coming to Shizuoka from other regions. When providing guidance in the development of products, Kawamura maintained a stable policy of adhering to the peculiar characteristics of the yeast and to market trends. He also gathered and analyzed sake brewing data obtained from breweries that were engaged in processes of trial-and-error. He then provided advice and incentives to the Tojis in order to spur competition among them. Exchanges of technical know-how and the creation of new organizations were accomplished through the

use of his technical expertise. This led to the establishment of know-how related to the use of the unique Shizuoka yeast in sake brewing, which in turn led to success in getting Shizuoka yeast to be used by more sake breweries in the prefecture. The new use of Shizuoka yeast and the introduction of new know-how was a kind of "open innovation" by many of the sake breweries in the prefecture. According to Rosenbloom and Spencer (1996), in order to ensure that open innovation succeeds, there is a need for those who accept new factor technologies and know-how to maintain high standards in their base technologies and in the newly introduced technology. What lay behind the impressive performance of the Shizuoka brand sake varieties at the NNSA 1985 was the high level of base technological skill that had been maintained at the breweries in Shizuoka Prefecture that took on the new technology. This in turn was due to the fact that in Shizuoka Prefecture there were a considerable number of full-time Kurabitos who had come from the Shida Toji tradition. It brought to the Shizuoka sake brewing cluster of the time a unique three-member set consisting of the highly skilled Tojis who came to Shizuoka Prefecture from regions around the country that were in competition with each other, the Shizuoka Prefecture engineers who consolidated their efforts in order to make the use of Shizuoka yeast more widespread, and the regional brewers' full-time employees, who were formerly seasonal migrant Shida Toji workers, demanding new technologies and know-how. This process includes the transfer of techniques and knowledge that are unique in the industry and by which Shizuoka Prefecture was recognized as an established sake brewing region.

5. The presence of customers (state of demand) was greatly affected by the fact that the Hasegawa Liquor Store in Tokyo appreciated Shizuoka yeast sake. It is a popular leader of locally produced high-grade sake varieties, local brews, and recognized the potential of Shizuoka *ginjo* sake. The Hasegawa company started selling Hokuriku *ginjo* sake at first, then put enormous energy into the discovery and sale of local brews from around the country that were still unknown. In the early 1980s, one of the Kuramotos who were involved in the early development of Shizuoka *ginjo* sake visited the Hasegawa Company on his own initiative in order to market the newly developed sake to them. Such an active engagement in the product marketing and selling was enabled by the Shinkansen ("bullet train") because Shizuoka was located only two hours or less from Tokyo by train. The climate in Shizuoka, which disproved the stereotype that premium local sake production is synonymous with regions with harsh winters, was a notable factor in the popularity of the highest quality, locally

produced sake. Put another way, the location of Shizuoka Prefecture contributed to create customers.

6. Competition between companies exists around the country in the sake brewing industry. In the case examined here, during the stage at which new technologies were established, the competition to develop new varieties of sake was intensified within the Shizuoka Prefecture. One reason that explains why a vibrant intra-Prefecture competition arose was the fact that there were several very active Kuramotos in Shizuoka Prefecture. However, these factors were not unique to Shizuoka, but existed in many other regions as well.

10.   CONCLUSION

Consequently, this case study showed the drastic changes during the 20th century affected Marshall and Porter's six clustering factors in many ways.

For example, the industrial policy established public technical support centers in every prefecture and made the difference in factor (3) smaller. Advanced transportation systems made the nationwide logistics easier and made factor (5) less important.

On the other hand, factor (1) was still important despite the highly developed transportation and communication infrastructure. It was recognized in this case that the skilled workers or the knowledge workers, those who were eligible for factor (4), like Toji or Kurabito had more freedom than before to live where they belonged and to do satisfying work. So, it can be concluded that factors (1) and (4) became more important, as well as the fact that conditions in a region where high-level workers wished to live and work had also changed.

As for factor (2), Kawamura's strategy was not so novel because it was a creative adaption of successful predecessors like the *kyokai-kobo* of the Brewing Society of Japan or the Danish Carlsberg case. Although the strategy was classic rather than innovative, the Shizuoka yeast was effective enough because the yeast was supposed to be a new strain which has enough character to brew its own differentiated *ginjo* sake. This suggests that the importance of scientific advance and new findings as factor (2) is verified.

Furthermore, factor (6) is a complicated issue in the Japanese sake industry because there are several licensing requirements and some anticompetitive regional establishments like the prefectural brewers' associations and so on. In particular, the multilayer contest system like NNSA, regionally and by prefecture, is unique because it makes the focused specific qualitative competitions harder. This provided Kawamura with a foundation for his leadership, though in this case, it is not certain whether it provoked appropriate innovations for the sake industry as a whole, because the total sake production had been decreasing for decades. Anyway, administrative interventions to industries are so common nowadays that factor (6) can be subdivided into the result of natural competitions and the outcome of policy inducements when considering competitions as a contemporary resource from a cluster to its innovation.

Finally, the factors that led to the establishment of a regional sake cluster in Shizuoka were the presence of Shizuoka yeast, a bioresource that was exclusive to the prefecture, as well as an open-innovation-style technological factor in the form of transferable brewing know-how regarding the unique Shizuoka yeast sake. Another unique factor was the presence of Kurabitos who were associated with the Shida Toji system, which had a technological base that allowed them to accept this new technology. In the history of industries there have been many examples of next-generation innovation occurring based on factors such as the legacy and leftovers from the previous generation. The case discussed here certainly represents one of these examples.

NOTES

1. See the last sentence of the first paragraph of section 7 below. There are several kinds of *kyokai-kobo* that are all numbered as "K#". The typical *ginjo kyokai-kobo* yeast strains were K7, K9, K10, or K14 at the time of this case.
2. Kishida (2005, pp. 126–7).
3. Kurose (2003).
4. Brewing Year, BY for short, is the fiscal year for the liquor industry in Japan. A BY starts in July and ends in June.

REFERENCES

Akiyama, Y. (1994) *Nihonshu.* Iwanami Shuppansha [in Japanese].
Gibbons, M., Limoges, C., Nowotny, H., Schwartzman, S., Scott, P. and Trow, M. (1994) *The New Production of Knowledge: The Dynamics of Science and Research in Contemporary Societies*, London: Sage Publications.
Kawamura, D. (1988) "The ginjo sake brewing in Shizuoka Prefecture", *Journal of the Brewing Society of Japan*, **83**(11), 723–8 [in Japanese].
Kishida, N. (2005) "The product developments and the technology management led by the public technology testing organization: The Shizuoka yeast sake case". Master's thesis, Graduate School of Asia Pacific Studies, Waseda University [in Japanese].
Kishida, N. (2006) "Innovations in new product developments of premium sake with Shizuoka sake yeasts", *Japan Venture Review*, No. 8, pp. 51–4 [in Japanese].

Kurose, T. (2003) "The separation and usage of the sake yeast monoploids", *The Studies of Sake Yeasts: The Studies in 1990s*, Brewing Society of Japan [in Japanese].

Marshall, A. (1923) *Industry and Trade: A Study of Industrial Technique and Business Organization, and of their Influences on the Conditions of Various Classes and Nations* (4th edn), Macmillan.

Nishimura, Y. (2003) *Sangaku-renkei – Beyond "The era of the central laboratories"*, Nikkei Business Publications [in Japanese].

Porter, M. (1990) *The Competitive Advantage of Nations*, New York: Free Press.

Rosenbloom, R.S. and Spencer, W.J. (1996) *Engines of Innovation*, Boston, MA: Harvard Business School Press.

Yoshikawa, T. (2001) "Industrial clustering for R&D based startup firms: Limits of Professor Marshal and Porter's industrial clustering", *Japan Venture Review*, No. 2 [in Japanese].

11. The empirical study on the emergence and diffusion process of design-driven innovation initiated by knowledge creation: from the field study in the industrial cluster of the Sumida Ward, Tokyo

Mutsumi Okuyama, Toshiyuki Yasui,
Takashi Maneo and Kyosuke Sakakura

1. INTRODUCTION

Japanese Small and Medium Enterprises (SMEs) account for 99.7 percent of companies, 70 percent of employment, 50 percent of added value as well as becoming an important economic entity of Japan as a player in innovation. However, as the economic environment changes, Japan's SMEs are exposed to a harsh business environment affected by factors such as: (1) a sluggish procurement ratio from Japan due to globalization; (2) shorter product cycles and a sharp change in market shares; (3) the Fourth Industrial Revolution, represented by the Internet of Things (IoT), big data, artificial intelligence (AI) and so on; and (4) the normalization of human labor shortages brought on by changes in the population structure due to declining birthrates and an aging population. However, we must accept these changes in the environment and take on the task of creating future industries and employment.

For this purpose, we shall focus on Design-Driven Innovation (DDI) and propose a means to solve the problem by expanding upon it. A previous study (Verganti 2003) defined the occurrence of DDI as "innovation driven by new meaning (a reason for human use, which can be created by design), not technology (physical characteristics)".

The purpose of this chapter is to extend DDI to a horizontal network providing a creative solution for SMEs. DDI is an activity that creates new meaning in the market, and innovation in meaning is the concept of "creative problem solving" required for future strategies. The research question of this chapter centers on how SMEs can be productive and innovative at the same time, because it is to be noted that the superiority of a company lies not only in technical ability. In general, the competitive advantage for companies is to be able to bring about "problem solving" and improvement of productivity for customers. In addition to that, bringing new meaning to the market is also an important factor for companies in gaining an advantage. It is considered effective for SMEs exposed to particularly severe business conditions.

The key contribution to this research is the design discourse as an expanded model of DDI theory with a horizontal network. Design discourse is said to be a concept that analyzes what a design means in a social context and why it is necessary through dialogue with various stakeholders.

It is the process of creating a concept through dialogue with human networks that makes it easier to innovate meaning. This is because in the discussions among those who talk with the same logic, it is pointed out that the view to innovation tends to narrow.

2.   LITERATURE REVIEW

2.1   Genealogy of Innovation Research

In this chapter, we first organize existing innovation research and then clarify how DDI relates to the innovation indicated in that research. By doing so, we will clarify the theoretical features of DDI and the reasons used in this research.

It was J.A. Schumpeter (1912) who clarified the concept itself regarding innovation, which is interpreted as "innovation" or "new innovation". So, in the following, some representative areas of innovation research will be examined.

1.   Schumpeter's concept of innovation: Innovation by Schumpeter generally means the establishment of a new production function. It involves many aspects, such as the introduction of new products, the acquisition of new markets, and the implementation of new organizations, not merely innovation in production technology. At the same time, defining innovation as "discovery of new technological knowledge and practical application to industry" makes the distinction from invention clear. Based on the above points, Schumpeter said that the innovator is an entrepreneur. He also said that the economic development of capitalism is a process of creative destruction, which

suggested that the economic structure is transformed from the inside by the new combination of production factors.

2. Drucker's concept of innovation: P.F. Drucker (1955) developed Schumpeter's idea and held innovation to be a function of the enterprise. According to Drucker, the function of the enterprise is defined as "the function aimed at the management of productive resources and the improvement of productive use and productivity". The contents were divided into market development and innovation, and the latter was further broken down into product or service innovation and innovation of various skills and activities required for their supply. Innovations that in the past had only been captured in a very broad sense in economics are dealt with more specifically.

3. Research on innovation process: The innovation process refers to an approach in which innovation is understood as one process, and a new idea is embodied as a transformation process within the organization. Pioneering research on this approach was carried out by March and Simon (1958), who regarded innovation in an organization as an information processing paradigm, and raised two basic propositions: (a) An agent with an innovation avoidance tendency tends to start innovation when they feel dissatisfaction with the results of existing execution programs; (b) Innovation requires new research activities that impose an information processing load on the agent.

   Cognitive constraints on rationality affect program development, and as a result of performance gaps, exploration activities are initiated when dissatisfaction with existing activities occurs, leading to the discovery of new alternatives (programs). It is said that this is innovation.

   Research classified in this category includes Knight (1967). Knight emphasizes changes in output (new product development and new business expansion), making innovation a process of creating new programs.

   In addition, Rogers and Shoemaker (1971) divide the innovation process into the decision making stage and the implementation stage, specifically as follows: "knowledge → persuasion (attitude formation) → decision (recruit / reject) → communication → act".

4. Research on innovation organization: This research is a so-called organizational theory-based approach that attempts to capture innovation in relation to organizations. Representative studies include Burns and Stalker (1961), which focuses on implementing innovation in two separate organizations. The first is a mechanical (official bureaucratic) management system of centralized decision making, vertical duties, discrepancies, clear rules, division of duties, and decentralization into an organic organization with its own decision making. The second is

an organization with decision making, horizontal personality interactions, and job and rule elasticity. The analysis of 20 UK sites shows that innovation has been effective in the following research: Burns and Stalker (1961).

5. Research on innovation management: This approach can be roughly divided into the following:
    (a) Entrepreneurs and entrepreneurship for innovation: entrepreneurs and entrepreneurship are closely connected and are regarded as a factor in the efficient generation of innovation.
    (b) Capture a company in its life cycle and claim the need to manage innovation in relation to its stages.
    (c) Connect innovation directly to "technology", and use strategies such as research and development (R&D) and in-house ventures.

Innovation focuses on managing the products and market strategies that appear in the market.

Regarding approach (a) above, the study by Quinn (1979) is given as a representative example. Quinn defines innovation as "creating and introducing unique solutions to already recognized or newly recognized needs and requirements."

Furthermore, in connection with entrepreneurs, Quinn (1979) tried to demonstrate that in historical considerations of American business management. And, as a conclusion, it is clarified that the existence of entrepreneurs at the initial stage of the enterprise, especially the personality of the individual, strongly influences the innovation.

As a study from the viewpoint of the life cycle in point (b) above, Moore and Tushman (1982) divide innovation into product innovation and process innovation, and in each case, the change itself was due to the structural change in the company's competition base, strategy and organization.

The continuous emergence of innovation is said to be made possible by adopting an organization and strategy that fit the stages of the product life cycle.

2.2 Future Challenges of Innovation Research

In the previous section, five major areas of innovation research are outlined: (1) Schumpeter's innovation concept; (2) Drucker's innovation concept; (3) innovation process research; (4) innovation organization research; and (5) innovation management research. The representative results of each study are described.

Therefore, in this section, we will refer to the challenges of innovation research and future directions.

Innovation research is specific and practical, such as how it will be achieved in reality, and what kind of measures are needed for the organization, rather than as theoretical things that are needed. Therefore, innovation needs to be considered from multidimensional concepts. Therefore, not only business science but also research from the surrounding area is desirable. At the same time, the approach in business science needs to be integrated in the interrelationship.

2.3   Positioning of DDI in Innovation Research

The reason that the approach of innovation needs to be integrated in the relationship is that in recent years as global competition has intensified, flexible innovations are required in accordance with the business environment of a company.

In addition, with the intensification of international competition, the cycle from the concept stage of new products and services to market launch has become shorter, and the life cycle of new products and services has also become shorter. In order to respond to such a business environment, there is a trend in product development methods that differs from conventional methods. As an example, a method of product development focusing on the meaning brought by the product has been highlighted in recent years. One of them is DDI, proposed by Verganti (2009).

It is said that it is important to innovate this meaning by giving meaning to the product rather than simply enhancing the design of the product. Verganti (2009) cited the Swiss watch "Swatch" as an example of DDI. "Swatch" is a "fashion accessory" that can take the form of many pieces and change according to Time, Place and Occasion (TPO), like a tie, without competing with the conventional product method of improving watch technology and functions. The Swatch manufacturers incorporated new meaning into products and adopted a design that made consumers feel the meaning. By innovating meaning through design, they succeeded in fighting their competitors on a completely different ground.

Increasing the ability to introduce intelligence into products will be a weapon to expand business in an advantageous manner even in a globalized business environment. However, there are still only a few studies on intelligence activities regarding the meaning of goods.

So, in this research, we explain it using the case of what happened in Sumida Ward, which is a Japanese industrial development with high spatial proximity.

3.   THEORETICAL FRAMEWORK

Maskell and Malmberg (1999) stated that knowledge-based theory of spatial clustering was important for innovation formation. The problem-solving process employed by enterprises and regions includes elements that are strengthened by the spatial and cultural clustering of participants. The theory is that if related industries concentrate in a specific space, and an Industrial Milieu is built and succeeds, it is then sustainable. In this study, based on the preceding research mentioned above, we shall use Sumida Ward, Tokyo as an example. As a region, Sumida Ward has the highest concentration of business locations in Japan, and its spatial clustering is high.

Until now, it has not been possible to explain what has motivated the generation of DDI in industrial clusters. Due to this lack of explanation, DDI was not easy to apply as a policy for promoting regional innovation.

For this reason, in this research, we extend DDI, focusing on how the model starts with industrial accumulation, and obtain effects, and verify the effectiveness in the generation of innovation using text mining.

4.   METHODOLOGY

Text data is a representative of "qualitative data". The purpose of text mining is to collect high value-added information from this qualitative data. Therefore, we carried out text mining using KH Coder software, which automatically analyzes and classifies text information.

This software automatically extracts words from text data, and uses the results as a correlational approach in which multivariate analysis such as factor analysis and cluster analysis is performed, and words and documents according to the criteria are created by the analyst. It has the feature of being able to interpret in an integrated manner a Dictionary-Based approach that classifies. In addition, it has a morphological analysis function that divides text into parts of speech, and can perform multivariate analysis.

These analyses can provide an overarching presentation of the factors and correlations that lead to DDI.

We thought that it was important to analyze the current situation of Sumida Ward by text mining in multiple ways.

5.   THE EMPIRICAL WORK

5.1   Case Study

In this study, we shall use Sumida Ward, Tokyo as an example. As a region, Sumida Ward has the highest concentration of business locations in Japan, and its spatial clustering is high. In Japan, the spatial clustering is the highest in Sumida Ward, having an office location density (total area divided by number of establishments) of 252.1; with 3466 establishments; and total area (kilometers) of 13.75, compared to, in second place, Higashi Osaka City: density of 102.3; with 6321 establishments; and 61.78 total area, and in third place, Ota Ward: density of 79.0; with 4699 establishments; and 59.46 total area (2014).[1] As industries continued to cluster for over 100 years, factory owners began using collaborative design out of fear that they may not survive if they couldn't break away from the subcontracts focused solely on technological superiority which had been imposed on Japanese SMEs.

The following case is representative of this study where a factory owner who had operated within the isolated, single-line relationship structure of a parent enterprise and a subcontracting company pointed fellow industrial companies and various stakeholders such as local governments, financial institutions and universities in the direction of DDI.

5.2   Outline of Sumida Ward

5.2.1   From the reconstruction of Tokyo's largest afflicted area to the projected forecast of business losses

Let us first take a look at the regional characteristics of Sumida Ward. Sumida Ward is a region that is representative of the common people's culture from the Edo period (1603–1867), with the development of various traditional crafts being the driving force behind modern light manufacturing industries.[2] And then, in 1923, the Great Kanto Earthquake[3] hit the area, causing a lot of damage. About 90 percent of the ward's area was burnt and destroyed, killing 70 000 people throughout Tokyo. As a result, 80 percent of Tokyo's Sumida Ward died. In addition, World War II[4] turned 70 percent of the area into ruins, resulting in 63 000 deaths and nearly 300 000 injuries.

And again, due to dramatic changes in business environments across the world, there has been suffering in recent years too. According to the "Forecast of trends in manufacturing factories in Sumida Ward" published in 2013 by Sumida Ward, the number of SMEs in the ward has gradually dropped from 9703 at their peak in 1973 to 3391 in 2008, and, if this continues, a wipe-out is predicted by 2030 (Figure 11.1).

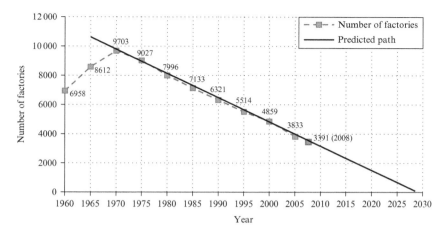

Source: Sumida Ward, "Sumida Ward Industry Promotion Master Plan" (2013, p. 10).

Figure 11.1 *Forecast of trends in manufacturing factories in Sumida Ward*

5.2.2 Collaboration between diverse stakeholders and Sumida Ward SMEs

As stated in section 5.1, as the largest area in Tokyo affected by the earthquake, Sumida Ward needed to create industries from the ground up. Opinions were voiced both from the local municipalities' managers for industrial promotion, "industrial promotion will lead to improving the residents' welfare", and the owners of SMEs in the ward, "naturally, we need to keep an eye out for and call out to our neighbors, especially after the ward experiencing such a disaster". Aside from the "Knowledge-Based Theory of Spatial Clustering" from the Innovative Milieu theory, the ward's resilience[5] is thought of as one of the factors that strengthened the region's bond.

In order to promote industries on a zero basis in this way, the following three are listed as distinctive approaches of local governments' industry promotion.

1. Establishment of basic principles for promotion of SMEs (1979): Improving the welfare of residents living in Sumida Ward, having a high percentage of people working in the same ward, and enacting ordinances before Japan are the most important tasks in boosting the industrial vitality of Sumida Ward's manufacturing industry. In 1977 to 1978, a massive survey was conducted by mobilizing about 180 staff members in the entire manufacturing and commercial investigation.

2. Establishment of Industry Promotion Master Plan (1987): Through the formulation of this master plan, Sumida Ward has created: the Sumida Small and Medium Enterprise Center, the International Fashion Center, and the "frontier Sumida Juku" for training human resources (a private business school aimed at training successors of SMEs and young talent who will be responsible for the next generation). By designing a policy program to revitalize local industries, we have expanded various possibilities in Sumida Ward. Aggressive municipal assistance on such industrial promotion also helped, making a new trend within the ward by designing a policy program for revitalizing local industries.

3. Establishment of Sumida Ward Industry Promotion Master Plan, Stay Fab, (2013): In Sumida Ward, they will change the idea of "vertical division" and "equal support for all business operators", and they will work on industry promotion by fusing commerce, industry and tourism. By intensively supporting highly conscious managers, they will train managers who will lead other managers, and as a result will improve the overall industry.

Aggressive municipal assistance on such industrial promotion also helped, and as a result, various stakeholders and SMEs in Sumida Ward cooperated to launch a number of advanced projects.

Edokko No. 1 Project The "Edokko No. 1" is a compact, unmanned deep sea research vehicle capable of diving to the depth of 8000 meters, collecting mud and life forms from the sea bed, and using its 3D video cameras to capture 3D imagery (see Figure 11.2). With SMEs from Sumida Ward, Katsushika Ward and Ota Ward at its center, it was developed in 2013 by Shibaura Institute of Technology, Tokyo University of Marine Science and Technology, Japan Agency for Marine-Earth Science and Technology (JAMSTEC), Shin-Enoshima Aquarium, volunteers from Sony Corporation, Tokyo Higashi Shinkin Bank, and others (see Figure 11.3). The project's objective was to allow SMEs suffering from a challenging business environment, such as a strong yen and the recession, to gain product development and market development capabilities with the aim of "moving away from the subcontracting company stance".

In November 2013, they succeeded in obtaining the world's first 3D high-definition video recording at 8000 meters below sea level in the Japan Deep. The development of Edokko No. 1 cost 20 million yen, and a single machine can be reused by simply replacing small parts. Because it can be submerged and collected by a small fishing boat, the cost of a single experiment can be kept to between tens of thousands of yen to several hundred

Source: Edokko No. 1 Project.

Figure 11.2   Photographs taken under the sea

thousand yen. Up until then, the development costs of larger research vehicles had been over 10 billion yen, with a single experiment costing tens of millions of yen. When compared to that, its greatest characteristic is that the production was achieved at a considerably lower cost.

In July 2014, the same project was awarded the 2014 Prime Minister's Award in the Excellent Contribution to Industry–Academia–Government Collaboration Award and The Seventh National Maritime Award.

The Edokko No. 1 Project is a typical project cited as a successful example of collaboration between Japanese industry, government agencies and financial institutions in academia. This project has enabled university students to support SMEs smoothly. SMEs have strengths in their respective technologies, but there are many that lack information capabilities in terms of how to use these technologies and how to introduce them into products. These university students complemented the SMEs' strengths. They have become catalysts that make "innovation of meaning" more possible.

48-hour commercialization design marathon project   The project aims to promote "research that has manufacturing that emphasizes user-centered thinking and creating the social environment while deeply respecting and

Source: Edokko No. 1 Project.

Figure 11.3   Project members aboard

supporting the dignity of humans as its goal", as praised by "International Universal Design Declaration in Japan 2002" (UD), and its goal is the exploration and dissemination of UD as well as the nurturing of human resources capable of creating future UD.

Within a time limit of 48 hours, designers, engineers and marketers from large corporations ventured into town with disabled people, coming up with new findings through repetitive observation and experience, and incorporating these into the production process of "experience, discover, design, verify".

Held by the International Association for Universal Design (IAUD), with the backing and support of the Tokyo Higashi Shinkin Bank, SMEs centered in Sumida Ward were introduced to this approach and SMEs who expressed their desire to participate in the project were supported. Participating SMEs can gain from this by learning the product development process and theories of major manufacturers.

From this project, prototypes of "fitting rooms that are easily accessible even for those in wheelchairs" (Figure 11.4) and "shop signs that

Source: Tokyo Higashi Shinkin Bank.

Figure 11.4   Dressing room easy to use for wheelchair users

can provide information to the blind" were completed and, in December 2016, were displayed at the International Conference for Universal Design exhibition.

This project will carry out the following: (1) Hold a productization meeting (Figure 11.5) once a month, and confirm and report on the progress of productization; (2) IAUD and Shibaura Institute of Technology provide support for businesses that develop products. A commercialization review committee will be organized consisting of Tokyo Electric University coordinator, specialists such as patent attorneys, and Hamano Manufacturing Co. Ltd (metal processing) in Sumida Ward, and advice given on development at the time of the commercialization conference; (3) Raise issues each time until the next meeting and productization will be carried out according to the issues; (4) By holding a product development step-up seminar in conjunction with the productization conference, we have gone through four flows of learning about product development and market development.

Shitamachi canoe   A project was started to develop competition-standard canoes for the 2020 Tokyo Olympics (see Figure 11.6). The production of the canoe is handled by Hamano Products Co. Ltd, a metal processing firm from Sumida Ward. The same company is credited with having led the structural design of the deep sea research vehicle Edokko No. 1 in 2013. In 2016, the Tokyo Higashi Shinkin Bank and Toyo University agreed to

Source: Tokyo Higashi Shinkin Bank.

Figure 11.5   Presentation for product development

Source: Tokyo Higashi Shinkin Bank.

Figure 11.6   Project members of Shitamachi canoe

an industry–academic collaboration in order to advance joint research between the university and the city's SMEs.

As the same bank does business with many of these SMEs, SMEs having the skillsets that can be of use in developing the canoe are introduced to Hamano Products Co. Ltd. Support is also provided with communicating and coordinating with local governing bodies and applying for subsidies and other such tasks related to fundraising.

Since canoeing mainly takes place in Eastern Europe, such as the high-powered Slovakia, Japanese canoeists are slow to get used to it. Once a domestic canoe has been completed, the advantage will be that canoeists can concentrate on practice because they do not need time to get used to the canoe, and a canoe frame suitable for the physical size of Japanese canoeists can be developed (Figure 11.7).

As described above, based on the success of Edokko No. 1 and 48 HDM projects, we are aiming to develop new products in collaboration with industry, academia and government, and financial institutions.

Garage Sumida   Opened in 2014 on a small scale and then reopened in 2017 at about seven times the size, Garage Sumida is a facility run by Hamano Products Co. Ltd that supports entrepreneurship in manufacturing. Digital machine tools such as 3D printers and laser cutters

Source: Tokyo Higashi Shinkin Bank.

Figure 11.7   Shitamachi canoe

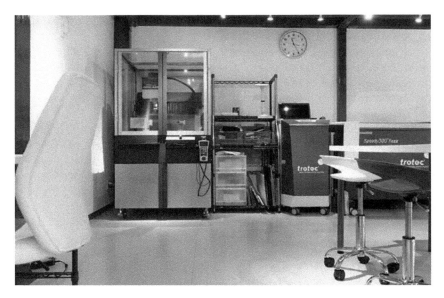

Source: Authors.

Figure 11.8 *Digital machine tools such as 3D printers and laser cutters are available*

are available (Figure 11.8). Also, it is possible to use the office, and one can even use it as a registry office. Events and workshops are held regularly, and, with free space where visitors can read or relax at the bar (Figure 11.9), it is also a place for exchange that anyone with an interest in manufacturing can visit freely.

The facility and the equipment, as well as the technical coaching, are provided by Hamano Products Co. Ltd. Financial support such as investment is carried out by Glocalink Co. Ltd, a subsidiary of Leave a Nest Co. Ltd. (Shinjuku Ward, Tokyo) who are capital participants (Figure 11.10).

Consultations for new businesses, whether large or small, are often received daily, and total more than 200 (as of April 2018).

In industry, there are many consultations on saving labor and the labor of robots, transportation, agriculture and food. By project, development accounts for 20 percent and part processing accounts for 60 percent.

Garage Sumida has made it possible for venture companies to develop their ideas rapidly by consulting SMEs' excellent ideas and technologies from the design stage. In general, parts processing that takes about one week when carried out at the factory can be done in about one hour.

Source: Authors.

Figure 11.9   Free space where visitors can read or relax at the bar

Sumifa   Having first taken place in 2000, Sumifa is an event where visitors can walk around the manufacturing factories of Sumida Ward, discussing with craftspeople and touching on technology, experiencing the process of how products are manufactured (Figure 11.11).

In 2017, 19 SMEs from Sumida Ward participated and 13 original tours were also organized. For instance, you can visit an oil and fat manufacturing factory and make your own bar of soap (Matsuyama Oil and Fat Company), visit a glassware manufacturing factory, do some glassware shopping (Iwasawa Glass Company), or visit a plastic products factory (Figure 11.12: Chiba-plas Company) where you will be given a plastic convertible plate/chopping board as a gift, followed by a "Food on your plate" walking tour of Kirakira Tachibana Shopping Street (Figure 11.13) where you'll be able to fill up your plate with local food. Another interesting tour is the "Bicycle tour with a Sumida specialist" (Figure 11.14), where the chairman of KUME SEN-I Co. Ltd (a domestic T-shirt manufacturer) will take you around hand-selected Sumida factories, back alleys and shopping streets by bicycle. The chairman is also director of Sumida

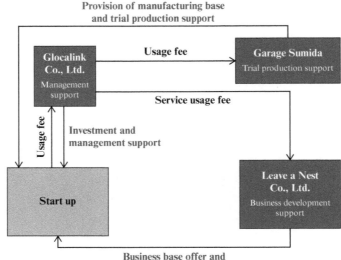

Source: Authors.

Figure 11.10   System in Garage Sumida

Sightseeing Association DMO (Destination Management Organization). Many unique events have been held.

During the tour, participants eagerly take notes about the engineer's story, take photos with their smartphones, and actively ask questions such as "what is this part used for?" The participants want not only the artifacts that are there, but also to hear an explanation of "intangible value" including the story behind the artifacts, such as how they are used and why they have been made. Also, from hearing the participants' opinions, the SMEs may rediscover the "meaning" of things anew, which can promote intelligence activities.

We explain further an overview of these five projects and their success factors. Verganti (2003) advocated a method called design discourse in DDI. His study involved engaging human resources with diverse values inside and outside the company in the product design and development stages and forming collective discussions to give new meaning to products. Diverse stakeholders are perceived as interpreters of meaning that can bring new meaning to products.

Interpreters range from artists working to bring out new values, researchers and educators who have insight into society, and designers

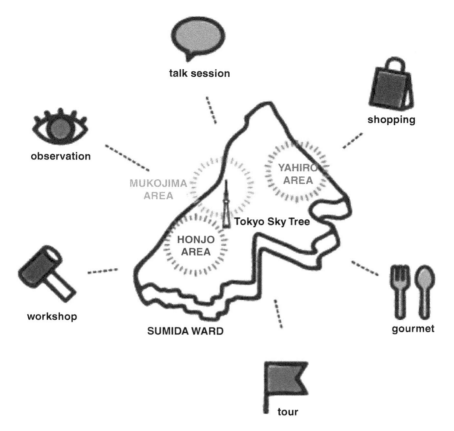

Source: Sumifa Executive Committee.

Figure 11.11   Schematic of Sumifa

and engineers outside the company. Interpreters discuss the formation of networks and the creation of new meanings and they share new knowledge with each other to create new product development.

A dialogue, such as the inability to apply existing technologies to other areas, or the inability to apply technologies in other industries in their own fields, is an opportunity to give products new meaning.

These five projects in Sumida Ward are the cases where DDI is created by design discourse.

Source: Sumifa Executive Committee.

Figure 11.12   Food on your plate tour (plastic plate/chopping board)

5.3   Outline of Survey

5.3.1   Purpose of survey

The purpose of this survey is to define the conditions that generate DDI in order to develop regional industries. For this purpose, a semi-structured interview survey was conducted with four owners of SMEs in Sumida Ward, two local government officials, one chairman of a financial institution, and three facility personnel.

5.3.2   Target attributes

The interviews were conducted with 10 people from the 5 project stakeholders evoked in section 5.2.2 (some were involved in all aspects whilst others were only involved selectively), from 22 December 2017 to 12 April 2018. The attributes of the targets are as shown in Table 11.1.

Source: Sumifa Executive Committee.

Figure 11.13   Kirakira Tachibana Shopping Street

5.3.3   Question items
The question items take into account the objectives of the survey and are categorized as seen in Table 11.2: I: Regional characteristics, II: Involvement in project, III: Effect of project, and IV: Future prospects.

5.3.4   Method of analysis
In this study, text mining (KH Coder[6]) was used in conducting the analysis. This involves automatically extracting words from text data and analyzing them quantitatively. The analyst's analytical skills often have an influence on the analysis' point of view and how its interpretation, concept and philosophy are generated. However, KH Coder can exclude the analyst's predictions as far as possible when digging through data and presenting results. It was used for this very study for that reason.

5.3.5   Results of analysis of frequent words
Frequent words   To begin with, words that were used frequently during the survey interviews were extracted (see Table 11.3). Results show that the

Source: Sumifa Executive Committee.

Figure 11.14   Bicycle tour with a Sumida specialist

Table 11.1   Attributes of the targets

Number	Attribute	Main activity
A	CEO of a SME	Mental processing industry
B	Chairman of a SME	Domestic T-shirt manufacturing industry
C	CEO of a SME	Printing industry
D	CEO of a SME	Manufacturing support, shared factory
E	Local goverment official	Industry promotion officer
F	Local goverment official	Industry tourism officer
G	Shinkin Bank chairman	A financial institution of a cooperative organisation aimed at mutual aid of the region
H	Art gallery staff	Katsushika Hokusai's exhibition
I	Workshop staff	Edo Kiriko exhibition
J	Museum staff	Sword exhibition

Source: Authors.

Table 11.2   Question items

Category	Question items
I Regional characteristics	Q1. What are the characteristics of Sumida Ward?
II Involvement in project	Q2. Please tell us about the contents of the projects you have been involved with.
	Q3. Please tell us about your purpose in participating in the project
III Effect of project	Q4. Was collaborative design born from your participation in the project?
	Q5. Has participating in the project had an effect of expanding sales channels?
IV Future prospects	Q6. Please tell us about your vision of the future
	Q7. Is your answer to Q6. something that can be achieved by participating in the project?

Source: Authors.

Table 11.3   Frequent words

Frequent words	Number of use	Frequent words	Number of use
Factory	33	Process	13
Make	29	Technology	13
Think	23	New	13
Company	21	Sumida	12
People	18	Things	12
Now	17	T-shirt	11
Myself	16	Have	10
Town	16	Era	10
Design	15	Employees	10
Work	14	Information	10
Consider	13		

Source: Authors.

following words ranked highly: "Factory" (33), "Make" (29), "Think" (23), "Company" (21), "People" (18), "Now" (17), "Myself" (16), "Town" (16), "Design" (15), and "Work" (14).

Co-occurrence network   Next, we check the co-occurrence network, a network diagram of extracted words that share a similar appearance pattern (Figure 11.15). The co-occurrence network is a diagram where words

Diversity, innovation and clusters

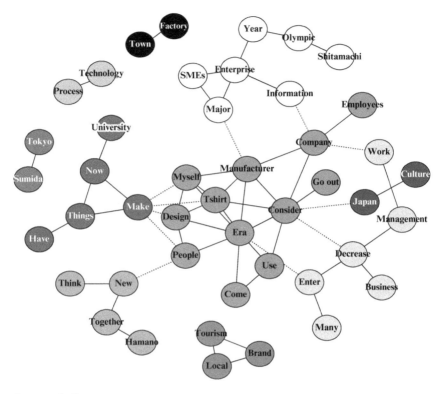

Source: Authors.

Figure 11.15   Co-occurrence network

with similar appearance patterns are joined by lines. The more frequently a word is used, the larger it is, and the stronger the appearance similarity, the thicker the lines.

As a result, we can confirm the presence of words that act as the core of appearance similarity, such as "Era", "People", "Consider", "Myself", and "Manufacturer". Also, "Tourism", "Brand" and "Local" were bundled together, and "Hamano" (the name of the owner of Hamano Products Co. Ltd who participates in all projects), "New", "Think" were bundled together, with "New" being linked to "People".

Self-organizing map   We then studied a self-organizing map where the clustering of the words is relevant to the similarity of their meaning (Figure 11.16). The results show the words "Information", "Cooperation",

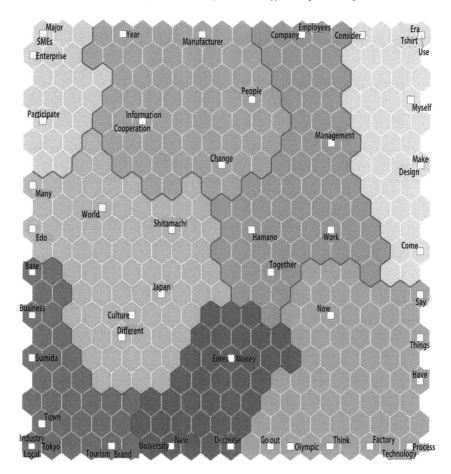

Source: Authors.

Figure 11.16   Self-organizing map

"Change", and "People" placed in the same hierarchy along with "Manufacturer" and "Year", although they appear further away. Also, the word "Participate", belonging in the same hierarchy as the words "Enterprise", "Small and Medium Enterprises", and "Major (corporation)", appears near the words "Information" and "Cooperation". The words "Together", "Hamano", "Work" and "Management" are placed close together in the same hierarchy, and the words "Design", "Make", and "Myself" are placed in a hierarchy close to the word "Management".

"Small and Medium Enterprises", and "Major (corporation)", appear near the words "Information" and "Cooperation".

6. RESULTS AND CONSIDERATIONS

6.1 Results

The purpose of this survey was to define the conditions that generate DDI in order to develop regional industries. Through analysis, we revealed that the words "Factory", "Making", "Thinking", "Company", "People", "Now", "Myself", "Town", "Design" and "Work" rank highly in the list of frequent words.

In the co-occurrence network, the word "Era" was linked to the words "People", "Design" and "Consider", and "Local", "Tourism" and "Brand" were bundled together.

According to the results from an analysis of the self-organizing map, "Change" and "People" appear in the same hierarchy as "Information" and "Cooperation", and "Design" and "Make" appear in the hierarchy close to "Management".

Through these analyses, at the town factory in Sumida Ward, design is currently created in collaboration with information, which serves as a response to change as one of the creative problem-solving mechanisms in management. This result can be considered a story when you look at the co-occurrence network and the self-organizing map comprehensively.

On DDI, thought by Sumida Ward as being created by groups of individual designers and designer–customer teams, this research has newly revealed the tendency for it to happen from collaborative design through the horizontal relationship between owners of factories in industrial clusters of high spatial clustering.

6.2 Considerations

According to Mr A, who owns a SME and who participates in all the projects,

> There are 3 directions, and one of this region's characteristics is its stance in wanting to commit to the Upstream of manufacturing. The second is its will to move away from subcontractor mentality. That is not to say ill of working as a subcontractor, but rather the will to move away from the simplistic one-way schematic of 'big company to small company' and build partnerships that go beyond the boundaries of industry and company sizes.

SME owner B said,

Meeting people and networking, these are things that spread unexpectedly but, when you think about it, you kind of feel like it happened because it was meant to be. The people you meet will bring out facets of yourself that you didn't know you had. Doing this will help broaden your possibilities and lead to even more encounters. I am truly grateful to these connections and wish to continue meeting all kinds of people. In Sumida Ward, the overwhelming clustering of the professional and personal lives makes this even easier.

In addition, Mr E, the local government official, said,

We formulated the 'Sumida Ward Industry Promotion Master Plan' in March 2013. In order for the economy of Sumida Ward to gain traction, we defined the ward's basic stance of intensively supporting highly aware operators who wish to boost the industry. The leader enterprises will then pull the SMEs of Sumida Ward up in a bottom-up approach. 'If you're going to start something, go to Sumida'. That is the message written on the back cover of the master plan's brochure. New manufacturing creation bases like Garage Sumida embody these words.

Shinkin Bank's chairman, Mr G, said,

Just looking at one corner of Ryogoku, we have the Sumo Museum, the Japanese Sword Museum, Edo-Tokyo Museum, and Sumida Hokusai Museum. There are 4 cultural facilities. And they are all cultural facilities that are among the most important in Japan. And there are other smaller museums such as the Tobacco & Salt Museum, or the Seiko Museum. All these makers have left things here as cultural facilities. There is history and culture that is unique to this ward. There is also Sumida Triphony Hall which is a Japan Philharmonic Orchestra franchise. We really take immense care of culture.

From the above interviews and the results of the analysis, we can consider the following points:

1. Collaborative design can happen from a horizontal relationship (as opposed to a vertical relationship as shared between a parent company and its subcontractor) between factory owners within an area.
2. Collaborative design coming from the horizontal relationship of factory owners occurs from factory owners living and interacting within the extreme geographical and emotional clustering called an "economies of scope".
3. The meaning of collaborative design, which is a major incentive for the occurrence of Innovation in Design-Driven Innovation, is neither

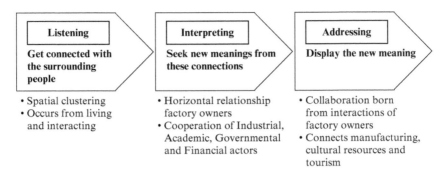

Source: Authors, adapted from Verganti (2003).

Figure 11.17   Structure of DDI occurrence in Sumida Ward

an individual idea from an individual designer, nor a bilateral idea from a designer and a client, but a cooperative creation coming from exchanges between factory owners.
4.   To foster this, collaboration between industry, academia, government and financial institutions has been developed in the region.

As a result of the above four considerations, the DDI process that occurs in Sumida Ward is represented as in Figure 11.17.

In the case of Sumida Ward, the process of creating DDI is organized from these research results. At the "Listening" stage, it can be understood that the connection with people around you, which is generated by living and interacting in the area with high spatial proximity, can be achieved. Subsequently, at the "Interpreting" stage, the factory owner has a horizontal relationship, and in cooperation with various stakeholders such as industry, government, academia and financial institutions, interprets the new meaning in manufacturing.

Finally, at the "Addressing" stage, the factory owners interact with each other to create co-creation power, and combine with the cultural resources and tourism resources of Sumida Ward to present products with new "meanings".

As described above, it is important to clarify the source of innovation by dissecting the system inherent in the region's DDI, and future challenges for this research would be to generalize this and lead on to solutions for an industrial revitalization in other regions.

6.3 Future Research Agenda

This study is to construct the model of a DDI-based horizontal innovation platform with the network of SMEs and to apply it for verification of this model to a field of manufacturing sites in downtown Tokyo. Based on this research, the authors will further proceed to developmental research with greater originality and theoretical implications for public policy on innovation.

NOTES

1. "Economic census basic survey", Ministry of Internal Affairs and Communications, available at http://www.stat.go.jp/data/e-census/2014/kekka.html.
2. Spinning, precision manufacturing, soap and shoes are especially popular, and toy manufacturing and rubber industries were developed in the Taisho era (1912–1926) for export. In addition, many major manufacturers of everyday commodities in Japan (Seiko Watch Corporation, Kanebo Cosmetics Inc., Lion Corporation, Kao Corporation, etc.) were founded here. To that end, small and medium manufacturing businesses gathered and developed, leading to the creation of diverse consumer goods for every need, "for every waking moment".
3. Disaster caused by a major earthquake (the Kanto earthquake) that occurred in Sagami Bay, Japan, at 11:58 a.m. on 1 September 1923. The earthquake was measured at magnitude 7.9. With Tokyo at its center, the disaster spread to many other prefectures such as Chiba, Saitama, Shizuoka, Ibaraki, Nagano, Tochigi and Gunma. The number of deaths and missing persons reached 105 000.
4. A large-scale worldwide war fought between the Axis camp, centered around the alliance of Japan, Germany and Italy, and the allied camp of Britain, the Soviet Union, the United States and the Republic of China. The invasion of Poland by the German army in September 1939, the ensuing invasion by the Soviet army and the declaration of war on Germany by Great Britain and France all had Europe as its battlefield. This was followed by the war between Japan and Great Britain, France and the Netherlands in December 1941, spreading the war over the whole world and becoming the greatest war in human history.
5. A word that describes resilience, elasticity or recuperation of vitality. The term was used to describe the wish that the Treaty of Amity and Cooperation in Southeast Asia, signed during the 1st ASEAN summit held in Bali, Indonesia in February 1976 would bring the member states strength coming from elasticity, like the way in which branches from a willow tree can withstand rain and wind.
6. Free software for content analysis (quantitative text analysis) or text mining. Developed and produced by Kiichi Higuchi (Associate Professor at Ritsumeikan University, Japan) in order to quantitatively analyze various Japanese text data such as answers to open-ended questions in surveys, interview recordings and newspaper articles.

REFERENCES

Burns, T. and Stalker, G.M. (1961) *The Management of Innovation*, London: Tavistock Publications.

Drucker, Peter F. (1955) *Practice of Management*, New York: William Heinemann.

Knight, Kenneth E. (1967) "A Descriptive Model of the Intra-Firm Innovation Process", *The Journal of Business*, **40**, 478.

March, J.G. and Simon, H.A. (1958) *Organizations*, New York: John Wiley & Sons.

Maskell, P. and Malmberg, A. (1999) "Localized Learning and Industrial Competitiveness", *Cambridge Journal of Economics*, **23**, 167–85.

Moore, W.L. and Tushman, M.L. (1982) "Managing Innovation Over the Product Life Cycle", in M.L. Tushman and W.L. Moore (eds), *Readings in The Management of Innovation*, Colombia: University Graduate School of Business, Pitman.

Quinn, J.B. (1979) "Technological Innovation, Entrepreneurship and Strategy", *Sloan Management Review*, Spring, 19.

Rogers, E.M. and Shoemaker, F.F. (1971) *Communication of Innovation: A Cross-Cultural Approach*, New York: The Free Press.

Schumpeter, J.A. (1912) *Theorie der Wirtschaftlichen Entwicklung*, Graz: Quadriga.

Sumida Ward (2013) *Sumida Ward Industry Promotion Master Plan*, Tokyo: Sumida Ward industrial promotion department industrial economic section [in Japanese].

Verganti, R. (2003) "Design as Brokering of Languages: Innovation Strategies in Italian Firms", *Design Management Journal*, **14**(3), 34–42.

Verganti, R. (2009) *Design-driven Innovation: Changing the Rules of Competition by Radically Innovating What Things Mean*, Boston, MA: Harvard Business Press.

Index